The White Devil

ARDEN EARLY MODERN DRAMA GUIDES

Series Editors:
Andrew Hiscock , University of Wales, Bangor, UK and Lisa Hopkins, Sheffield Hallam University, UK

Arden Early Modern Drama Guides offer practical and accessible introductions to the critical and performative contexts of key Elizabethan and Jacobean plays. Each guide introduces the text's critical and performance history, but also provides students with an invaluable insight into the landscape of current scholarly research, through a keynote essay on the state of the art and newly commissioned essays of fresh research from different critical perspectives.

A Midsummer Night's Dream edited by Regina Buccola
Doctor Faustus edited by Sarah Munson Deats
King Lear edited by Andrew Hiscock and Lisa Hopkins
1 Henry IV edited by Stephen Longstaffe
'Tis Pity She's a Whore edited by Lisa Hopkins
Women Beware Women edited by Andrew Hiscock
Volpone edited by Matthew Steggle
The Duchess of Malfi edited by Christina Luckyj
The Alchemist edited by Erin Julian and Helen Ostovich
The Jew of Malta edited by Robert A Logan
Macbeth edited by John Drakakis and Dale Townshend
Richard III edited by Annaliese Connolly
Twelfth Night edited by Alison Findlay
and Liz Oakley-Brown
The Tempest edited by Alden T. Vaughan and
Virginia Mason Vaughan
Romeo and Juliet: A Critical Reader, edited by
Julia Reinhard Lupton

The White Devil

A Critical Reader

Paul Frazer and
Adam Hansen

Bloomsbury Arden Shakespeare
An imprint of Bloomsbury Publishing Plc

B L O O M S B U R Y

LONDON • OXFORD • NEW YORK • NEW DELHI • SYDNEY

Bloomsbury Arden Shakespeare

An imprint of Bloomsbury Publishing Plc

Imprint previously known as Arden Shakespeare

50 Bedford Square	1385 Broadway
London	New York
WC1B 3DP	NY 10018
UK	USA

www.bloomsbury.com

BLOOMSBURY, THE ARDEN SHAKESPEARE and the Diana logo are trademarks of Bloomsbury Publishing Plc

First published 2016

British Library Cataloguing-in-Publication Data
A catalogue record for this book is available from the British Library.

ISBN:	HB:	978-1-4725-8739-8
	PB:	978-1-4725-8740-4
	ePDF:	978-1-4725-8742-8
	ePub:	978-1-4725-8741-1

Library of Congress Cataloging-in-Publication Data
A catalog record for this book is available from the Library of Congress.

Series: Arden Early Modern Drama Guides

Cover image taken from the 1615 title page of *The Spanish Tragedy* by Thomas Kyd

Typeset by Fakenham Prepress Solutions, Fakenham, Norfolk NR21 8NN
Printed and bound in India

CONTENTS

SERIES
INTRODUCTION

The drama of Shakespeare and his contemporaries has remained at the very heart of English curricula internationally and the pedagogic needs surrounding this body of literature have grown increasingly complex as more sophisticated resources become available to scholars, tutors and students. This series aims to offer a clear picture of the critical and performative contexts of a range of chosen texts. In addition, each volume furnishes readers with invaluable insights into the landscape of current scholarly research as well as including new pieces of research by leading critics.

This series is designed to respond to the clearly identified needs of scholars, tutors and students for volumes which will bridge the gap between accounts of previous critical developments and performance history and an acquaintance with new research initiatives related to the chosen plays. Thus, our ambition is to offer innovative and challenging guides that will provide practical, accessible and thought-provoking analyses of early modern drama. Each volume is organized according to a progressive reading strategy involving introductory discussion, critical review and cutting-edge scholarly debate. It has been an enormous pleasure to work with so many dedicated scholars of early modern drama and we are sure that this series will encourage you to read 400-year-old play texts with fresh eyes.

Andrew Hiscock and Lisa Hopkins

ACKNOWLEDGEMENTS

The editors would like to extend thanks and praise to the contributors for their efforts and positive responses to feedback. We would also like to express our gratitude to Andrew Hiscock and Lisa Hopkins for approaching us, and for their patience, support and insights during the process. The publishers and copy-editors (especially Aruna Vasudevan) made the book much better than it might have been, for which we are very grateful. Colleagues and students at Northumbria University did the same, by providing helpful suggestions, guidance, perspective and good humour, especially Monika Smialkowska, Megan Holman, Inmaculada Sánchez-García, Pete Newbon, Amanda Patten and Graham Hall.

Adam dedicates this with love to Lars, Mila and Angela, and to Joe, Leon and Katie, whose curiosity about a play with multiple murders, infidelity and a white devil in it provoked some interesting questions and some not always satisfactory answers from their dad before school. Paul thanks his family for their support and love, saving especial gratitude for Liam – for enduring his father's devilry with levels of amusement that only he understands.

Note on text

Early modern spellings and punctuation have been modernized in the text, where required, for clarity and fluency.

NOTES ON CONTRIBUTORS

Jem Bloomfield teaches at the University of Nottingham, UK, having studied at Oxford and Exeter universities. He has published on Webster's production history in a range of centuries and is currently preparing a volume on *The Duchess of Malfi* which uses the play's rich afterlife to call into question our framing of early modern drama's past and present. His other research interests include the canonical debates surrounding Shakespeare and the New Testament, and the dialogue between performance studies and theology.

David Coleman has held academic posts at Nottingham Trent University and at Queen's University Belfast, UK, where he currently works in the Directorate of Academic and Student Affairs. He is the editor of *Region, Religion and English Renaissance Drama* (2013) and the author of *Drama and the Sacraments in Sixteenth-Century England* (2007) and *John Webster, Renaissance Dramatist* (2010).

Paul Frazer is Senior Lecturer in English at Northumbria University, UK. He has published work on Shakespeare's *Henry IV* in *Shakespeare* (2013), Dekker's *Old Fortunatus* in *Philological Quarterly* (2010) and Elizabethan Protestant propaganda in *Region, Religion, and Renaissance Literature* (2013).

Eva Griffith is a seventeenth-century theatre historian, researcher and writer who has published extensively on the Red Bull playhouse. She has written about the Red Bull, its repertoire and its first company of actors, Queen Anna's men, for Richard Dutton's *Oxford Handbook of Early Modern Theatre* and *Huntington Library Quarterly*. Her book about this subject, *A Jacobean Company and Its Playhouse: the Queen's Servants at the Red Bull Theatre c.1605–1619* was published by Cambridge University Press in 2013. She acted as Durham University's AHRC Research Associate on *The Complete Works of James Shirley* (forthcoming from Oxford University Press) and has written on Shirley in England and Ireland for *The Times Literary Supplement* and for Four Courts Press. She is currently researching for a *Times Literary Supplement* article about the scholarship behind the Sam Wanamaker Playhouse built at the Shakespeare's Globe complex.

Adam Hansen is Senior Lecturer in English at Northumbria University, UK. He has published widely on early modern literature, including *Shakespeare and Popular Music* (2010), 'Cities in Late Shakespeare' in *Late Shakespeare, 1608–1613* (2013), 'Shakespeare vs. The BNP' in *Literary Politics* (2013) and 'Marlowe and the Critics' in *Marlowe in Context* (2013). He is co-editor of *Shakespearean Echoes* (2015) and *Litpop: Writing and Popular Music* (2014)

Brett D. Hirsch is ARC Discovery Early Career Research Fellow and Assistant Professor of English and Cultural Studies at the University of Western Australia. He is an editor of the Routledge journal *Shakespeare* and serves on the executive committees of both the Australian and New Zealand Shakespeare Association and the Australasian Association for Digital Humanities. His current projects include a computational study of early modern dramatic style, repertory and genre (with Hugh Craig), an electronic critical edition of *Fair Em* (with Kevin Quarmby) and a monograph study of the editing and publishing of English Renaissance plays since the eighteenth century.

James Hirsh is Professor of English at Georgia State University, USA. He is the author of *The Structure of Shakespearean Scenes* (1981), *Shakespeare and the History of Soliloquies* (which won the 2004 South Atlantic Modern Language Association Book Award) and of articles published in journals such as *Shakespeare Survey*, *Shakespeare Quarterly*, *Shakespeare Newsletter*, *Medieval and Renaissance Drama in England*, *Modern Language Quarterly* and *Papers of the Bibliographical Society of America*. Dr Hirsh is a recipient of the Georgia State University Distinguished Honors Professor Award for teaching excellence.

Christina Luckyj is Professor of English at Dalhousie University in Halifax, Nova Scotia, Canada. She is the author of '*A Moving Rhetoricke:*' *Gender and Silence in Early Modern England* (2002) and '*A Winter's Snake:*' *Dramatic Form in the Tragedies of John Webster* (1989) as well as editor of *The Duchess of Malfi: A Critical Guide* (2011) and the New Mermaids edition of *The White Devil*. She has published many essays on early modern drama and women's writing, including 'Gender, Rhetoric and Performance in *The White Devil*' in *Enacting Gender on the Renaissance Stage*. She is currently completing a monograph entitled *Reasonable Libertie: Early Modern Women Writers and the Politics of the Female Voice 1603–1636*.

TIMELINE

1537: Probable birth year of Paolo Giordano Orsini, later Duke of Brachiano.[1]

1558 (3 October): Orsini wedded to Isabella (daughter of Cosimo de Medici). Between 1560 and 1572, three children are born. A few days after the wedding, Orsini is made Duke of Brachiano by Pope Paul IV.

1557 (February): Birth of Vittoria Accoramboni at Gubbio in the Italian province of Umbria.

1564: Christopher Marlowe born in Canterbury (d. 1593). Shakespeare born in Stratford-Upon-Avon (d. 1616).

1565–7: Arthur Golding's translation of Ovid's *Metamorphoses*.

1572: Ben Jonson born (d. 1637). John Donne born (d. 1631).

1573 (28 June): Marriage of Vittoria Accoramboni to Francesco Peretti, nephew of Cardinal Montalto. The couple settle in Rome, but have no children.

1576 (16 July): The Duchess of Brachiano dies at Cerreto Guidi near Florence, 'probably strangled by her husband',

---

[1]Details of the Accoramboni events have been taken from Gunnar Boklund, *The Sources of The White Devil* (Cambridge, MA: Harvard University Press, 1957).

Paolo Giordano, 'who had made one of his rare visits to the Medici court' (Boklund, 16).

1576: First public theatre built in London, called The Theatre.

1577–80: Francis Drake circumnavigates the globe.

c. 1578–9: John Webster born in London; the son of a wealthy coachmaker, he grows up in St Sepulchre, near Smithfield.

c. 1580: Giordano (Duke Brachiano) makes the acquaintance of Vittoria Accoromboni.

1581 (16 April): Murder of Francesco Peretti. Vittoria and Giordano (Duke Brachiano) are married within two weeks.

1584: Roanoke Colony founded in America by the English – abandoned by 1586.

1585: One version of the events of Vittoria and Brachiano's relationships in 1580–1 is related in *A Letter Lately Written from Rome, by an Italian Gentleman* (translated into English by John Florio). Thomas Kyd's *The Spanish Tragedy* enjoys great success and proves to have a lasting influence.

1587: Execution of Mary Stuart, Queen of Scots.

1588: Defeat of Spanish Armada.

1595: Approximately 15,000 people attend London theatres weekly.

1599: Globe Theatre erected.

1600: London's population c. 200,000. East India Company founded. There are twenty-two printing houses and fifty-four licensed presses in London.

1601: Essex's Rebellion (and execution).

1602: Webster mentioned in the diary of the theatre entrepreneur Philip Henslowe, recording money paid for plays.

1603: Death of Elizabeth I; accession of James VI of Scotland, Mary, Queen of Scots' son, to the English throne as James I.

1604: Hampton Court Conference on religion. Webster writes the Induction to John Marston's *The Malcontent*. *Westward Ho!* by Thomas Dekker and Webster first performed. Elizabeth Cary writes *The Tragedy of Mariam* between 1604 and 1606.

1605: Gunpowder Plot. Webster writes *Northward Ho!* with Dekker. Webster marries Sara Peniall in this year or the next.

1606: The 'Act to Restrain the Abuses of the Players' is passed. Webster's first child, John, is born.

1607: John Smith founds English colony in Jamestown, Virginia, in the New World. Midlands Revolt against dearth.

1609: Earls' Rebellion in Ireland. Ulster Plantation begins.

1610: James I creates ninety baronets. James I imprisons his cousin, Arbella Stuart (to which *The White Devil* alludes at 5.4.36–40), prompting accusations of tyranny.

1611: *Authorized Version* of Bible published.

1612: *The White Devil* first performed (probably in February), at the Red Bull Theatre in Clerkenwell, north of London. Published later in the year. Webster contributes the poem 'To his beloved Friend Master Thomas Heywood' to Thomas Heywood's *Apology for Actors*. Prince Henry dies (6 November).

1613: Webster writes the elegy *A Monumental Column* to commemorate the death of Prince Henry, dedicated to Sir Robert Carr.

1613 (7 March)**:** Thomas Adams preaches sermon titled 'The White Devil, or The Hypocrite Uncased at St Paul's Cross, London' (published in 1614).

1613 (14 September)**:** Death of Sir Thomas Overbury. Overbury was poisoned by the King James's favourite, Sir Robert Carr and his wife Frances Howard.

1613–14: Webster's *The Duchess of Malfi* first performed by King's Men at the Globe and Blackfriars Theatres.

1614: Parliament dissolved and not convened again until 1621.

1615: Webster edits and contributes to a set of descriptions of *Characters* to the sixth edition of Thomas Overbury's bestseller *The Wife* – memorializing its author's murder.

1616: King James sells aristocratic titles to raise funds (again). Ben Jonson publishes *Works*.

1617: Henry Fitzjeffrey publishes *Satyres: and satyricall epigrams*, in which he terms Webster 'crabbed Websterio/The Play-wright, Cart-wright'.

1619?: Webster's *The Devil's Law Case* is first performed by the Queen's Men.

1623: *The Duchess of Malfi* printed by John Waterson. First Folio of Shakespeare's *Works*. *The Devil's Law Case* printed by Augustine Mathewes for John Grismand.

1624: Webster composes *Monuments of Honour*, a lavish and expensive pageant for Sir John Gore on his becoming Lord Mayor of London.

1631: Second edition of *The White Devil* printed by John Norton for Hugh Perry.

1632: Webster dies (cause, circumstances and burial place unknown).

1642: Theatres closed at start of civil war.

c. 1650: Abraham Wright (a royalist clergyman) mentions *The White Devil* in his commonplace book intended for his son's edification, terming it 'an indifferent play', whose lines are 'too much rhyming'.

1651: Samuel Sheppard writes the poem *Epigrams Theological, Philosophical and Romantic*, commenting on 'Vittorio Corombona, that famed whore' and Webster's treatment of her story.

1661: On 2 October, Samuel Pepys attends a production of *The White Devil*. He is not impressed and thinks it 'a very poor play'. On seeing it again two days later, he thinks it even worse.

1665: Third edition of *The White Devil* printed by G. Miller for J. Playfere and William Crooke.

1672: Fourth edition of *The White Devil* printed for William Crooke.

1707: Nahum Tate rewrites *The White Devil* as *Injur'd Love, or, The Cruel Husband*. Vittoria is tempted by Brachiano, but does not betray Camillo and praises Isabella.

1830: Alexander Dyce publishes *The Works of John Webster*, terming *The White Devil* 'a play of extraordinary power'.

1831: George Darley writes letter to Allan Cunningham praising *The White Devil*: 'there are passages [...] almost worthy of the Angel Gabriel'.

1856: Charles Kingsley, the novelist and social reformer, asserts in *Plays and Puritans* that 'The whole story of [*The White Devil*] is one of sin and horror'.

1886: Algernon Swinburne celebrates Webster's 'genius' in *The White Devil*.

1887: George Saintsbury, Regius Professor of Rhetoric and English Literature at Edinburgh University, suggests *The White Devil* indicates 'the punishment of female vice'.

1920: *The White Devil* staged at Cambridge, UK, by the Marlowe Society.

1925: Edith Craig directs the Renaissance Theatre Company's production at the Scala Theatre, London.

1947: Michael Benthall directs *The White Devil* at The Duchess Theatre, London.

1965: Jack Landau directs *The White Devil* at Circle in the Square, New York.

1969: National Theatre production of *The White Devil* at the Old Vic, London, directed by Frank Dunlop with set design by Piero Gherardi.

1976: Michael Lindsay-Hogg directs *The White Devil* at the Old Vic, London, with Glenda Jackson as Vittoria, working from an edition of the text prepared by the dramatist Edward Bond.

1977: Michael Blakemore directs *The White Devil* at the Guthrie Theatre, Minneapolis, US.

1979: Michael Kahn directs *The White Devil* at Saratoga Springs, New York.

1983: John McMurray directs *The White Devil* at Bristol Old Vic, UK.

1991: Philip Prowse directs *The White Devil* at the Olivier Theatre at the National Theatre, London, having staged the play at Glasgow's Citizens Theatre in 1971.

1996: Gale Edwards directs *The White Devil* with the Royal Shakespeare Company at the Swan, Stratford-upon-Avon, the first time a woman directed the play at a major theatre.

1999: Jason Byrne directs *The White Devil* with the Loose Cannon Theatre Company, Dublin.

2000: Philip Franks directs *The White Devil* at the Lyric Theatre, Hammersmith, London.

2014: Maria Aberg directs *The White Devil* for the Royal Shakespeare Company at the Swan, Stratford-upon-Avon, UK.

Introduction

Paul Frazer and Adam Hansen

The making of art is never itself in the past tense.
It is always a formative process, within a
specific present.[1]

The White Devil: Modern tragedy?

Why read *The White Devil* and a collection of essays about it now? Perhaps because you are studying or teaching this provocative and challenging play, with its compelling 'glorious villains' (5.6.268).[2] *The White Devil* is set by several exam boards and universities and this collection is partly intended to help make learning about it even more enjoyable and engaging. This involves focusing on some of the provocations, challenges and concerns that make the play so appealing to students and teachers, as the materials provided by one examining body suggest:

> The title itself is a paradox and […] is assumed to refer to the nature of Vittoria. Is she vicious or virtuous? Magnificent or vulgar? Is she a glamorous courtesan, an anguished moralist, or an impoverished noblewoman on the make? […] This sense of ambiguity, even duplicity, is not confined to Vittoria. It is reflected in every major

character of the play [...] even individual speeches are hard to interpret.[3]

All the contributions assembled here offer their own analyses of the play, exploring the 'peculiar glamour', 'unexpected patterns' and 'moral ambiguity' in its parts or as a whole, or reflecting on what others have done with or said about these things.[4] In this way, this collection is meant to be a valuable resource for both teachers and students in many contexts.

However, that does not mean that analysis necessarily makes the play's paradoxes, challenges and provocations easier to interpret or that the kinds of analyses presented here aim to do nothing more than help you prepare for an exam or essay. On the contrary, sometimes asking questions about a text creates more questions and resolving one particular ambiguity generates others. This is because the play is much more than a set text and also because we are reading – or seeing it – now. As Raymond Williams' epigraph above suggests, and as many of the chapters in this collection prove, what people do with the play in their own 'specific present' makes the play mean new and different things.

Creative reworkings of the play exist in many forms. To some film critics, Webster's worldview and aesthetics informed Mike Hodges' iconic crime thriller set in the north-east of England, *Get Carter* (1971).[5] Quoting liberally from Webster's plays throughout his study of the film, Steve Chibnall explicitly links characters from the film to the malcontents identified by critics of tragedy like Jonathan Dollimore.[6] Chibnall suggests:

> [*Get Carter*'s] most salient ancestry is the dark and violent theatrical tradition of revenge tragedies that begins with Jacobean plays like John Webster's *The White Devil* [...] In Jacobean tragedy, the centre of violence and corruption is generally the court of the city state. *Get Carter* updates this trope by depicting Tyneside as a local state in which venality and the rule of force go largely unchallenged.[7]

Beyond such 'local' resonances, the play also lives on in the ramblings of Francis Mirković in Mathias Enard's epic single-sentence novel *Zone* (2008). A French ex-spy, crypto-fascist and volunteer veteran of the Yugoslav wars, Mirković is 'crossing Italy at full tilt', remembering the conflicts and degradations that have afflicted Europe for aeons, heading to Rome by train with the 'life insurance' that he plans to sell 'to feverish cardinals': a suitcase 'wherein is written the fate of hundreds of men', 'names testimonies secret reports memos', akin to Monticelso's list of 'notorious offenders' (4.1.51) in the play.[8]

The best recent stagings, like the Royal Shakespeare's Company's UK version in 2014, have similarly tried to impress the play's continuing relevance upon audiences: 'Maria Aberg's bold new production [...] illuminates the misogyny coursing through the decadent corridors of the Italian establishment.'[9] Erica Whyman's use of the present continuous tense ('coursing') here invites us to see the production's Italy as a rendering of a near-contemporary Italy, that of Silvio Berlusconi's notorious sex-and-prostitute-fuelled Bunga Bunga parties, papal intrigues, exploitative priests and a notorious drug-smuggling 'white lady'.[10] Stimulating as such gestures are to continuities between past and present, are they also limiting? Webster's Italians spoke English; so did Aberg's. If this play is more than a set text, it is also about more than Italy, past and present, and recognizing this provides another answer to the question: 'why read *The White Devil* now?'

Modern relocations of the play – on stage, in film or in collections like these – can, and perhaps should, have a wide scope, reflecting on Webster's work in its own time and in others. This is why this introduction and contributions to the collection explore both early modern contexts and what it means to study or stage Webster now, or at specific moments after the play was first performed. For early modern authors themselves used 'anatopism' to think about real life places through fictional ones: 'remote locations – in terms of geography, period or myth – were readily understood to represent English society in general, and even specifically London'.[11] In other words, while *The White Devil*'s Italy may have confirmed English stereotypes about conniving continentals, audiences would also have had occasion to reflect on what the play might have been saying about themselves.

'think on what hath former bin' (5.4.20): Reading the past in *The White Devil*

Thus, it is important to recognize that for all of its apparent connections to our present, *The White Devil* is a play that looks obsessively at its own moment of production and the histories buried there. Helen Wilcox explains how the textual culture of 1611 (the year preceding *The White Devil*'s first performance) was 'a remarkable year of textual riches' in which 'readers could have pored over newly published works of magnitude such as [George] Chapman's complete *Iliad* in English verse, [Edmund] Spenser's collected *Works*, Robert Bolton's *Discourse about the State of True Happinesse*, [John] Florio's *Queen Anna's New World of Words*, [John] Speed's *History of Great Britaine*, *Coryat's Crudities* and (among many printed guides to this year) *Savage 1611: A New Almanack and Prognostication*'.[12] We could add to the list to mention the completion of the Authorized King James Bible project and the first known performances of Middleton and Dekker's *The Roaring Girl*, Shakespeare's *The Tempest* and *The Winter's Tale*, Aemelia Lanyer's *Salve Deus Rex Judaeorum* and the first printed poems by John Donne. Webster was a writer who borrowed heavily from his contemporaries: '[m]ore than three fourths' of Webster's writing could be traced to other literary sources, claims R. W. Dent.[13] So several essays in this collection demonstrate that we should not be surprised to find echoes of many other authors within the dialogue of his *The White Devil*.

The title of the play itself was derived from Martin Luther's 1535 *Commentary on the Galatians* ('And no marvail: for Satan himself is transformed an Angel of light', derived from 2 Cor. 11.14), which centres upon the dangers of hypocritical religious behaviour. According to Emma Rhatigan, in coining the image of 'the white devil', Luther 'articulates a paradox whereby good works pursued without an understanding that only Christ can save are actually more dangerous than open sins [...] [I]t is within this paradox that the white devil is born'.[14] Luther's image of the hypocrisy of sinners who delude themselves with vain belief in the value of their 'good works' was echoed by Swiss reformer Pierre Rivet in 1575 and English Protestants like Lancelot Andrews in 1592; it resonated with 'a long-standing association of metaphors of concealment and anti-Catholic polemic stemming out of concerns with the role of visual beauty within the Catholic Church'.[15] Indeed, Annaliese Connolly and Lisa Hopkins extend their reading of *The White Devil*'s preoccupation with the colour white to the Catholic paragon Mary, Queen of Scots and her 'iconography of white mourning'.[16] This suggests that lurking beneath the play's anatopic explorations of Catholic Rome, Venice and Padua is a deep-rooted interest in the memories (and cultures of memory) of English Catholicism.

Despite the Church of England's efforts to separate itself from Roman Catholicism over the course of the century that preceded *The White Devil*'s first performances in 1612, those memories were still radically present in Webster's time. Furthermore, that preoccupation surfaces in noteworthy ways where Webster's play recalls and imitates Shakespeare. For example, Brachiano's Ghost comically fails to haunt Flamineo ('Are you still like some great men / That only walk like shadows up and down / To no end[?]' (5.3.126–8) Flamineo calmly enquires). Here, *The White Devil* remembers and parodies Old Hamlet's purgatorial doom 'for a certain term to walk the night' (1.5.91).[17] And Ophelia's madness certainly reverberates within Cornelia's grief for her murdered son,

Marcello, not least in her forlorn recollection of her grand-mother's grieving song:

> Call for the robin-red-breast and the wren,
> Since o'er shady groves they hover,
> And with leaves and flow'rs do cover
> The friendless bodies of unburied men.
> Call unto his funeral dole
> The ant, the field-mouse, and the mole
> To rear him hillocks that shall keep him warm
> And (when gay tombs are robbed) sustain no harm,
> But keep the wolf from thence that's foe to men,
> For with his nails he'll dig them up again. (5.4.89–98)

These lines suggest that as Old Hamlet – a ghostly 'old mole' (1.5.161) – haunts the younger prince, so Webster remembers the older Shakespeare. Moreover, Webster's imagery of subterranean entities and the allusion to the grave-digging wolf also carry Catholic associations. The White Devil's obsessive return to issues of how the dead should be remembered, and the perils of what look like Catholic performances of commemoration rites, was in dialogue with volatile Jacobean debates about the nature of English mourning at this time.[18] This is important because Catholic practices of commemoration – which involved thinking about the dead as though they still lived, and praying for their deliverance – were being prohibited by the Church of England in these years. The men and women who first experienced The White Devil were being taught to remember their dead in new ways, despite the fact that many of their forbears died in the Catholic faith. So Cornelia's use of the imagery of wolves also chimes with the mythic origins of the play's setting, as the mythological founders of Rome (Romulus and Remus) suckled at the teat of Lupa the she-wolf. Moreover, when Brachiano moans 'How miserable a thing it is to die / 'Mongst women howling' (5.3.37–8), he invokes the origins of Roman religion, and the mourning and commemorative habits of its 'white devils'.

Such thorny issues of Catholic memory and commemoration relate closer to home, too. Webster would return to Cornelia's grave-digging wolf in *The Duchess of Malfi* (1613–14), in Ferdinand's paranoid descent to lycanthropic madness: 'Oh, I'll tell thee; / The wolf shall find her grave, and scrape it up, / Not to devour the corpse, but to discover / The horrid murder' (4.2.298–9).[19] Whatever else these lines might mean, they seem likely to relate to the controversy surrounding James VI/I's commemorative project to exhume and reinter his mother, Mary, Queen of Scots, at Westminster Abbey – an expensive process that was concluded by 8 October 1612, but had been planned since at least January 1605/6 (with approvals and payments recorded for Mary's tomb dated to this time).[20]

The White Devil's first performance (estimated in February 1612) pre-dates Mary's exhumation by around six months, but such was the cost (around £2,000) and controversy of the plans, that Webster could well have been aware of them at the time that he was composing his play. When James had his mother's remains translated to the Tudor burial site (directly facing the sepulchre of Elizabeth I) where they still reside today, he not only performed the kind of elaborate commemoration practice that the Jacobean Church attempted to outlaw, but he very successfully rewrote history by conditioning the memory of his mother in overtly politicized ways: 'the sum allowed for [the mason Cornelius] Cure's fee and the larger number of people involved in the project, suggests that from the outset James intended the monument to be substantially larger than Elizabeth's'.[21] This is yet another instance of what David Coleman and Christina Luckyj's contributions to this critical companion emphasize: *The White Devil*'s engagement with its immediate cultural moment and how this draws repeated emphasis to the darker shades of Jacobean political culture and its conflicting modes of ritualistic memory.

We can also link this Catholic–lupine–mnemonic imagery to the play's various elaborations on Irishness. When (Othello-like) Brachiano jealously accuses Vittoria of deceiving him, he speaks of how, 'Thou hast led me, like an heathen sacrifice, / With music and with fatal yokes of flowers / To my eternal ruin' (4.2.85–7). In the next line, he rages, 'Woman to man / Is either a god or a wolf' and then scorns Vittoria's tears: 'Ye'd furnish all the Irish funerals / With howling, past wild Irish' (93–4).

Elsewhere, when Francisco contemplates revenging his sister Isabella's death, he praises Monticelso's book of knaves as, 'Better than tribute of wolves paid in England', compares the bounty he will offer Lodovico to how 'th'Irish rebels were wont to sell heads' and asserts his readiness to reap vengeance on Brachiano: 'Like the wild Irish I'll ne'er think thee dead / Till I can play at football with thy head' (4.1.71; 79–80; 136–7). His reference to the tribute of wolves evokes more memories connecting Englishness with Catholicism, this time to the Celtic tradition of paying tribute to foreign emissaries with the Irish domestic wolfhound. Irish Chieftain Shane O'Neill bestowed 'a brace of wolfhounds' upon Elizabeth I in 1562, at a time when wolves had been extinct in England, Scotland and Wales for several centuries.[22] Wolves held wider ideological significance with Irish military rebellion, through Celtic mythological figures like Cúchullain (the 'Hound of Ulster') and, according to Luckyj, Elizabeth paid bounties for Irish rebel heads in the years of Irish rebellion.[23] Ever resistant to English control, Irish space was itself associated with lupine wildness. In 1617, for instance, English traveller and writer Fynes Moryson would personify the wild openness of Irish land as comparable to (and populated by) unruly wolves:

> For four vile beasts Ireland has no fence:
> Their bodies lice, their houses rats possess;
> Most wicked priests govern their conscience.
> And ravening wolves do waste their fields no less.[24]

The four unfenced beasts refer to the Irish provinces (Ulster, Munster, Connaught and Leinster) and his allusion to 'wicked priests' could well instance memories of Jesuit priest Father

David Wolfe (1528–78/9), who was instructed to 'visit the chief churches in Ireland; congratulate them, in the pope's name, on their constancy; and urge them to persevere' in their resistance to English persecution, colonization and reform.[25] The wolf images Webster activates, therefore, held complex and multi-layered associations with Catholic memorial cultures of devotion, resistance and rebellion.

When we map these lupine associations onto *The White Devil* and its historical moment, however, we find a surprising connection to the type of erotic discourse that Adam Hansen explores in his essay in this collection. As Flamineo engineers the sexual union of his sister and Brachiano, he warns the Duke not to be 'unwisely amorous', like the 'Irish gamester [gambler] that will play himself naked, and then wage all downward, at hazard', rendering himself 'unable to please a woman' (1.1.37; 29–31). This reckless eroticism encapsulates material links to the overarching black-white imagery of the play, but also to issues of Irishness. For when Zanche talks of sleep and dreaming with Francisco (disguised as Mulinassar the Moor, again in homage to Shakespeare's *Othello*), their flirtations centre once more upon the notion of (lupine) Irish secrecy and concealment:

> [ZANCHE]   Fie, sir! As I told you,
> Methought you lay down by me.
> MULINASSAR   So dreamt I;
> And lest thou shouldst take cold, I covered thee
> With this Irish mantle.   (5.3.228–31)

The mantle was a heavy sheepskin pelt (worn as a cloak and blanket) and was firmly associated in the English imagination with the rebellious Irish. The mantle is an important national emblem of insubordination, referred to by Edmund Spenser's Irenius as 'a fit house for an outlaw, a meet bed for a rebel, and an apt cloak for a thief [...] When it raineth it is his pent-house; when it bloweth it is his tent; when it freezeth it is his tabernacle'.[26] Stephen O'Neill reads important colour symbolism into this scene from the play: 'In this erotic fantasy, blackness is temporarily displaced by the fetishized Irish cloak, an equally potent signifier of alterity and, to the English imagination, a symbol of Gaelic male wildness and female promiscuity.'[27] Webster presents us with a clandestine union of base nakedness, thinly veiled by the material signifier of Irish (Catholic) resistance and subterfuge. At this moment, Webster leads us back to the ambiguous theological coding of his play's title; for Matthew 7.15 warns 'Beware of false prophets, which come to you in sheep's clothing, but inwardly they are ravening wolves', once again confounding any stable association between whiteness and purity in this darkest of tragedies.[28] Time and again, *The White Devil* stretches and blurs memorial boundaries of national, sexual, theological and political agency, presenting variously horrible yet attractive reflections of the histories and cultural memories that dominated its Jacobean moment of production.

The White Devil and 'the present time' (3.2.258)

Webster's interest in the dramatic immediacy of surveillance and spying in his time animates his depiction of a world of espionage and 'intelligencing ears' (3.2.229), where the authorities compile lists of 'notorious offenders / Lurking about the city' (4.1.31–2) in preparation for 'th'bloody audit' (4.1.19). Clearly, though, 'voyeurism' and eavesdropping are as 'pervasive' in our world as in the world of the play.[29] Edward Snowden's revelations have shown us how Western authorities do something similar in the name of protecting us from terrorizing bad guys and from ourselves.[30] However, as Snowden suggests, 'a super-state that has unlimited capacity to apply force with an unlimited ability to know [...] that's a very dangerous combination'.[31] Like Snowden, and many more people, Webster is vexed by what such intelligencing and invasive investigations do to the boundaries between behaviour and morality in 'private' and 'public' contexts (3.1.17–18). How easily, in the 'th'condition of the present time' of our internet age, can an intimate or personal failing become a 'public fault' (3.2. 257–8)? We endure the web and the 'hypermediacy' or multiple versions of reality it creates; Webster's characters suffer intrusive papal power where 'Religion [...] is commeddled with policy' (3.3.35) and where 'a reverend cardinal' tries to 'play the lawyer' (3.2.60–1); Webster's audiences, too, endured the pervasive corruption of the Jacobean court, a place that might make you 'More courteous' but more likely makes you 'more lecherous by far' (1.2.307–8).[32] We are not the first to make these kinds of connections, and they have been obvious to critics of Jacobean drama (and the state we are in) since at least the 1970s:

> In the present-day world, alienated in poverty and affluence, dehumanised by state bureaucracies and military machines, the most urgent study of mankind would seem to be [...] the prospect of survival in the face of impersonal power drives.[33]

How does reading Webster help in that 'survival'? Perhaps by reminding us that someone's private faults are not what causes tragedy:

> Webster does not allow us to telescope the problem of conflict back into the individual – that is, to see social dislocation as solely the responsibility of the hubristic hero/ine possessed by evil, deranged by passion, fatally flawed or whatever.[34]

To put this another way: compelling as Webster's characters are, they are made more so by being shown to exist within (and against) structures and forces that make them act, and make them die, and kill, in the ways they do. One of these structures, of course, is gender. How often those at 'fault' in the play (and now) victimized and targeted because of their gender, and because the way they embody their gender does not conform to the expectations of those around them (virtually and otherwise)? Is what happens to Vittoria a version of early modern 'slut-shaming', that is 'where a girl's [or woman's] reputation can be invoked and scrutinized to discipline her through codes of sexual conduct'?[35] Now, when it can seem as though there is one rule for boys and another for girls, so the play exposes the difference in power between men and women. Dismissing his sister's anguish as 'slight wrongs' (2.1.240), Francisco polices Isabella's body and sexuality in order for her to submit to her husband: 'keep your vow / And take your chamber' (2.1.267–8). Yet this suggests that it is not entirely true that, as Vittoria asserts, 'woman's poor revenge / [...] dwells but in the tongue' (3.2.283–4). This form of revenge can be dismissed as 'but grammatical laments / Feminine arguments' (5.6.66–7), yet power also lies in the body. In turn, the play emphasizes that power is not exclusively men's, as Isabella's 'or' here suggests:

ISABELLA   O that I were a man, or that I had power
             To execute my apprehended wishes (2.1.242–3)

Just as girls and women now respond to such shaming through reclaiming the terms of abuse thrown at them by misogynists (of either gender), so *The White Devil*'s women may be repeatedly disempowered, but they do not go quietly, and recognizing the ways they are disempowered exposes the corrupt and partial motivations of the conniving schemes and rough justice to which they are subjected.

Such are the play's ambiguities, however, that women like Vittoria and Zanche are at times actively involved in such schemes: their participation can be understood as being motivated by the insecurity of being a woman in a man's world. The fact that *both* genders connive suggests that corruption has material motivations: 'there's nothing so holy but money will corrupt and putrify it' (3.3.24). Some try to resist such motivations. The older, outmoded, Cornelia wonders: 'What? Because we are poor, / Shall we be vicious?' (1.2.296–7). Her son responds with the words of someone who knows his generation has lost the gains, security and comforts of those before:

> Pray what means have you
> To keep me from the galleys, or the gallows?
> My father proved himself a gentleman,
> Sold all's land, and like a fortunate fellow
> Died ere the money was spent. (1.2.297–301)

Flamineo's future is either death or dispossession, because obedience and conformity furnishes a servant like him with nothing but a query about 'how shall we find reward [?]' (3.1.46). In the context of such indignation, people start asking awkward questions about privilege and social distinction, just as the *Indignados* did in Spain in the early 2010s:

FRANCISCO What difference is between the Duke and I? No more than between two bricks; all made of one clay. (5.1.103–4)[36]

What is the point of following the 'great': feeding their 'victories' with your 'blood', asks Flamineo, 'What hast got?' Nothing but a 'frail reward' (3.1.36–41). Why, then, defer, serve, submit? The question matters now, as much as then, and informs and alters political debate.

'a politician imitates the devil' (3.3.15): Political critique and *The White Devil*

This is an era – you decide which or when – where politics is up for debate and it is, therefore, fitting that this play insistently repeats the word 'politic' and its cognates. Yet, as with

Shakespeare – think of *Romeo and Juliet*'s 'civil blood makes civil hand unclean' (Prologue 6) – the more a word is used the less it means just one thing; repetition unsettles rather than confirms significance.[37]

Luckyj's chapter in this volume explores some of the early modern contexts for the play's interrogation of politics, but what the play has to say about that speaks to us now, too. As an adjective 'politic' can be applied more specifically by misogynists, to women who increase male desire 'by the difficulty of enjoying' (1.2.20) or as Brachiano condemns Vittoria's 'politic ignorance' when he assumes she plays dumb in concealing further infidelity (4.2.77). However, restraining the power and mobility of women by putting them in 'politic enclosures' makes even more 'rebellion' (1.2.90–1). Moreover, men are themselves 'politic'. Monticelso's list of 'notorious offenders' contains details of 'politic bankrupts' (4.1.51), scoundrels pretending to be penniless so as to evade the attentions of people they owe money. Being 'politic' can mean being cunning, back-stabbing and dangerous, as Flamineo says to Brachiano: 'I would not go before a politic enemy with my back towards him' (4.2.66). Men like Flamineo orchestrate murders 'by [...] politic strain' (2.1.312), just as he conceives that it is the defining feature of 'politicians' never simply to 'kill the effects of injuries', while letting 'the cause live' (5.6.42–4). His murderous, desperate cynicism does not go unchallenged: he is told by own his brother to 'stride over every politic respect', and instead act with decency, to 'bear an honest heart' (3.1.55–6). Being 'politic', however, Flamineo does not heed the lesson, as he resolves later to offer Francisco some 'politic instruction' (5.1.127), and says he will for a time 'appear a politic madman' (3.2.307–8), that is, pretend to be insane for deceitful purposes.

Perhaps Flamineo's words hint at the instability of being 'politic': it is something only a madman would try to be. A madman or a statesman, as Flamineo observes to the Savoy Ambassador when in this disguise: 'a politician imitates the devil' (3.3.15). Behind such figurings lurks the Florentine political theorist Niccolò Machiavelli, someone the dying Brachiano hints at when he terms Francisco 'that politician Florence' (5.3.93). After his death Brachiano is himself damned as 'the famous politician / Whose art was poison' (5.3.152). The meaning of 'politic' shifts and squirms so much it ends up being used ironically, in reverse as it were: the hapless cuckold Camillo is described as having a 'politic face', that is, he looks smart but is not (2.2.35).

Read or seen now, then, *The White Devil* appeals to more than just our despair at or distance from institutional politics, where the bleeding together of powers that should be separate (the state, religion, brutalizing corporations) jeopardizes freedoms and dignity (in Italy, Britain or anywhere else), and where regime change reflects 'politics as the work of death'.[38] Accordingly, the play also evokes for us what Achille Mbembe identified as 'necropolitics', the idea that 'the ultimate expression of sovereignty resides, to a large degree, in the power and the capacity to dictate who may live and who must die'.[39] As Flamineo reflects on Brachiano's death, after so many others, we hear that 'princes', 'have unpeopled towns, divorced friends, and made great houses unhospitable', creating what Mbembe sees in our time as '*death-worlds*'; perhaps it is some 'justice', or some working out of what tragedy is, that such figures die in 'solitariness' (5.3.43–5).[40]

'But this allows my varying of shapes' (4.2.237): Postmodern tragedy?

As this collection shows, *The White Devil* has provoked diverse responses as a tragedy:

> Critical opinion cannot speak with certain or united voice about Webster's purposes; it has proved possible to talk of him as an old-fashioned moralist, as a sensationalist, as a social dramatist, as an imagist or dramatic symphonist, as

a man fascinated by death, or a man halting between his inherited and his individual values.[41]

Some have found hope in the confusion, cynicism and morbidity:

> *The White Devil* may lead us to the edge of despair, but it stimulates enough pride in the depths and capacities of human nature to keep despair from being the obvious or easy course.[42]

We might not share such optimism, but as David Coleman has argued, and as the essays here by Jem Bloomfield, Brett D. Hirsch and Eva Griffith suggest, critics and audiences remake the play in their own image, informed by – even when in contrast to – 'the particular interests of their own historical era', whether that is late Victorian morality or the horrors of the First or Second World War.[43] Surveying critical responses to Webster, Dena Goldberg appreciates that forgetting the ways his 'intellectual disequilibrium can be invigorating' is probably due 'to the growing dread of the future in contemporary society'.[44] As the threats of mass annihilation and environmental disaster have grown post-1945, who can blame people for being unsettled by Webster? When Ian Jack claimed, in 1949, that Webster did not offer a '*balanced* insight into life', he was conscious of how the world had just been horrifically unbalanced, and of the role he thought culture should take in setting things right.[45] Yet, what he disliked in Webster made Webster attractive to others a few years later, as these comments from 1955 indicate:

> many twentieth-century poets have found Webster congenial because they saw in their world a correspondence with the world depicted by the dramatist. Values crumpled in their hands as they had for Webster and his contemporaries three centuries earlier. From the very lack of values there sprang an affinity.[46]

Hereward T. Price made a similar point in that same year:

> [Webster's] sombre rendering of life's terrors provides
> something that our generation can respond to immediately
> and with perfect comprehension.[47]

This reminds us that, as Jonathan Dollimore and Alan Sinfield
note in the introduction to their edition of Webster's plays,
a critic's assertions about Webster all too often 'directs us
as much to the critical assumptions – and eventually the
ideological position – of the critic as they do to Webster's
theatre.' Dollimore and Sinfield have no problem with critics
bringing 'ethical, religious and political beliefs into their
criticism', because it is impossible not to (as *this* introduction
attests); the problem comes when scholars 'have been less than
explicit about their presence', when, in other words, inevitably
subjective and partial views masquerade as total and universal
ones. Such criticism still has its uses, though, if only to prompt
searching questions from others more upfront about their
perspective:

> So, when a critic complains that 'In Webster's work
> the proper relations between the individual and society,
> between God and Man, are overthrown', we might remark
> that this judgement begs the question: what are those
> 'proper relations'?[48]

Where does this leave Webster now? As Coleman suggests,
'eras which prized the concept of absolute truth […] found
Webster puzzling'; 'our own era', however, has 'enthusiastically
adopted' Webster because 'relativism' (the lack of absolute
values) is 'fashionable'.[49] Summing up his own reading of
and approach to *The White Devil*, Stephen Purcell argues
something comparable: 'critics tend to resist the temptation to
come to a definitive conclusion, recognizing instead that as we
reread historical texts through the prisms of our own priorities
and belief systems, we rediscover neglected meanings just

as we reinvent new ones.'[50] Webster's early adopters always
reckoned he would be future-proof, with *The White Devil*'s
characters '[g]azed at as comets by posterity'.[51] Given such
views, must he now adapt to become the poster-boy for
Western postmodern normlessness and moral relativism?

Not necessarily.

In one important recent account of the play, Andrew
Strycharski has asked: 'What is the ethical status of the
pleasures twenty-first century readers might take in such a
morally bankrupt Jacobean tragedy?'[52] Strycharski argues that
'recent scholarship on *The White Devil* has tended to focus
on acute, local questions, whether historical or performed,
rather than the moral questions that previous critics found
imperative.'[53] The play does not offer any '*exemplary* morality
to hang our hat on'; this means there is no single, solid take
on who or what is right or wrong.[54] He concludes: '*The White
Devil* denies the familiar comforts of revenge, instead leaving
shock, groping, confusion.' In an age of apparent moral
relativism, how might we respond in any other way?

Perhaps like this: Strycharski also adds 'pain' to the play's
impact and legacy, suggesting that this pain 'echoes from one
historical horizon to another'; in turn, he suggests that the
ethical questions and responses that might help us understand
and lessen such pain cannot be articulated by 'the individual
outside history', but only by 'community'.[55] In coming to
this conclusion about *The White Devil* and tragedy more
generally, Strycharski builds on a position outlined by Terry
Eagleton:

> In one sense, to be sure, all tragedies are specific: there
> are tragedies of particular peoples and genders, of nations
> and social groups [...] not to speak of those hole-in-the-
> corner calamities of obscure individual lives which lack
> even the dignity of a collective political title. And none
> of these experiences is abstractly exchangeable with the
> others. They have no shared essence, other than the fact
> of suffering. But suffering is a mightily powerful language

to share in common, one in which many diverse life-forms can strike up a dialogue. It is a communality of meaning.[56]

Despite the different approaches and emphases evident in the contributions to this collection, we hope that they too attain some kind of community, if not 'communality', of meaning. The opening three survey chapters encompass a range of scholarly and critical materials, to provide a solid grounding in how *The White Devil* has been understood and performed in the past, and might be in the future. Jem Bloomfield applies a series of lenses to look at *The White Devil*, seeing how perceptions of the play alter as critical principles shift. The narrative of the play's critical reception is interrupted and knotty, and complicated by the play's neglect between the seventeenth and nineteenth century and recurring perceptions of it as abnormal, obscure, dense or even misshapen. Bloomfield's chapter is, therefore, arranged around three 'problems' that have attracted repeated critical attention across the centuries: the problem of Vittoria's guilt, the problem of Webster's skills and the problem of not being Shakespeare. Eva Griffith's history of the play in performance asks: what makes a particular production possible, and successful? Griffith makes performers a focus, especially those involved in the play's earliest productions. From there, we learn how the concerns of succeeding eras were mapped out on stagings of the play. Griffith concludes showing how the play has developed into one fit for exploring gender issues. In his contribution, Brett D. Hirsch surveys twenty-first century scholarship on *The White Devil* in order to identify recurring themes and areas of concentration as well as opportunities for future study. His chapter, therefore, covers: textual studies and editions; race, cosmetics and colour; the law and analogous cases; death and the dumb show; adaptation, source study and style.

Following these surveys, the collection presents four chapters set on stimulating debate about new directions in the study of the play. These are, by definition and design, questioning and provocative. David Coleman's chapter begins by noting that it has long been recognized that Webster's drama displays an interest in ritual and ceremonial form. Coleman suggests, though, that too often it has been assumed that Webster's approach to ritual is what one critic has called 'desecration'; that is, that the dramatist's scepticism towards ritual practice leads to a challenge to its importance, a parody of its structural forms and an evacuation of its meaning. While Webster is sceptical of some effects of ritual, he is nevertheless aware of its impact. Using Freud's notions of the relationships between 'doubling', the 'compulsion to repeat', and the 'Uncanny', Coleman shows how Webster's rituals contribute to the dramatic effects of this play.

In contrast to Coleman's interest in ostensibly Catholic, traditionalist ritual ceremonies, Paul Frazer's chapter explores the Protestant hybridity of *The White Devil*, in relation to how Webster used this play to explore vexed issues of selfhood, subjectivity, and death. Beginning with a reading of the text's Calvinistic representation of sin and reprobation, Frazer focuses attention on the conceit of the 'moving subject', which Calvin appropriated from the writings of St Augustine. Frazer describes how another of Webster's key sources, the *Essays* of Michel de Montaigne, also used this Augustinian model. Frazer argues that understanding how *The White Devil* used these sources can help us comprehend some of the ways in which the Jacobean stage was developing and attempting to reconceive concepts of selfhood and death in unsettling yet didactic ways.

Politicizing the religious angle, Christina Luckyj argues that *The White Devil* mounts an ultra-Protestant critique of monarchical authority. The play counters its own misogynistic rhetoric with a carefully constructed defence of women, illuminating female transgression as a product of masculine economic and social oppression. The figure of Vittoria as a 'famous Venetian Curtizan', moreover, taps into contemporary notions of Venice as a site of political liberty and challenge to popery. The figure of Giovanni, indebted to the chivalric Protestant ideal embodied in Prince Henry, whose death Webster later mourned in print, emphasizes by contrast the debased masculinity in the rest of the play. Linked to both the hyper-Protestant printer Thomas Archer and the rival court of Queen Anne, *The White Devil* activates a rich web of contemporary political allusions.

In his chapter, Adam Hansen asks a seemingly unanswerable question: is *The White Devil* pornography? This question generates some discomfiting answers, and further questions. If *The White Devil*'s Vittoria is a 'whore' (3.2.78), and is punished as such, does this play conform to the etymological roots of pornography, that is, 'writing about prostitutes'? And what happens if we see early modern pornography a way of obsessive reading as much as representation? *The White Devil* depicts voyeurism, speculation and scrutiny, yet the love of looking does not make for loving looks, and the play destabilizes viewers (on- and off-stage).

This introduction began by asking: why read *The White Devil* now? The volume concludes with James Hirsh asking: why and how might we teach it now? Drawing on long experience of the teaching the play (and his own publications about doing so), Hirsh contends that Webster dramatizes the complexities of human experience in ways that make the play challenging. However, complexities matter, and disregarding them might have negative consequences. While also considering individual characters, Webster's artistry and resources for working on the play, this chapter explains and illustrates methods by which a teacher can raise the abilities of students to understand complexity; to 'read between the lines' of a work of literature; and to engage in rigorous empirical analysis.

1

The Critical Backstory

Jem Bloomfield

In 1651, Samuel Sheppard declared that after reading Webster's *The White Devil*, people would no longer bother with the classical tragedies of Euripides and Sophocles.[1] In 1856, Charles Kingsley opined that Vittoria Corombona was exactly the sort of criminal young woman that London magistrates had to deal with every week. In 1989, Dympna Callaghan suggested that Webster's play showed that the entire genre of tragedy was inherently flawed. As these few examples imply, the critical backstory of *The White Devil* is both a dramatic and eccentric one. The play has been subject to a range of critical paradigms and frameworks in the centuries since the first printing of 1612; at different times commentators have valued aesthetic smoothness, moral aptness, conceptual coherence, realism of representation, rounded characters, thematic unity, moral vision, chaotic alienation and ironic distance. Webster's work is likely to be accorded a higher valuation under some of these criteria than others, but it is striking how often *The White Devil* transgresses these canons or resists explanation by them. The play is so very frequently 'wrong', when judged according to a shifting array of aesthetic and moral standards, and critical appreciation of it often takes on the character of apology, explanation or justification. Just as the stage history of Webster's plays is marked by productions which declare themselves as 'revivals', their critical history involves a series of conscious 'recuperations' or 'revaluations'. This does not account for the entire history, but it is frequent enough to feature as a significant factor in any account of that history. Judgements on *The White Devil*, whether positive or negative, are often arranged around an implicit (or explicit) 'but'. Therefore, what follows is not a comprehensive history of what has been said about the play but rather an account of some of the tragedy's most critical 'problematic' focal points. I have directed attention towards the disagreements and complications which form such a part of the play's critical history. This should both provide a more accurate account of how the play has been regarded than a simple account of description and exegesis, and help to avoid (as much as possible) a narrative of how people in the past gradually came to understand the play better as they became more like us. It should also provide the reader with some sense of what has been going on in the generations before they turned up, orienting them in the turmoil whose aftershocks continue to shape the landscape of thought and practice around this play.

Perhaps the first piece of literary criticism we should take into account is by Webster himself, in a bad tempered and defensive epistle to the reader attached to the play's initial printing in 1612. The play's performance at the old-fashioned and open air Red Bull had been a flop for which the author clearly felt justification was necessary, or for which blame should be apportioned. He begins with this declaration:

> In publishing this tragedy, I do but challenge myself that liberty, which other men have taken before me; not that I affect praise by it, for, *nos hæc novimus esse nihil* [we know that these things are nothing] only since it was acted in so dull a time of winter, presented in so open and black a theatre, that it wanted (that which is the only grace and setting-out of a tragedy) a full and understanding auditory.[2]

Webster also staves off several expected criticisms, including the suggestion that he has broken poetic conventions and that his writing practice is overly laborious:

> To those who report I was a long time in finishing this tragedy, I confess I do not write with a goose-quill winged with two feathers; and if they will need make it my fault, I must answer them with that of Euripides to Alcestides, a tragic writer: Alcestides objecting that Euripides had only, in three days composed three verses, whereas himself had written three hundred: Thou tellest truth (quoth he), but here's the difference, thine shall only be read for three days, whereas mine shall continue for three ages.[3]

Whether or not we accept the goose quill (or its absence) as a valid standard of canonicity, we can recognize Webster's preface as an attempt to control the criteria by which his work has been judged. As Zachary Lesser and Douglas Brooks have demonstrated, this authorial passage before the main text was part of an attempt within in the early modern book trade to create a category of 'literary playbooks'.[4] These volumes frame their contents in terms of aesthetic value and the appreciation of a discriminating readership, defining themselves apart from – and in some cases in direct opposition to – the theatrical popularity which was cited proudly on other title pages. Webster's epistle makes an effort to involve the reader in a narrative of cultured judgement, retrospectively relocating his play from the Red Bull theatre to the more exclusive Blackfriars or even to the imagined library of the book buyer. In presenting a standard by which to evaluate his play, Webster tacitly gives the reader a standard to live up to. His classical references offer them a literary game to play if they will accept the legitimacy of his work.

Despite the paucity of formal literary criticism in the seventeenth century, Webster's epistle appears to have succeeded in at least one case. In 1651, Samuel Sheppard included a commendatory poem on *The White Devil* in his *Epigrams Theological, Philosophical and Romantic*:

> We will no more admire Euripides,
> Nor praise the tragic strains of Sophocles;
> For why? Thou in this tragedy hast framed
> All real worth that can in them be named.
> How lively are thy persons fitted, and
> How pretty are thy lines! Thy verses stand
> Like unto precious jewels set in gold
> And grace thy fluent prose. I once was told
> By one well skilled in Arts he thought thy play
> Was only worthy fame to bear away
> From all before it. Brachiano's ill –
> Murdering his Duchess hath by thy rare skill
> Made him renowned, Flamineo such another –
> The Devil's darling, murderer of his brother.
> His part – most strange! – given him to act by thee
> Doth gain him credit and not calumny.
> Vittoria Corombona, that famed whore,
> Desperate Lodovico weltering in his gore,
> Subtle Fransisco – all of them shall be
> Gazed at as comets by posterity.
> And thou meantime with never-withering bays
> Shall crowned be by all that read thy lays.[5]

Sheppard's references to classical tragedians praise Webster by accepting his self-description as their equal, in the preface to *The White Devil*. Indeed Sheppard goes one step further, using the familiar metaphor of the 'never-withering bays' to imagine art as a transhistorical competition, in which Webster has surpassed his exemplars. The rather bland hearsay opinion of 'one well skilled in Arts' chimes with the epistle's stress on individual judgement by properly qualified readers, rather than appealing to popularity or the general voice. Sheppard also introduces a couple of themes which were significant in the play's ensuing critical reception:

the unusual construction of Webster's dramaturgy, and the sexual culpability (or otherwise) of Vittoria. In the rest of this chapter, I will use these themes to organize my discussion of *The White Devil*'s critical backstory and also add another from Webster's own epistle: his perennial comparison with Shakespeare.

The problem of Vittoria's guilt

Over the centuries Vittoria's character and, in particular, her culpability, have provided a problem around which commentary and criticism have gathered. It is not simply that she is a powerful central figure who commits morally wrong acts – though this has, in itself, been enough to provoke anxious and elaborate commentaries – but also that the play seems to ascribe fluctuating characteristics to her. In some scenes, Vittoria appears both devious and calculating and yet, in others, she speaks with apparent sincerity and integrity. Arguments about Vittoria's character are, thus, often concerned with questions of moral blame and justification, as well as with the theatre's ability to represent the world in accurate and realistic ways.

Sheppard's poem dismisses the titular character of the tragedy, referring misogynistically to 'Vittoria Corombona, that famed whore'; it reflects the later critical tendency to reduce the role's complexity to her sexual transgressions. We should perhaps read 'famed' not solely as a reference to her public shaming within the play or the notoriety of the historical Vittoria Corombona, but also as a natural complement to 'whore'. Early modern concerns around women's sexualities and their proper place in the social order come together in assumptions about the unchastity of women who are 'public' in some sense. To be spoken of too much, on whatever basis, is to attract suspicion (hence the paradox of women famous for their private virtues), and Sheppard's phrase performs the easy slip between meanings: Vittoria is not only 'famed' for being a 'whore', she is also a 'whore' because of her 'fame'.

No sustained discussions of the play have survived between the mid-seventeenth and early nineteenth centuries. However, when it then reappears in critical commentary, Vittoria's conduct and character are once again a significant factor. William Hazlitt gives a remarkable and impressionistic description in *Lectures Chiefly on the Dramatic Literature of the Age of Elizabeth* (1820):

> the insulted and persecuted Vittoria darts killing scorn and pernicious beauty at her enemies. This White Devil (as she is called) is made as fair as the leprosy, dazzling as the lightning. She is dressed like a bride in her wrongs and her revenge.[6]

Hazlitt seems to admit her guilt while also feeling that the audience should (or does) side with her. Violence and disease are made beautiful, and even justified by the greater evil of those around her: she is 'persecuted' and magnificent.

By the time Hazlitt described this 'killing scorn and pernicious beauty', Charles Lamb had already, in 1808, introduced a phrase into criticism of *The White Devil* which would serve as touchstone and stimulus for subsequent commentators:

> This White Devil of Italy sets off a bad cause so speciously, and pleads with such an innocence-resembling boldness, that we seem to see that matchless beauty of her face which inspires such gay confidence into her, and are ready to expect, when she has done her pleadings, that her very judges and her accusers, the grave ambassadors who sit as spectators, and all the court, will rise and make proffer to defend her in spite of the utmost conviction of her guilt.[7]

That 'innocence-resembling boldness' clearly distinguishes between the guilt that the audience is aware of (because they witnessed her crimes) and the character's demeanour within the trial scene. Though Lamb seems to intend a tribute to Webster's characterization here, his emphasis on the admiration provoked in the onstage audience (the judges and ambassadors) towards the guilty women (Vittoria and Zanche) seems to have unsettled some other critics, as we shall see below. Lamb's description taps into the concerns around the possibility of male knowledge of women's motives, and the necessity of justice being performed publicly. In suggesting that the off-stage audience, or even the reader, might find themselves equally taken in by this 'matchless beauty' and skilful pleading, Lamb implies there was something in the play which troubled the operations of moral and theatrical judgement – all without implying that Vittoria was innocent in any sense.

The Reverend Alexander Dyce is similarly enthusiastic in his praise of Webster's character-drawing when he discusses Vittoria in his 1859 edition of Webster's *Works*:

> What genius was required to conceive, what skills to embody, so forcible, so various, and so consistent a character as Vittoria! We shall not easily find, in the whole range of our ancient drama, a more effective scene than that in which she is arraigned for the murder of her husband.[8]

Having praised the skill with which the dramatist held together the variety of the central figure with such consistency, Dyce goes on to differ from Lamb's assessment. Where Lamb thought her 'boldness' resembled innocence, Dyce suggests that Webster has written the character to demonstrate the 'forced and practised presence of mind' typical of a 'hardened offender'.[9] He insists that there is a difference between the 'simple confidence' which 'the innocent manifest under the imputation of a great crime' and the way Vittoria appears at her trial. For him, Vittoria 'surprises by the readiness of her replies', but never produces 'any words which were likely to have fallen from an innocent person'.[10] Her 'high-wrought and exaggerated boldness' has 'none of the calmness which belongs to one who knows that a plain tale can put down his adversary', and instead seeks to 'act the martyr though convicted as a criminal'.[11]

The drift of his argument essentially seeks to rescue Webster's moral quality via the supposed realism of his characterization and dialogue. (It is worth noting that these are not aspects of Webster's work which the critical tradition has generally applauded as 'realistic'.) *The White Devil* is not an immoral play, but one which explores individuals' immoralities. The contrasting perceptions evident in Hazlitt's and Lamb's responses are firmly banished and Dyce argues that our moral sympathies are not overthrown if enough attention is paid to the particular texture of the writing. The doubt which had been cast on truth's ability to sustain its distinctive quality through the confusions of theatrical representation is banished by reference to Webster's skill and the audience's capacity to discriminate. In contrast, that same emphasis on Webster's supposed realism was used by Charles Kingsley to condemn the play in 1856. Discussing the same 'confest master-scene', he declares that Lamb's belief in the 'innocence-resembling boldness' was a result of that critic's knowledge of 'the world from books, and human nature principally from his own loving and gentle heart'. For those more familiar with the 'real world' and its vices, 'the knowledge of character shown in Vittoria's trial scene is not an insight into Vittoria's essential heart and brain, but a general acquaintance with the conduct of all bold bad women when brought to bay'.[12] He calls the depiction 'perfectly just and true, not of Vittoria merely, but of the average bad young woman in the presence of a police magistrate' and suggests that this simply proves the lack of benefit to be gleaned from Webster's art, whose flair 'lies simply in intimate acquaintance with vicious nature in general'.[13] Though disagreeing with Lamb about what sinners look like under questioning, Kingsley takes a different route out of the dilemma to Dyce. For Kingsley, Webster is realistic, but morally vacuous, depicting Vittoria accurately as a corrupt woman without producing any wise or tragic insight. For Dyce, Webster is realistic in showing how a guilty person in Vittoria's situation would act and thus allows us to discriminate between true innocence and guilty bluster. In both cases, however, these authors reassert the theatre's ability to represent wickedness without involving the audience in it, and we are assured that audiences can tell good from evil in the great drama of the British tradition.

At the cusp of the twentieth century, Algernon Swinburne also wrestled with these issues of innocence and guilt on the grounds of realism, suggesting, in 1886, that Webster's portrayal of Vittoria was likely to have been influenced by the trial of Mary, Queen of Scots and her 'shallow and fiery nature', in which 'ambition, self-interest, passion, remorse and hardihood' are only connected by an 'indomitable courage'.[14] He 'hesitate[s] to agree' with Dyce's verdict that 'he had never once made his accused heroine speak in the natural key of innocence unjustly impeached'.[15] When Rupert Brooke surveyed the scene in 1917, he redirected the debate by denying the relevance of innocence in the play:

> The trial scene is prodigiously spirited. There is no hero to enlist our sympathy; it is merely a contest between various unquenchable wickednesses. The rattle of rapid question and answer, sharp with bitterness, is like musketry. Vittoria is wicked; but her enemies are wicked and mean. So one sides with her, and even admires. Her spirit of ceaseless resistance and fury, like the wriggling of a trapped cat, is astonishing.[16]

Where Dyce, Lamb and Kingsley seem concerned with whether Vittoria might persuade the audience to side with her despite her guilt, Brooke revels in the possibility. He and the play's earlier critic Hazlitt both value her vitality and energy over the moral impact these might have in the production of the play. Neither, unlike many later critics, seems much interested in the prospect of Vittoria's guilt providing a moral critique of the society around her.

The mid-twentieth century offered a pair of attitudes which contrast with this instructively. In 1951, Clifford Leech recalled the older moral criticism: 'The impression we are left with is of beauty, adroitness, a brave spirit, but Webster would not have us forget that she is the devil of the play's title'.[17] However, Roma Gill's 1966 study directly addressed this judgement, asserting that Leech had 'succumbed to the ever-present temptation to fit Vittoria into a recognizable pattern'.[18] The simple moral contrasts provided by reading her as an 'admirable adultress', who shows that 'beauty is not inevitably accompanied by virtue and that one may praise and condemn the same person for different qualities in turn',[19] are too straightforward in her view. Gill stresses the dislocation of the 'different angles' from which 'Webster photographs' the character, 'leaving it to the boy-player to create the whole being from these partial views'.[20] That whole being, when recognized, is 'one of the "new women" on the English stage', breaking away from the Elizabethan ideal of the silent woman (which 'seems to have died with Cordelia') and presenting instead 'a creature of suffragette eloquence who suffers [...] agonies of sexual and social ambition'.[21] 'When such a being comes on stage', she declares, 'she brings with her all the ambiguity of response that men can give to a woman whose head is as strong as her heart.'[22] Gill admits that this reading 'owes more to post-Freudian psychology than to Jacobean writings on the passions', yet insists it is the only way of reconciling the angles the play shows of her.[23]

The political framing of Vittoria's 'character' was extended by M. C. Bradbrook's 1980 assertion that: 'The rôle of a woman, even when, like Vittoria, she initiates so much of the action, is one of frustration in each of her five scenes.'[24] The action of the trial scene means that the 'comparison of the defined "Character" of a Whore with that of a Wife, of the Bad Woman with the Good Woman, is exploded', but after these dichotomies have been collapsed 'Vittoria can be found neither innocent nor guilty'.[25] Her rhetorical and moral force is displayed in the 'power to transform the Cardinal's trial of her into her trial of the Cardinal', but 'this is not the reward of innocence but of courage'.[26] Ultimately, for Bradbrook, Vittoria's revolt against the social order, which seeks to define and constrain her, is powerful – and has broader political implications – in its disruption of the categories it places around her:

> Prisoners may gain ascendancy over their jailors, and Vittoria demonstrates the disgraceful political rôle of a corrupt Church, leaving a sceptical gap that is to be unresolved even in the final scene.[27]

Gill's interest in the social location of Vittoria's role, and Bradbrook's reading of it as a critique of social oppression, are themes picked up in Jonathan Dollimore's *Radical Tragedy*.[28] Dollimore demonstrated a similar concern with the defining power of social and moral languages: Vittoria is caught in a 'society in which women are subordinate to men', but in which men who are not confident in their power 'require that women acquiesce'.[29] Resisting this requires using 'the language of the dominant' in order to fight against the way that language can 'confer identity on the subordinate' – hence Vittoria claims 'masculine virtue' which can 'only go so far' since it involves accepting, or at least employing, the categories constructed by male power.[30] In Dollimore's analysis, the play 'does not idealise Vittoria', and even 'alienates our sympathy for her', but 'if it does not invite sympathy it invites even less judgement', particularly judgement which 'forecloses the play by relegating problematic figures like Vittoria and Flamineo to the realm of the morally defective'.[31] Dollimore's account of *The White Devil* sketches out the pressures which society exerts on Vittoria, though he does not go as far as the next critic in reading the play as a radical critique of that society.

Dympna Callaghan's *Women and Gender in Renaissance Tragedy* (1989) locates the 'problem' of Vittoria as central to the entire play, and indeed more broadly to tragedy as a genre.[32] She shares Catherine Belsey's sense of gender and subjectivity as *the* critical lenses through which tragedy should be understood – an approach which Belsey harnessed in her earlier *The Subject of Tragedy*.[33] The questions of 'structural coherence' and 'moral vision' which previous critics had posed when discussing Webster's work should not be seen as proof that the playwright could not handle his material effectively, or was ineffective in writing a good tragedy. Rather, that apparently confused construction and blurred moral vision are 'a demonstration of certain flaws in the critical construction of tragedy' itself.[34] Callaghan finds in Webster's female protagonists a force which 'decentr[es] the tragic hero' and 'destabilizes the tragic paradigm as it has been constructed in criticism from fatal flaw to tragic catastrophe, and, finally, to apotheosis'.[35] This decentring of the tragic drama universe goes alongside a 'radical discontinuity' in the female protagonist, 'at times displaying a degree of sexual autonomy and at others utterly idealised'.[36]

Female characters 'oscillate uneasily between their functions as objects of uncertainty and embodiments of perfect truth', and 'even the almost irredeemable Vittoria shifts being from the wanton adulteress to the stoic victim'.[37] In her discussion of the trial scene, Callaghan sees Vittoria 'tak[ing] up contradictory subject positions', as both '(phallic) speaker, and [...] the ravished woman'.[38] Her intrusion into the 'public, male sphere' of language puts her in a 'double bind' in a system in which women's 'loquacity and lasciviousness are equated', and thus she is 'damned by every word she utters'.[39] For Callaghan, the question of Vittoria's guilt opens out the inconsistency of her character; this, in turn, calls into question the assumptions about subjectivity, gender and the self which underpin traditional understandings of tragedy. When an entire vision of the world has been based on the perspective of only one gender, other people's actions may appear inconsistent or even inexplicable. Vittoria is one of the figures to produce a breach in tragedy's presentation of the world, revealing it to be sustained by gendered ideologies. In Callaghan's analysis, the 'problem' of Vittoria is in fact a problem with the realities that Vittoria embodies and reflects.

Ann Rosalind Jones's 1991 reading of Vittoria locates her inconsistency or incomprehensibility in the social discourses of the early modern era, reading her in terms of ethnic and nationalistic rhetoric as well as gender concerns.[40] In her account, 'if Vittoria comes across as "less" (or indeed more) than a "natural woman", it is because she "distils English fantasies of Italianate excesses into an unstable personification of Venetian vice and allure".[41] Vittoria's characterization is, thus, a result of the 'psychic contradiction' which is 'maintained in a constant state of play by the political and sexual systems of representation'.[42] Brachiano's rhetorical attack on Vittoria also locates her as the 'target for a simpler xenophobic discourse' as 'she is associated with the uncivilized behaviour of the Irish'. Sketched as at once too sophisticated and too barbarous, Vittoria is attacked via 'two available though contradictory vocabularies of contempt', namely 'misogyny's suspicion of feminine insincerity and English disdain for the unbridled emotionality of the Irish'.[43]

Thus, the 'problem' of Vittoria reveals a great deal about the ways in which critics have engaged with the play via its central figure. It shows a series of contrasting readings of the character, which throw light back onto the presuppositions and paradigms being employed by critics, displaying not only assumptions about sexual morality and theatrical performance, but about the purpose of drama and criticism. Some justify Webster by condemning Vittoria, some seek to justify both, some justify her by condemning him, and some want to pull the whole world down around Vittoria's ears.

The problem of Webster's skill

Exploring the critical controversy over Vittoria's guilt leads to the issue of *The White Devil*'s dramatic and aesthetic coherence. Several of the critics discussed above are also concerned with Webster's skill in depicting the world. A great deal of critical commentary has started from the perception that *The White Devil*'s construction and artistry is unusual, whether that commentary is engaged in condemning it, singling out passages which rise above their surroundings, or justifying the whole play by offering a framework within which it makes more sense. When, in the seventeenth century, Sheppard referred to the verse passages of *The White Devil* as 'precious jewels' set into the 'gold' of the prose, he praised an aesthetic coherence which few subsequent critics have echoed. Later traditions have been more attracted to the 'problems' posed by the strange dramaturgical textures of the play.

To paint with very broad strokes, this appears to have been caused by two major forces across the centuries. We might first consider the inevitable shifting of aesthetic principles and assumptions, which made Webster appear deeply dysfunctional at times and more satisfying at others. This includes assumptions about what early modern drama was and should be used for: valuing *The White Devil* as a series of poetic passages for reading produces a different perspective from viewing it as a practical performance score, and will inevitably result in a different evaluation of its worth and success. Secondly, the growing dominance of Shakespeare as a paradigm for drama, and literature, in general, established a set of criteria for artistic value within which Webster could never comfortably reside. The more Shakespeare became the standard against which all art was expected to be measured, the more Webster's artistry would look like a 'problem' to be dissected or explained away. (This, however, enables writers such as Swinburne to frame their appreciation for Webster as part of an oppositional attitude towards the dominant culture represented by Shakespeare.)

Such reliance on Shakespeare as an exemplar of how drama should be written is evident in the writing of John Wilson, in 1818. Wilson produced a near definitive statement of one position on Webster in *Blackwood's*, when he held the dramatist up as the exemplar of all that was wrong with

non-Shakespearean early modern drama. Here, he admires
Webster's power and invention, but finds it only in isolated
moments: 'some single scenes are to be found in his works
inferior in power of passion to nothing in the whole range
of the drama' but they are spoiled by 'incompleteness and
imperfection'.[44] *The White Devil* in particular is identified as
'so disjointed in its action', with 'incidents [that] are so capri-
cious and so involved' and 'such a mixture of the horrible
and the absurd, the comic and the tragic – the pathetic and
the ludicrous'.[45] Wilson finds that this inconsistency prevents
the audience from being drawn into the correct forms of
sympathy and moral response, leaving the play as shocking
and impressive at times, but lacking the structure which would
develop an edifying and tragic experience. His critique is no
doubt undertaken as a reaction against the enthusiasm for the
'old dramatists', and a vindication of the supposedly unique
qualities of Shakespeare in the face of it.

Towards the end of the nineteenth century, J. A. Symonds's
1888 edition of Webster and Tourneur offered measured
praise of the dramatists' craft, identifying what was powerful
and effective, while acknowledging a range of problems.[46]
Part of the lack of appreciation of Webster, he suggests, had
been caused by the 'condensation of thought and compression
of language' which 'offer considerable difficulties to readers
who approach them for the first time'.[47] Webster's major
tragedies present 'many fantastic incidents' all 'crowded into
a single action', along with dialogue 'burdened with so much
profoundly studied matter', that the effect is blurry, though
powerful.[48] The reader is likely to come away with 'a deep
sense of the poet's power and personality, an ineffaceable
recollection of one or two resplendent scenes, and a clear
conception of the leading characters', but 'the outlines of the
fable, the structure of the drama as a complete work of art'
will be elusive.[49] Symonds's image of the plays as 'a mosaic'
of brilliant and sensational effects on 'a murky background'
contributes to the strain of criticism which sees Webster as a
considerable but disjointed talent. The reader who perseveres

past the initial problem will find that Webster 'treats terrible and striking subjects with a concentrated vigour special to his genius'.[50] Having assumed that those buying his edition would automatically be concerned with Webster's poetic qualities (an assumption that fits with the previous century's consumption of the early modern dramatists), Symonds foreshadows later critical developments with a speculation which tempers some of the problems with this brilliant 'mosaic': 'It is probable that able representation upon the public stage of an Elizabethan theatre gave them the coherence, the animation and the movement which a chamber-student misses'.[51] Though Symonds might find *The White Devil* blurred and murky, he suggests that the play might have been more clear and focused in its original performance context.

As the nineteenth-century revival of the 'old English dramatists' develops into the twentieth-century enthusiasm for 'the Elizabethan', commentary on Webster increasingly locates him in the past, whether in positive or negative terms. It might be helpful to characterize the shift in this period as one from antiquarianism to historicism. Antiquarian attitudes involved selecting small sections of his works to be regarded as intriguing but isolated poetic artefacts. Historicist approaches sought to understand those works more thoroughly via considering them within the period in which they originated. F. L. Lucas insisted, in 1927, that understanding Webster is only possible through appreciating the conditions and mentalities of his audiences.[52] The reader who does not 'look at his tragedies as his audience saw them – less as whole than a series of great situations' will consistently 'under-rate his stage-craft', and condemn it by its lack of a 'close-knit logical unity'.[53] Instead, Lucas insists that Elizabethan audiences 'lived […] far more in the moment for the moment's sake than the cultured classes of today' and thus desired 'a succession of great moments […] great situations, ablaze with passion and poetry'.[54] They would not, argues Lucas, have understood the 'chilly sort of pedantry' that 'peered too closely into the machinery' of the drama.[55] The middle-class and mid-century self-consciousness, which this account displays, comes into focus with Lucas's suggestion that Elizabethan audiences were 'in fact, very like a modern cinema-audience, with the vast difference that they also had an appetite for poetry'.[56] Though Webster worked 'predominantly in scenes', with material that is 'often childishly irrelevant' and characters who can be 'wildly inconsistent', Lucas holds that the dramatist's work is 'more than a mere chaos of dramatic fragments', since it comes from 'a highly successful playwright in his own Gothic style'.[57] The impulse to reconstruct the mental and moral world of Webster's contemporaries shares much with E. M. W. Tillyard's attempt to reveal *The Elizabethan World Picture* in the 1940s, though Lucas is concerned less with entire organizing systems of metaphor and more with the imagined conditions of theatrical production.[58]

By contrast, in 1936, Una Ellis-Fermor argued that Webster's dramaturgy could be recognized as that of 'a good theatre-man', without recourse to an entirely different ethos and audience mentality.[59] Rather than being inconsistent, the variation in tone 'leaves his producer free to unbrace the tension of the audience's mood here or there', which Webster provides by grim humour and emotional shifts.[60] The 'variations of mood, tempo and force' preserve the 'elasticity of the emotions' and the interjection of poetic elements into a more prosaic section provides 'the imaginative relief of [...] poetic imagery, the momentary escape into the world called up by the images'.[61] However, this imagery is 'interwoven with the concept of the play' to such an extent that 'it is impossible to isolate passages without losing that essential part of their effect which they draw from their dependence upon the whole preceding drama'.[62] This must be a deliberate reaction against the anthologizing and selective approach of nineteenth-century appreciation, as Ellis-Fermor insists that it is the 'range and interplay of mood, thought and imagery' in the poetic passages which 'gives them their richness and their variety' as well as 'that impression of width and universality which is an essential of great tragedy'.[63] For her, Webster's control of tempo and rhythm are not confined to a distant past or an archaic mentality, but could be admired by the practical producers of the contemporary theatre.

In the 1960s, Roma Gill had accepted the long-standing orthodoxy on Webster as incoherent and patchy, ('the tragedy is disjointed and seems to have been written in episodes, not as a whole') while accounting for it in terms of the theatrical culture of the time.[64] She describes Webster as 'possessed of the dangerous tendency to focus his attention on the smaller unit instead of, and sometimes at the expense of, the larger'.[65] She discusses his extensive borrowings as evidence that he wrote with a commonplace book to hand, exacerbating this tendency to concentrate 'on the single image or line instead of the speech' and risking that 'without strong emotional pressure to fuse them into a new whole the separate particles will remains distinct'. However, Gill moves on from this image of a lone authorial figure amidst his obscure books, to a parallel suggestion which locates his work more in the theatre industry, blaming 'Webster's early experience as a collaborator' which 'encouraged a natural weakness'. Having been 'the junior partner writing single scenes at the instruction of a more experienced colleague' would have stunted his ability to 'take responsibility for the total structure', meaning that critics can 'use his inexperience as a dramatic architect as one excuse for the rickety scaffolding, forever needing to be propped up with the first thing that comes to hand'.[66] Thus, Gill perpetuated both the older opinion that *The White Devil* was composed of individually excellent moments within an incoherent structure, and the critical evaluation that this was proof of a failed attempt in mainstream dramaturgy, while seeking to excuse it in more historicist terms which emphasized Webster's place in a theatrical (rather than literary) process.

In the early 1970s, Ralph Berry argued that much criticism of Webster's work had originated in two impulses: neo-classicism, which assumes that all early modern drama should conform to the model of Jonson; or in a 'distrust [of] the violence, the emotional excess, the philosophical doubt of the early seventeenth century' that regards these elements as evidence of a decline (moral and aesthetic) from the era of Shakespeare.[67] Berry, instead, proposes to read the playwright 'within the mainstream of the arts, in Europe' in his period, and to frame Webster as a baroque poet.[68] Placing Webster within this context, Berry argues that the dynamic quality of painting requires the use of dramatic vocabulary in this era and that the vocabulary of visual arts may elucidate the drama in turn. The central concept he borrows is that of 'movement', both in terms of emotional impact and of physical motion; and he compares the characteristic mode of early modern drama with the Catholic mass of the same era: a multisensory, overpowering spectacle intended to surround, involve and convince those present, both 'seeking [...] urgently to convince the spectator of the reality' presented.[69]

This baroque aesthetic is also the key to appreciating another apparent inconsistency in Webster's play: that he 'aggressively asserts the problematic nature of 'character'.[70] With a striking proviso, Berry claims that nowhere in early modern drama can one 'find behaviour that oscillates so wildly, evidence that appears so contradictory, "final" statements that are so disturbingly provisional', except for in 'the realms of hack dramaturgy'. The 'portraiture' of Webster's work 'is, and is meant to be, blurred', demonstrating his 'profoundly baroque appreciation of the indefinability of the human essence'. Evidence of this baroque quality can be found in the aspects of *The White Devil* which have caused past critics to dismiss or question the author's achievement: 'intense emotionality; extravagance of language and behaviour, bordering on the bizarre; a fascination with the intricacies of the human mind; a profound sense that man lives in a context of time, and death'.[71]

In 1980, M. C. Bradbrook's *John Webster: Citizen and Dramatist* continued the line of aesthetic appreciation via comparison with other arts, but was critical of the 'comparisons' with Italian mannerist or baroque painting on the grounds that 'Webster would not have known these paintings and he certainly could not have relied on any mutual appreciation to establish their conventions with his audience'.[72] She finds Webster's artistic judgement 'distinctly provincial' and argues for the English baroque of Inigo Jones, and 'the movement and perspectives of his masques', as the defining context for understanding his works.[73] Though she obviously differs from Berry on the scope and form of the baroque context, she also relies for her analysis on a highly metaphorical application of terms across art forms. The articulation of a 'character divided within itself, playing a double game', such as Flamineo, is only possible within the conditions of the new indoor theatres, where 'intimacy and concentration' are possible, 'so that gradually, through many contradictions and inner divisions, by the finer touches of modelling' the coherence and integrity of the character can be revealed.[74] Having referred to the material conditions of the theatre, and how they differ from those available to previous drama, Bradbrook states that the 'development by gradual revelation, within the character itself, closely resembles the actual scenic development of the masque under Inigo Jones'.[75] The concepts of revelations, angles and contrasts exist in this account both as physical actions within the world of stage fixtures and furniture, and as metaphors inhabited by the actor (or perhaps cognitive processes carried out by the audience). 'The unfolding of character, and the disjunctive movement of his plot', which (as we have seen) earlier critics regarded as 'Webster's weaknesses' provide the actor with 'the equivalent of Inigo Jones' carpentry', with which, perhaps, Webster, 'the coach-maker's son', had 'some sympathy'.[76] Thus, the context of Webster's familial profession is used to construct guiding metaphors to understand its unusual dramaturgy.

At the other end of the decade, in 1989, Christina Luckyj was equally concerned with the way Webster's dramatic construction shared elements with the work of his contemporaries, but she moved away from the material metaphors to focus on issues of repetition and rhythm. She stresses the way in which criticism through the eighteenth, nineteenth and into the twentieth centuries understood dramatic construction in terms of 'conventional expectations of cause-effect, linear plot development, typical of classical drama', and how more recent work has identified the analogical and repetitive features of early modern drama.[77] Dramatists 'selected events which would mirror or contrast with other events, repeating and varying their material, as did the rhetoricians'; rather than producing a 'linear, causally connected narrative proceeding logically like a lawyer's brief from point to point' they 'built a broadly analogical framework for the action'.[78] The repetition connected disparate elements and events while stressing and developing the central movement of the drama as the play's 'central experience' is 'explored and intensified'.[79] Luckyj emphasizes that these strategies of construction are closely connected to the imperatives of theatrical performance, and that 'broad rhythms of repetition' are more likely to be 'grasped – consciously or unconsciously – by an audience in the theatre' than 'elaborate verbal echoes or image links'.[80] For this reason, she draws on reviews and records of modern performance, situating her work here within the stage-centred criticism of the late twentieth century, at a point between the major works of J. L. Styan in the 1970s and the opening of Shakespeare's Globe in the 1990s. In identifying and handling repetition, she distinguishes a series of different ways in which it can operate, including 'parallel, contrast, intensification, recapitulation and reversal'.[81] Luckyj comes to argue that *The White Devil* moves (like Webster's other works) in a coherent development from 'a series of brief ominous episodes, interrelated through parallel and contrast' to a climax where a 'clear and sustained dramatic experience incarnates the play's central paradox'.[82]

Another way of reading Webster's plays as both coherent and part of their own dramatic tradition was provided in the 1980s by Jacqueline Pearson in *Tragedy and Tragicomedy in the Plays of John Webster*.[83] She locates three strands of dramatic influence which Webster had available when producing *The*

White Devil as a 'mixed play': one, 'Tudor tragical comedy' which was 'based on tragedy undercut or disturbed'; two, 'the grotesque tragedy' represented by *King Lear* and *The Revenger's Tragedy*; and, lastly, 'Fletcherian tragicomedy'.[84] She reads *The White Devil* as producing a 'tragicomic web of repetition and parody' which juxtaposes characters and incidents, to effectively 'undermine the tragic status of the noble characters'.[85] Here comedy and comic elements test, challenge and disturb tragedy throughout the play. Humour serves both to carry 'suggestions of aggression, detachment and isolation' as audiences laugh at appalling events, but also to 'suggest a genuinely comic world' beyond the horrific world of tragedy, where a more complete and thorough truth is to be found.[86] One of Webster's most powerful techniques in bringing these clashing elements together is creating 'a dichotomy between an event and the reaction to it'.[87] Pearson suggests that 'murder is greeted by laughter, celebration is torn apart by violence'[88] and the normal processes of developing and receiving the tragic experience via character, theme and plot, are disrupted. This is not simply for the purpose of nihilism, however, as on one side the comedy suggests the possibility of that greater truth which simple tragedy cannot depict, and the 'ironically inverted or incomplete' tragedies of Camillo, Isabella, Brachiano, Marcello and Flamineo are 'poised to allow and to emphasize the laborious and painful achievement of tragedy by Flamineo and Vittoria'.[89]

Perhaps the final significant shift in discussions of the dramaturgy of *The White Devil* in the period covered by this chapter was brought to bear by the work of Catherine Belsey and Dympna Callaghan, discussed above with reference to their reading of Vittoria. It is characteristic of Websterian criticism that issues of gender, dramatic traditions, stagecraft, ethics and literary value will not stay in separate categories, but blur and blend into each other, and even more true of the feminist critical tradition within which Belsey and Callaghan operate. As we have seen, Callaghan argues that what appear to be flaws in the construction of the play in fact reveal points of strain within the ideology of tragedy itself, showing up the asymmetries which sustain a gendered and hierarchical vision of the world. For Callaghan the apparent 'problem' of *The White Devil* – and Vittoria – is in fact a revelation which should cause us to reassess every other play which has implicitly been regarded as normative. The history of disagreement over Webster's skills as a poet and dramatist, like the similar critical debate over Vittoria, reveal a great deal about the prior assumptions made by the critics involved in it. The history is, in its way, a narrative of certain critical tendencies and impulses, clashing across the territory of Webster's play, but it is also a testament to the knottiness of *The White Devil* and the resistance it poses to being easily explained or accounted for.

The problem of not being Shakespeare

Just as investigating Vittoria's guilt or innocence led into questions of Webster's dramatic abilities, the discussion of *The White Devil*'s stagecraft has already thrown up comparisons to Shakespeare. As the critical history I am sketching progressed through the centuries, Shakespeare increasingly became the defining figure against which any early modern dramatist – or even any verbal artist – would be measured. After listing the criticisms that have been levelled against Webster over the years, James Calderwood (in 1962) noted one last charge: 'a fault for which some of his critics have been unable to forgive him – his plays were not written by Shakespeare'.[90] Calderwood flippantly characterizes one of the major forces which have shaped critical approaches to Webster over the last two hundred years or so: the growing significance of Shakespeare. The development of the Shakespeare icon has had a vast impact on the ways in which Webster scholarship has developed, whether in terms of crowding out the space and attention available in theatrical and academic institutions, producing a dominant model of literary value against which other works would appear lacking if they operated upon different principles or acting as a touchstone of authentic 'British' culture and values. This has been increasingly visible through the progress of the previous two problems, and in this section I will discuss it directly. This will involve a more general discussion of Webster's qualities, but I have tried to concentrate on critics who discuss *The White Devil*, even if they do not explicitly state that their comparison with Shakespeare is drawn from observations about the play. This matters not only because it is a major part of the critical backstory of this particular play, but also because tracing the traditions of interpretation surrounding works such as *The White Devil* can demonstrate how contingent and non-inevitable Shakespeare's status is. The difficulty of Webster's play, and the friction produced when it is discussed and analyzed within a Shakespeare-dominated context, can help make that dominance seem less obvious and natural.

The very first critic to make the comparison with Shakespeare is Webster himself, in the epistle to the reader which I quoted at the opening of this chapter. While defending himself both from the failure of the play in its first performances at the Red Bull and also from literary fault-finding which he hopes to disarm by forestalling it, he declares that:

Detraction is the sworn friend to ignorance: for mine own part, I have ever truly cherished my good opinion of other men's worthy labours, especially of that full and heightened style of Master Chapman, the laboured and understanding works of Master Jonson, the no less worthy composures of the both worthily excellent Master Beaumont and Master Fletcher; and lastly (without   wrong last to be named), the right happy and copious industry of Master Shakespeare, Master Dekker, and Master Heywood, wishing what I write may be read by their light: protesting that, in the strength of mine own judgment, I know them so worthy,

that though I rest silent in my own work, yet to most of
theirs I dare (without flattery) fix that of Martial:
— *non norunt hæc monumenta mori* [these monuments
         do not know death] ('To the Reader', 33–45)

Despite his statement that naming Shakespeare, Dekker and
Heywood last does not imply a slight on their qualities,
Webster does seem to be relegating them to a latter rank of
talents, especially given the declension from 'laboured and
understanding works', through 'no less worthy composures'
to 'happy and copious industry'. Composed four years
before Jonson's notorious Folio publication drew scorn for
laying claim to the title of *Works* for his plays, this epistle
was at pains to assert the value of careful and laborious
composition in creating literature which the discerning reader
would appreciate. So, the contrast between 'laboured and
understanding works' and 'happy and copious industry' here
seems to mark a genuine distinction. In placing himself within
the literary fellowship (rather than the theatrical marketplace)
of the era, Webster makes the first comparison between his
own work and that of Shakespeare, putting himself on a level
which few subsequent critics would quite allow.

When Hazlitt came to consider Webster's relation to
Shakespeare, as one of the 'race of giants' among whom
the greater dramatist lived and worked, he was seeking to
remedy what he saw as Shakespeare's domination of the
public imagination.[91] In discussing Webster himself, Hazlitt
judges the *White Devil* and *The Duchess of Malfi* as 'upon
the whole perhaps [...] the nearest to Shakespear [*sic*] of any
thing we have upon record'.[92] In fact, this comparison tends
to undercut Webster's major tragedies even while praising
them: the plays 'are too like Shakespear, and often direct
imitations of him, both in general conception and individual
expression'.[93] Despite feeling that 'there is nobody else whom
it would be either so difficult or so desirable to imitate' and
that 'Webster's mind appears to have been cast more in the
mould of Shakespear's, as well naturally as from studious

emulation', Hazlitt nonetheless values the originality to be found more evidently in the writings of Thomas Dekker.[94] *The White Devil* is caught in a near-paradox here, which runs through the reception of non-Shakespearean drama: in displaying similar characteristics to the exemplar of literary value the play gains approval and value, but at the cost of demonstrating its redundancy, since what it offers has already been supplied in more perfect form by the greater artist. Since no-one can be more Shakespearean than Shakespeare, Webster's work both gains and loses from its proximity to the figure who 'towered' over his fellow giants.

Nathan Drake displayed a similar judgement a couple of years earlier, in 1817, though explicitly beginning from Shakespeare: where Hazlitt was discussing the 'Age of Elizabeth', Drake considered 'Shakespeare and his Times'. Surveying the playwrights of the era, 'we are astonished that even the talents of Shakespeare should, for so long a period, have eclipsed their fame'.[95] The 'predilection for the terrible and strange' that he found in Webster provides 'very striking, though, in many respects, very eccentric, proofs of dramatic vigour'. Webster's epistle to the reader in *The White Devil* is used to balance this impression, showing that 'our author was well acquainted with the laws of the ancient drama' and that he consciously and deliberately 'adopted the Romantic or Shakespearean form'.[96]

It is even less clear in Drake than Hazlitt where 'Shakespearean' is a description of artistic influence, specific aesthetic characteristics or just general excellence, though he also finds Webster's similarity to Shakespeare a sticking point, specifically in *The White Devil*. The 'fifth act of his *Vitoria Corombona*' demonstrates an ability to 'imbibe the imagination of Shakespeare, particularly where its features seem to breathe a more than earthly wildness', but Webster 'has not escaped' the risks which accompany 'such an aspiration after, what may be called inimitable excellence'.[97] To Drake, Webster seems to have been 'laboriously striving to break from terrestrial fetters' in following 'where his master moves free and ethereal', and when Webster does take flight his work displays 'an extravagant and erring spirit'. The borrowing from *Hamlet* has the same effect as Hazlitt's more explicit account of Webster's supposedly Shakespearean qualities, by folding the whole issue within the space defined by Shakespeare. Even the words which the critic uses to evaluate *The White Devil* are determined by Shakespeare, a fairly apt demonstration of the inescapability of the Shakespearean paradigm. When Drake declares in the next sentence that 'for all their faults', Webster's tragedies are 'stamped with' and 'consecrated by' the seal of genius', it seems likely that this supposedly holy impression consists in Webster's receptivity to Shakespeare's power and tendency to reproduce it in albeit blurred and imperfect forms.[98]

However, there was another strain of comparison with Shakespeare which did not involve such complex and nuanced forms of appraisal. In 1818, John Wilson wrote an article in *Blackwood's* generally disparaging the enthusiasm for reviving the non-Shakespearean dramatists and comparing them to their more famous colleague, which I have quoted in the previous section. He isolates Shakespeare, stating that,

> none of the predecessors of Shakespeare must be thought along with him, when he appears before us like Prometheus moulding the figures of men and breathing into them the animation and all the passions of life [...] the same may be said of almost all his illustrious contemporaries.[99]

Wilson rhapsodizes on the ways in which Shakespeare's characterization produces sympathetic and personal engagement, while in contrast his contemporaries 'have rarely indeed inspired us with such belief in the existence of their personages'.[100] Unlike Hazlitt and Drake, who stressed Shakespeare's influence on Webster and other contemporaries, Wilson denies that Shakespeare even raised the quality of those around him significantly:

And if we wonder at his mighty genius, when we compare his best plays with all that went before him, we shall perhaps wonder still more when we compare them with the finest works of those whose genius he himself inspired, and who flourished during the same splendid era of dramatic poetry.[101]

While he admits the power and originality of Webster's writing, Wilson levels at him all the criticisms which he has of the period in general: 'to none of our early dramatists do these observations more forcibly apply than to Webster'.[102] The playwright is intriguing, but flawed, and typifies the inadequacies of his contemporaries when their works are placed alongside those of Shakespeare. If Shakespeare transcended his contemporaries' weaknesses to an extraordinary extent, in Wilson's account Webster embodied them.

Later in the century, William Archer (1893) also produced a serious critique of Webster and the popularity he had gained since Lamb and Hazlitt's assessments. Though he appreciates the light which Lamb's *Specimens* cast on some neglected poetic jewels in forgotten works, Archer criticizes what he sees as the suspension of critical standards and a general desire to praise the tacky and badly made jewellery in which these poetic stones appeared. When it comes to comparing him with Shakespeare, Archer has not forgiven the epistle to the 1612 printing and describes Webster as having 'reverted to a stage of literary development which Shakespeare had outgrown', despite being younger than Shakespeare (whose 'right happy and copious industry' he bracketed with that of Dekker and Heywood).[103] The general tone of Archer's comments is one of impatience with dramatists who failed to produce decent plays according to the principles of dramatic construction and yet were enjoying a faddish cult following. His comments about Webster 'reverting' despite being born later than Shakespeare are even more critical given his involvement with the progressive theatre movement of the 1890s: it was the dramatist's duty to move forward.

Another voice of the late nineteenth century was in no doubt that Webster stood below Shakespeare on the scale of poetic greatness, but insisted that this was itself an extraordinary and unparalleled feat. Swinburne comes to the conclusion that 'we must admit, as an unquestioned truth' that 'Webster stands nearer to Shakespeare than any other English poet stands to Webster' when it comes to 'the deepest and highest and purest qualities of tragic poetry'.[104] While Webster is 'a good second', there is 'not one among the predecessors, contemporaries or successors of Shakespeare and Webster' who has 'given proof of this double faculty' which he values in both of them: 'this coequal mastery of terror and pity, undiscoloured and undistorted, but vivified and glorified by the splendour of immediate and infallible imagination'.[105] According to Swinburne's estimation, Shelley may possibly be accepted as a 'good third' to the pair of Shakespeare and Webster, but this addition to the rankings is doubtful, and they are more likely to stand on their own beyond the scope and achievement of the other poets of the English language. Swinburne's position is, thus, notable for praising Webster both for his similar mode of talent to Shakespeare (if not explicitly the similarity of their work) and for his distance from the rest of Shakespeare's contemporaries. He also displays the nineteenth-century tendency to praise Webster's abilities as another outstanding poet, rather than using his demonstrable quality to argue for a reassessment of the Shakespeare-dominated system of literary appreciation.

As criticism of early modern drama became more thoroughly historicist in approach during the twentieth century, the comparison between Webster and Shakespeare became less explicit. Even though Shakespeare is more culturally and academically dominant during this era, there is less appetite for picking out particular writers and setting them in a contest against him. The odd relationship which this century at times constructs between Shakespeare and Webster was exemplified by Hereward T. Price's 1955 essay on 'The Function of Imagery in Webster', which began from the premise that

Shakespeare is 'the center of a lively controversy about the exact function which he intended imagery to perform', and generalizes this to the literary scene of the time: 'we ought to approach this problem not as if it were something peculiar to just one writer but from the viewpoint of general Elizabethan practice'.[106] His assertion that '[n]ot enough work has been done on other Elizabethans' veered towards a call to study them for their own sake, though it turns again to a hope that critics 'may perhaps obtain some light on Shakespeare by studying the technique of his contemporaries', via 'establishing likeness or difference, by comparison or contrast'.[107] Webster is a suitable subject for this investigation since 'in the depth, the subtlety and the complexity of his imagery he comes nearer than any other Elizabethan dramatist to the power of Shakespeare', although '[w]hile Webster approaches Shakespeare in many aspects of his imagery, there can be no comparison between them in range'.[108] In a revealing piece of prefacing, Price states that the 'resolute consistency with which Webster elaborates an extended sequence of diverse but interrelated images' isolates *The White Devil* and *The Duchess of Malfi* 'not only from Webster's other work but also from the rest of Elizabethan drama'.[109]

Price appears to presume that many other studies will be undertaken of other 'Elizabethan' writers, focusing on their likeness and unlikeness to Shakespeare. The basis of this essay, however, does seem to involve a web of criss-crossing (and sometimes tangled) impulses. These are demonstrated again in the conclusion: as ever, the language of evaluation gleams through the descriptive project, and Price describes Webster's method as both 'unique' and 'tireless'.[110] Comparisons are also made in passing with the work of Marlowe, Jonson and Chapman, before concluding 'the only possible comparison is with Shakespeare'.[111] The author of *The White Devil* is implicitly derivative – 'There can be no doubt that Webster profited by Shakespeare's example' – though he also brought this particular technique to a pitch of excellence – 'even Shakespeare in his turn could have learned something from Webster's skill in interlacing long chains of figures and action'.[112] The subjunctive 'could' in that last clause is ambiguous and we are left to wonder whether Price is speculating on historical possibility or simply pointing out an area in which Webster was comparably talented. In the end, 'it is extremely important that all students of Shakespeare's art should familiarize themselves with Webster's technique', since appreciating 'the stern consistency with which Webster developed his elaborate imagery' would allow them to 'see that Shakespeare was doing very much the same thing'.[113] Thus an unusual quality in Webster is valuable for its potential to illuminate Shakespeare's practice.

For Price, the study of Webster is instrumentalized, in the sense that it is carried out in a way which directly enables an even higher appreciation of Shakespeare. Critics who understood Webster would 'no longer refuse to believe that Shakespeare used plan and system in the development of his imagery', and would be forced to admit that 'while he appears on the surface to be more simple than Webster, he plumbs to depths that Webster never reached'.[114] Price seems to exemplify the conflicting and complicated impulses which are involved in critical comparisons between Webster and Shakespeare during the twentieth century. While Webster has his value, he is ultimately useful to elucidate Shakespearean genius. It is the middle part of that process which can destabilize the process itself in some later work: the careful attention to Webster as dissimilar to Shakespeare and embodying different principles and potentials provides the impetus to critique the dominance of Shakespeare. This critique develops later in the twentieth century through the work on 'the Jacobean', 'not-Shakespeare' and non-Shakespearean performance studies carried out variously by Susan Bennett, Pascale Aebischer, Sarah Werner and others.[115]

Conclusion

As evidenced by the three problems I have focused on, Webster's play has so often been approached as problematic, or requiring explanation, that its critical backstory has assumed the character of a long-running argument. Even when new and radical critical perspectives appear, they are brought to bear on problems which were identified earlier; this is true for a great deal of literary criticism but perhaps even more so for Webster. For the general reader (or scholar from another area) who is not familiar with the years of previous criticism, this can provide an esoteric atmosphere, as critics address questions which the play might not seem to be posing, or indulge in elaborate proofs of apparently obvious opinions. This chapter should have provided some explanation of why people ever bothered arguing about whether the heroine of a play involved in adultery and murder is technically in the wrong or not. It has hopefully shown why critics feel the need to arrange their accounts of the play in ways which engage both with the work as it is reproduced in the present and with the critical tradition which has accompanied it in its journey into this era. At the same time, the issues I have discussed above, around which the critical debate has encrusted itself – sex and gender, dramaturgy and literary value, the overshadowing figure of Shakespeare – remain very lively parts of the contemporary critical scene. These are not abstruse or antiquarian concerns for anyone reading, performing and discussing early modern drama today. As soon as *The White Devil* appeared it provoked critical discussion and the first critical comment on it – Webster's own epistle – interposed itself between the first performance and the first readers' encounter with the play's text. That epistle sought to forestall certain other critical comments, implying that the author knew what readers would say, and attempting to silence them. That attempt proved splendidly unsuccessful, and continues to fail in fascinating ways today.

2

The White Devil in Performance

Eva Griffith

This chapter aims to demonstrate to what extent *The White Devil* has developed in the hands of actors and their companies. From the beginning, John Webster, like a modern-day critic, was able to acknowledge that *The White Devil*'s original company performed it well, in fact singling out one actor for particular praise. For decades after its first production in 1612, the play remained in the repertoires of successive companies of actors who were able to hand it on within a genealogy of knowledge or tradition. However, after the 1600s, due to many factors including sensitivities about staging sexuality, violence, or corruption, the play entered periods when leading companies did not – or could not – present it as Webster wrote it. In fact, it was not really performed in a form we would now recognize until the 1920s and 1930s – between the two World Wars – when understanding extreme violence or gender inequalities was more urgent for theatres and audiences. Consequently, this chapter is threaded with evidence regarding the effects of the social and ideological contexts (especially in the UK) in which the play was produced, during the rest of

the twentieth century.¹ This chapter asks, then: in what ways
have actors, producers and directors tried to present Webster
within changing contexts for altered audience needs?

First productions

The White Devil was Webster's first known tragedy, certainly
as a sole authored piece. It was probably first staged early
in 1612, at the Red Bull playhouse, and was published later
that year. That 1612 edition contained Webster's prefatory
address 'To the Reader', where he grouped himself among
playwrights who deserved notice, describing the 'full and
heightened style of Master [George] Chapman', 'the laboured
and understanding works of Master [Ben] Jonson', 'the no
less worthy composures of the both worthily excellent Master
[Francis] Beaumont, and Master [John] Fletcher', and 'lastly
(without wrong last to be named) the right happy and copious
industry of Master [William] Shakespeare, Master [Thomas]
Dekker, and Master [Thomas] Heywood' ('To the Reader',
35–41). The order Webster bestows upon this list of compet-
itors, in terms of their high- or low-brow status, is important.
Chapman, Jonson, Beaumont and Fletcher are seen today as
having catered to a university-educated, more 'elite' audience
in London, while Shakespeare, Dekker and Heywood are
viewed as producing plays for an open-air 'public playhouse'
crowd. Shakespeare was the central actor–playwright for
the King's Men at the Globe. Likewise, Heywood was a
shareholder and the main actor–playwright for the Queen's
Servants' company, whose main playhouse at the time was the
aforementioned Red Bull. Advertised on the title page of that
first Webster edition as *The Queen's Majesties Servants*, this
company was an acting troupe under the patronage of Anna
of Denmark, the wife of James I, who had come to the English
throne in 1603. The company had a reputation for catering
to the 'citizens' of London. Webster himself came from this

mixed class in London: those who earned their city status with attendant voting rights through apprenticeships and could rise to journeymen and masters within their working environs.[2]

We can see then that Webster uses his address 'To the Reader' to situate himself and his play in social and theatrical contexts. Yet in so doing he reveals tensions in those contexts, and his place in them. Webster felt that his work should be distinguished from writings that would not stand the test of time. Notably, when he invoked the longevity of Euripides' work elsewhere in his preface to this play, Webster used the verb 'read' and not 'acted' – suggesting, perhaps, a sensitivity to *The White Devil*'s suitability for staged success.

Crucially, that address contained a complaint that the play was produced 'in so dull a time of winter, presented in so open and black a theatre, that it wanted (that which is the only grace and setting out of a tragedy) a full and understanding auditory'.[3] Webster described those who came to this first airing at the Red Bull in rather derogatory terms: 'most of the people' who attended 'that playhouse' were like 'those ignorant asses (who visiting stationers' [bookshops], their use is not to enquire for good books, but new books)'.[4]

Some things clearly made Webster unhappy about *The White Devil*'s first production; however, we also know things about it which made him more content – and this had everything to do with performance. At the end of this first edition he described the play as 'generally well' acted:

> and I dare affirm, with the joint testimony of some of their own quality (for the true imitation of life, without striving to make nature a monster), the best that ever became them: whereof as I make a general acknowledgement, so in particular I must remember the well approved industry of my friend Master [Richard] Perkins, and confess the worth of his action did crown both the beginning and end.[5]

Thus, Webster thought the Queen's Servants' acting was a 'true imitation of life' in the way that Hamlet elucidated when he spoke of good acting as holding 'the mirror up to Nature' (3.2.21–3).[6] In Webster's words, we also see something quite unusual – the author of an early modern play giving a (positive) critique of his own play and of the performers involved, especially Richard Perkins.

Perkins started acting young and his talent drew two acting companies to fight over him when he was a teenager.[7] During 1602–3, he is mentioned in the accounts of Philip Henslowe, owner of the Rose playhouse on the Bankside.[8] From printed cast lists to plays of the time, we perceive that he performed leading adult male roles, including Sir John Belfare in James Shirley's *The Wedding* (London, 1629) and Captain Goodlack in Thomas Heywood's *The Fair Maid of the West* (London, 1631). Perkins was also associated with the role of Barabas in Marlowe's popular *The Jew of Malta*, which was resurrected in 1633 by Queen Henrietta Maria's Men; this gives us clues as to the kind of parts that he was given.[9] Most commentators have imagined him playing the speech-heavy part of Flamineo in *The White Devil*, the courtier who pimps his sister to Duke Brachiano.[10] Furthermore, we might argue that Perkins is likely to have reprised his role in the play some time in the late 1620s to 1630, from the reprint in 1631, when the play was again part of the repertoire of Queen Henrietta Maria's Men. Indeed, in the 1631 Queen Henrietta Maria text, Webster's opening address 'To the Reader' is the same as the 1612 Queen Anna edition and so also still includes Webster's praise of the actors and of Perkins at the end.

Unlike the 1612 edition, though, the 1631 title page gives the venue as 'the *Phoenix*, in Drury-lane.'[11] The Phoenix was a smaller, indoor playing space first occupied by Queen Anna's Men in 1616. Originally called the Cockpit, it was the property and responsibility of Christopher Beeston, another Queen Anna actor, but it was renamed the Phoenix after a destructive riot in 1617, invoking the idea of the bird that rose from the ashes. The company performing there at the time of the 1631 edition of Webster's play did so under the patronage of the new queen, Henrietta Maria. Perkins was a long-term friend and associate of Beeston and was apparently still in demand.[12] All this helps us realize some of the continuities between the original production in 1612 and stagings later in the 1600s.

Restoration devils

In February 1612, at around the same time that *The White Devil* was first performed, Thomas Killigrew was born. A man who would be important to the next stage of the play's history because of his connections to its 1630s' stagings, and because of his role in reviving it during the Restoration. A dramatist and theatre manager in later life, Killigrew was the son of Sir Robert Killigrew and became a page to Charles I. We know he was theatrically active earlier in the London area, since Samuel Pepys in his diary relates how, as a boy, Killigrew had answered the call for devil performers at the Red Bull.[13] Killigrew was to see his own first drama, *The Prisoners*, performed at The Phoenix in 1636 by Queen Henrietta Maria's Men – the company featuring Richard Perkins, and that had revised *The White Devil* at that theatre in the 1630s. It is therefore highly likely that Killigrew knew *The White Devil* by this time.

In about 1647, Killigrew followed the young Prince Charles into exile in Europe during the English Civil War. He returned to England in 1660, at the time of the restoration of the monarchy when the Prince became King Charles II. Along with William Davenant, Killigrew was given a royal licence granting rights over public entertainment in London. Killigrew took up residence at the Red Bull, one of the few available playhouses at the time, with his troupe, the (Restoration) King's Men. Soon afterwards, the company moved to a new theatre facility, 'Gibbons Tennis Court', in Vere Street, and this is, most likely, where Pepys first saw the production of *The White Devil*, which is reported in his diaries on

2 October 1661.[14] Pepys was not impressed: he called it 'Vittoria Corombona' and described it as 'a very poor play'. He was seated in 'an ill place' for the performance, and stated that he 'never had so little pleasure in a play in my life'. Two days later, he returned to see it again, arriving after curtain-up, which again upset him: '[it] pleased me worse then it did the other day'. Thus, he left the playhouse instead and 'went out and drank a bottle or two of Chana-ale, and so I home'.[15]

In 1663, Killigrew moved the company again, this time to the new 'Theatre Royal, Bridges Street', where The White Devil was performed once again. The title page of the edition of 1665 altered the description of Vittoria to 'A Lady of VENICE'. It was also much more clear about the play's immediate playhouse history and how it was acted, stating that it was '(formerly by Her Majesties Servants) at the Phoenix in Drury-lane' and now was '(by His now Majesty's) at the THEATRE ROYAL'. Perhaps oddly, considering the play had long ago moved from the original venue, whose staging and audience so offended Webster, Webster's complaining address about it was retained for this edition.

A list of the largest group of actors involved in the changing and developing Killigrew's company (and, therefore, those who could also have performed in the play) includes Richard Baxter, Theophilus Bird, William Cartwright, Charles Hart, Edward Kynaston, John Lacy, Michael Mohun, the Shatterells and William Wintersel. These men are notable for having varying connections to the different Queen's Men, The Cockpit/The Phoenix and the Red Bull. Of these, a Richard Baxter was a known original Jacobean Queen's Servant at the Red Bull playhouse who, in the 1620s, may have joined the King's men. If the Baxter of the Jacobean theatre was the same man as the Restoration player of the 1660s, then his stage career must have been, as Gerald Eades Bentley puts it: 'one of the longest of the seventeenth century'.[16] A Theophilus Bird was the son-in-law of Christopher Beeston and would have known the 1630s revival of The White Devil.[17] Michael Mohun or Moone, in turn, was the son-in-law of Bird, and also an actor with Beeston in his Queen Henrietta Maria days at the Phoenix.[18] In other words, there was a wealth of earlier actor and producer experience of performing *The White Devil* to draw from within this Restoration company that might create continuity with earlier productions of the play.

Despite these connections between productions, within lists of the 1660s' players available, however, comes an important innovation: actresses. Elizabeth Boutel, Katherine Corey, Nell Gwyn, Elizabeth (or Mary) Knipp, Anne Quin and Rebecca Marshall all stand as possible actresses for the Vittoria part once it could be given to a woman, in the more liberal world of Restoration theatre.[19] As hard as it is to imagine a male playing Vittoria – or Isabella, Cornelia or Zanche, for that matter – before this time, women were not allowed on the Jacobean stage; only men had performed the women's parts up to this period. With what extra kind of excitement, then, did a Restoration audience approach a play like *The White Devil*, as women now performed the key role? And what effects did this have on rendering a plot that explored sexual exploitation in a male-dominated court with a brother acting as his sister's pander?

We know from John Downes, a '*Book-keeper and Prompter*', that *The White Devil* was among a group of Killigrew plays that continued to be performed in repertory until 1682.[20] However, from that point, revivals of *The White Devil* – in its original text form, at least – seemed to come to a pronounced stop, until the twentieth century. Instead, writers and critics such as Lewis Theobald and Nahum Tate decided to adapt plays like *The White Devil* to better suit their own sensibilities, and those of their era. To what extent the introduction of women into public performance may have contributed to a heightened sense of propriety concerning what was on stage is uncertain, but by the 1690s, Tate himself had become more religious, and this certainly had an effect on his approach to the theatre; he wrote a letter to the Bishop of London (6 February 1699) outlining proposals for the 'Regulating of the Stage and Stage-plays'.[21]

Thus inspired, Tate decided to alter Webster's *White Devil* – and do this without crediting the original author. The following text appeared on the title page of the renamed *Injur'd Love*, the version Tate published in London, in 1707, which credited himself as the author of the piece:

Injur'd Love: | OR, THE | CRUEL HUSBAND. | A | TRAGEDY. | Designed to be Acted at the | *THEATRE ROYAL.* | *Written by Mr. N.* Tate, | Author of the Tragedy call'd KING *LEAR*.[22]

The cast list indicates the specific parts of Webster's drama that were modified by Tate. Brachiano is described as '*The cruel Husband, in Love with* Vittoria'; and Isabella '*The injur'd Wife*', showing the need to change perceptions of characters from the outset. Following Webster, Tate's Flamineo orchestrates Vittoria and Brachiano's secret liaison. He entices his sister with promises of a special night:

Thou shalt lie on a Bed stuff't with Turtle's
Feathers, swoon in Perfumes, stifled in
Roses [23]

Yet Tate then cuts Flamineo's speech up until where he tells Vittoria: 'Shalt meet him, 'tis fixt, with nails of diamonds to inevitable necessity' (1.2.143–4). Instead, Vittoria responds in an aside:

Yes I will meet him, but for other Ends
        Than their vile Purposes.[24]

Already we can hear the sound of a more virtuous and moral Vittoria than the woman who appears in Webster's original play; she is determined to deflect any possible adultery. After Camillo's departure, she meets Brachiano under Flamineo and Zanche's gaze: 'See now they Close', Zanche says.[25]

Much is cut from Webster's scene from this moment on. Gone is the sexually explicit jewel analogy, as well as Vittoria's manipulative dream of the yew tree which promotes the murders of Isabella and Camillo (1.2.212–37). Instead, Tate has Vittoria instigate a conversation which offers 'to quench and stifle / This hopeless Passion'.[26] 'That's too rough a Method,' Brachiano responds. 'And suits not with my Constitution'. Vittoria does not hesitate to make more headway:

> 'Twas that I purpos'd in this Interview,
> We now are wander'd to the brink of Ruin,
> And must turn short, or perish.[27]

Vittoria argues that despite her 'high born' status, which is brought down by misfortune and results in an unhappy marriage, she must confront the moral truth that marriage is a solemn sacrament:

> Yet still the Name of Husband's Venerable;
> My Vow was Sacred, and let Hope forsake me
> When first –

'Hold' says Brachiano,

>   'twas no Match,
> And I pronounce it void; unnatural Contracts
> Dissolve themselves.[28]

By contrast, at this point in Webster's original version, Vittoria's mother Cornelia has entered and is faced with her son playing pander to her adulterous daughter. In the 1612 to 1660s' productions, she witnesses both the jewel foreplay and the murderous yew tree dream. Tate, however, has her enter '*observing them at a Distance*'. She does not necessarily hear what they are saying, though, while Vittoria tries to convince Brachiano of the virtues of Isabella:

VITT You have a Princess, Sir, the Pride of Nature,
      And Paradise of Virtues; worth your Prizing
      If Monarch of the World; and Sir, this Charmer,
      Your Lover, and almost your Worshipper.
COR   My fears are fall'n upon me! Oh my Heart,
      My Son, their Pandar?
VITT Beware my Lord! Orphans and Widows cries,
      Defrauded Labour's starving Sighs are loud;
      But none, to draw down Vengeance from Above,
      No! None like the Complaints of injur'd Love.[29]

The extent to which Tate's version changes Webster's intention becomes obvious in this scene. By making Vittoria's sympathy lie with the betrayed wife, our perceptions of Vittoria alter radically in comparison with Webster's original play. Without even mentioning Webster on the title page, Tate decides that character complexity must be thrown over in favour of moral right.

Perhaps we might not feel surprised, then, that *Injur'd Love* did not make it to a London production. But the fact of its appearance as a script 'Design'd' to be performed represents the will to put much of Webster's rich text (however uncredited) onto the stage, even if with a misplaced hope of redemption. After *Injur'd Love* (1707) we see a strange moment in the history of *The White Devil*: the end of productions of any kind for almost 250 years, most probably because of the moral issues that Tate tried to address. However, evidence suggests that some continued to try and revive Webster's play for new audiences.

An eighteenth- to nineteenth-century void: 'too rough a flavour'

David Garrick, however, did not. The library of this important actor–producer, whose promotion of productions of Shakespeare in the mid-eighteenth century assured Shakespeare's staged prominence in times to come, reveals that *The White Devil* was certainly on his book shelves, if not on the stage of his theatre. All the copies of the play consulted at the British Library, in London, belonged to him – including Tate's *Injur'd Love*.[30] The perceived need for change to violent drama like this may have stopped him from attempting a production – or perhaps it was his pronounced efforts towards Shakespeare's advancement that deflected his mind from *The White Devil*.

There were attempts to produce Webster's play in the century to come, however, as evidenced in accounts given by Fanny Kemble, a distinguished actress, and also witnessed by newspaper reports of the time. Frances Anne (aka Fanny) Kemble was the daughter of the respected actor Charles Kemble and the niece of both John Philip Kemble and Sarah Siddons. One account of Fanny's day-to-day acting life was published in the form of her letters in *Record of a Girlhood* in 1878; and it was here that she recorded her play reading, including what she knew of *The White Devil*.

In a letter to 'H____' dated 5 March 1831, Fanny mentions 'Mr Procter's' play: 'It is extremely well written, but I am afraid it would not act as well as it reads.'[31] Later she writes again about Proctor, describing him as 'Bryan Waller Procter, dear Barry Cornwall'.[32] Getting the name of the original playwright wrong, Fanny goes on:

The play which I spoke of as his, in my last letter, was Ford's [sic] 'White Devil,' of which the notorious Vittoria Corombona, Duchess of Brachiano, is the heroine. The powerful but coarse treatment of the Italian story by the Elizabethan playwright has been chastened into something more adapted to modern taste by Barry Cornwall; but, even with his kindred power and skilful handling, the work of the early master retained too rough a flavour for the public palate of our day, and very reluctantly the project of bringing it out was abandoned.[33]

In Fanny's letter, obviously edited later because of the anachronistic literary references she gives, she demonstrates an astute knowledge of Webster's work in the Romantic era's context, for example, mentioning the rendering of the story in the 'magnificent historical novel' by the German writer Ludwig Tieck. This work, entitled *The Roman Matron or Vittoria Accorombona* in its 1845 English translation, had been published five years earlier in German and thus it was intelligent of her to hint at the play's economically successful possibilities in this context of literary fashion. It was hard for Fanny to say which was of the most interest in the story: the matter of 'the heroine's individual career' or 'the splendid delineation of the whole state of Italy at that period [...] and of the contemporary Medici in Florence'. She writes that the play 'is altogether a masterpiece by a great master-Superior in tragic horror, because unrelieved by the general picture of contemporaneous events'.[34] Fanny, dismissing the account of the story given by the French writer, Stendhal (Marie-Henri Beyle), in his *Italian Chronicles*, then goes on to describe the failure of another play, Mary Russell Mitford's *Inez de Castro*.

The point concerning Fanny's descriptions of failed productions in her time was that a number of innovative stage projects were falling to the wayside, including Barry Cornwall's adaptation of Webster. Cornwall's efforts were no doubt prompted by Rev. Alexander Dyce's publication of the first 'modern' edition of Webster in 1830; and this, in turn, was probably inspired by the earlier valorizing of the Romantic critics Charles Lamb and William Hazlitt.[35] Sensitivities to subject matter, however, were still an issue in the nineteenth century – too much so for productions of *The White Devil* to be mounted easily; thus, in practice, this did not happen at all.[36]

Twentieth-century re-emergence

Without evidence of any further attempt at production during these subject-conscious years, it is, perhaps, unsurprising that it wasn't until after the First World War that the play was revived. Following an absence of some 230 years from any professional repertoire in the UK, *The White Devil* emerged in 1920 at Cambridge University in a production by the Marlowe Society. This society was dedicated to presenting rarely played early modern drama, in reaction to the limitations of Victorian theatre, and it still functions today.[37] Their first production of Webster's play was directed by John Tresidder Sheppard, and comprised an all-male cast. The production was a noted success, with the *Cambridge Review* recording that anybody 'who enjoys hearing beautiful poetry beautifully spoken and tragic passion "with dignity put on" should not miss this wonderful opportunity. What a magnificent play!'[38]

In 1925, the first known full-scale professional production of the play since the latter seventeenth century was mounted and the context of its interwar revival is significant. The horrors seen in the First World War set the scene for an artistic detachment from the purely sentimental, bringing about a search for some kind of harder directive force and also of novel ways of perceiving subjects like death. As David Coleman asserts, it was only in 1919, a year after the war ended, that T. S. Eliot wrote about Webster's possession 'by death' and how the playwright 'saw the skull beneath the skin':

Daffodil bulbs instead of balls
Stared from the sockets of the eyes!
He knew that thought clings round dead limbs
Tightening its lusts and luxuries.[39]

The Renaissance Theatre Company's production of October 1925 was produced by Alice Fredman and J. T. Grein, and directed by Edith Craig.[40] An actor, theatre director and costumier, Craig was known as taking on experimental, often notably feminist theatre productions at a time when issues of equality for women, were vitally important.[41] She used the Scala, located in London's Charlotte Street (parallel to Tottenham Court Road), to stage the play. In contrast to the all-male university event of five years before, one part of the professional production partnership was female, with a female director – Craig. As well as being involved in the theatre, Craig was also an active member of the women's suffrage movement; she had joined ten related societies by April 1910 and claimed to have taken an organizational role in all of them.[42] It was three years after Craig's production of *The White Devil*, with its sexually confident and expressive heroine, that ordinary women over twenty-one finally achieved the vote in England. It is note-worthy, too, that with changing values and perspectives concerning female artists since that time, two of the more recent twentieth- to twenty-first-century productions have also been directed by women – Gale Edwards (1996) and Maria Aberg (2014), both for the Royal Shakespeare Company (RSC). One critic speculated (after the Aberg production) that the RSC should be labelling the play as one to avoid in part because of the way women are demonized by it, but suggested 'if you must do it, make sure a woman directs it', since they might defuse any misogyny.[43]

Craig's casting of Vittoria in the 1925 first professional production contains important references to the context's shifting conceptions of gender. Laura Cowie was a versatile and accomplished performer. According to an article in the *Tatler*, she had worked with Sir Herbert Beerbohm Tree at an early stage of her career.[44] In 1932, she was noted as having a 'genius for wearing period dress' – meaning, perhaps, that she knew how to hold herself well in straight-backed corseted costumes which could dictate the way in which a character moved.[45]

The Scala production also featured Esmé Percy as Brachiano, Cedric Hardwicke as Flamineo and Viola Tree as Isabella, with a sixteen-year-old Patricia Hayes, a distinguished actress until her death in 1998, as Giovanni.[46] A girl played a boy's part, then, in this first professional production for centuries. The first night was deemed a qualified success, with one critic passing comment that Webster 'came late in the lifetime of Shakespeare, and should have known much better'.[47] It seems, even at this stage, that there were still reservations about Jacobean drama, written by playwrights other than Shakespeare; and where such work existed, it was deemed necessary for it to know its place.

The next production we know of was that of 1935 by The New Phoenix Company, an outfit with which Edith Craig had been associated in the past. Reviews welcomed the return of this troupe, which – like the Marlowe Society – had focused on resurrecting old plays.[48] This company's production of the play was put on at St Martin's Theatre, West Street. From its programme, which specified an 'Invitation Performance' on 17 March of that year, Allan Wade directed it and Oriel Ross was cast as Vittoria.[49] Flamineo was played by John Laurie – the Scottish actor perhaps better known for playing Private Frazer in the BBC's popular *Dad's Army*. His performance as Flamineo was, however, pronounced as 'confident' by the *Observer* and 'easily the best' by W. A. Darlington of the *Daily Telegraph*.[50]

In the 1940s, the play was honoured with a longer run and a specific feel and style projected by the dancer–producer Robert Helpmann, along with Michael Benthall. Margaret Rawlings took the role of Vittoria to Helpmann's Flamineo in the production of 1947, which proved a hit with the critics. Kenneth Tynan wrote that Helpmann's performance was 'nasty and austere […] no heart or spleen in the curt aloofness of his voice. He is sinister, but without being wicked', and commented of the death scene that 'Mr Helpmann is tiptoe with nerves and topfull of power, and the result is splendid'.[51] Similarly, in his review, Harold Hobson referred to William Hazlitt and asserted that Rawlings as Vittoria was, 'dazzling as the lightning'. Continuing the natural allusions, Hobson also talked of snow and purity: 'the whiteness of Vittoria is the whiteness of corruption, the evil whiteness that terrified Melville, more horrible than all the redness that affrights in blood.'[52] James Agate quoted Lamb on Webster: 'To move a horror skilfully, to touch a soul to the quick, to lay upon fear as much as it can bear, to wean and weary a life till it is ready to drop, and then step in with mortal instruments to take its last forfeit: this only a Webster can do'.[53] Such were the Romantic responses to enjoying this stylized Webster on stage, produced by a dancer. Unlike Hobson who found the production a bit noisy, Agate was relieved about hearing every word:

> To the reader whose only interest in criticism is the answer to the question
>   'Shall I enjoy this play?' my answer is simple. If you get a pleasurable shudder at lines like 'Millions are now in graves which at last day / Like mandrakes shall rise shrieking' you will. If you think the Last Trump should sound to the strain of 'Oh What a Beautiful Mornin', you won't.

With the approval of two of the age's most prominent critics came an acceptance of the play, of a sort, into a canon worthy of establishment production.

Postwar productions

After the Second World War, an amateur company of good standing took up the reins of the play. The Maddermarket Theatre Association in Norwich staged it from 24 May to 4 June 1957. This theatre is said to be the first attempt at a reconstruction of an early modern playing space. Because of the ethos of the founder, Walter Nugent Bligh Monck, the promotion of the production was low key. Programmes were issued without the names of performers and the curtain call was banished, as Monck felt the play itself to be paramount.[54] To give an idea of the range attempted, the drama following Webster's *Devil* that season was Arthur Miller's *Death of A Salesman*.[55]

In 1961, a single performance of the play was held on Sunday 5 March at 7.00 p.m. by the Vic-Wells Association at London's Old Vic. This was the first of three occasions on which the play would be performed at the Waterloo-based theatre. The idea behind performing on Sunday was that it would give ordinary members of the company the opportunity to try out larger parts than they would usually play and also give others a chance to direct. It was in this way that company members already involved in, for example, Franco Zeffirelli's famed Old Vic production of *Romeo and Juliet*, took part – with Peter Ellis (who had been playing Benvolio) directing, as well as taking on the part of Brachiano. According to the *Daily Telegraph*, it was Ellis who was 'largely responsible for the scheme itself'.[56]

Other productions followed in the decade, in the UK and US, with *The White Devil* becoming a stylish play through which to explore interests in gender issues as they developed in an age of sexual revolution. In 1964, a first Royal Academy of Dramatic Art (RADA) attempt took place at the Vanbrugh theatre, featuring the future RSC director Terry Hands (as Flamineo). The play was also gaining significance in the US. In March 1955, the first American workshop production was held at the Phoenix Theatre in New York, co-ordinated by Jack Landau. In December 1965, Landau directed a full-scale production, this time at the Circle in the Square theatre, again in New York. This staging, featuring Carrie Nye as Vittoria in 'gangster mode' in a much cut version, was praised for its 'simple setting, modern dress' and 'clarity of verse speaking and terrific performance energy'.[57] In 1967–8, Richard Eyre's production of the play was staged at the Lyceum in Edinburgh, a staging described as 'highly successful' in the programme notes of the 1991 Royal National Theatre production. The successful amateur company the Tower Theatre also ventured to stage a production in 1969 and there was a Manchester professional production in that same year.[58] However, the play was about to be significantly stretched, most potently to its visual limits, in the production which followed: the second production at the Old Vic directed by Frank Dunlop in 1969.

In an interview with Leonard Pearcey for 'The Arts This Week' on Radio 3, Dunlop spoke about his decision-making process concerning the production. 'I can't talk about Jacobean tragedy as a whole,' he said, 'because the Jacobean writers all write in very different ways'. He continued:

> but with Webster the main difficulty is that we're all used to seeing Shakespeare who writes in a kind of golden glow and Webster comes along and writes white heat and it's a much more intense and extreme kind of writing than Shakespeare's so we had to find a style that fits this much more intense and complicated man.[59]

Dunlop's vision, in view of his perception of Webster, saw him having to find a style 'that was big enough, dramatic enough' to 'pull together' all the different elements of the play. Compared to Shakespeare, Webster was seen to have so much entertainment variety with 'funny bits, sadistic bits, sexy bits, mime bits, spectacle', which had to be 'brought together and made into a unit'. Channelling, as he claimed, Lawrence Durrell's *The Alexandria Quartet* ('because I thought it was a very oriental play that Webster had written'), and also William S. Burrough's *Naked Lunch*, he found a like mind in set designer Piero Gheradi's perspective. Gheradi regularly collaborated with the film director Federico Fellini, and had won two Oscars for his work on *La Dolce Vita* and *8½*. Pearcey, the interviewer, pushed Dunlop about the stone-strewn set which Gheradi had realized for the production, and then asked him about the outlandish costumes the actors had to wear 'with those fantastic ruffs'. Dunlop responded:

I asked him [Gheradi] to do something like extraordinary lascivious insects and reptiles and we looked at a lot of pictures and some of these things have enormous kind of flapping wings and hoods round their heads and rattle snakes have marvellous hoods [...] And he did some drawings and then we showed them to the actors and he made a lot of the costumes on the actors.

Despite Pearcey's assertion of the 'rave reviews' the play received, at least one critic saw no virtue at all in the strangely lacy, rocky, visual presentation of the play. The title of Ronald Bryden's 16 November review for the *Observer* summed up this feeling: 'Swamped by opulence'. Some critics were, however, convinced by the production. 'Frank Dunlop, the National's director, has approached Webster without fear – a bold attack is the only way – and his devices can frequently meet the demands' opined J. C. Trewin in a piece entitled 'Tightrope act'.[60] Trewin approved of the set, but found Gheradi's costumes 'less successful in their extreme fantastication', observing that 'Webster, above all, is for the ear.'

'Triumph for Designer in Jacobean Tragedy' was the headline for John Barber for the *Daily Telegraph*. Writing that the 'moving granite blocks' could have been 'stolen from Stonehenge', he also thought the actors were dressed in costumes 'as bizarre as any seen outside a Fellini film'.[61] Barber described the sight of Geraldine McEwan thus:

her frail body and naked back enveloped by a cobra-hood, her face evil with the mixed satiety and appetite, leer and snigger, coquetry and indecency of the consummate whore[...] Under a huge wig of ginger candy floss, her pretty vicious little head fascinates while her always-odd voice, twanging like a false 'cello, uses words like whips and sentences like scorpions [...] Towards the end of the play, dressed now as a corrupt Peter Pan in thigh-high boots and transparent lace, Miss McEwan dies chained to

a rock, expiring with a death-rattle of the whole body, as if
life were loth to leave a creature so rapacious. This was a
performance of bewildering power.[62]

What do such observations about the style of this production
in the age of the sexual revolution give to those studying *The
White Devil*? Perhaps a sense of how an English spin on the
Italianate could express the loucheness of an era. Any criticism
to do with making it awkward for actors to move, or any
puzzled comment about an environment where they were
supposed to appear like insects out of stonework, is immaterial
to the aesthetic priority. As a performance conundrum it
sounds as if the actors did their best in spite of the design,
aware that the vision was consciously big. 'Over-dressed, over
decorated, over-ripe, overdone as it all was and had to be, the
over-acting was kept remarkably in control' finished Barber.
'The National Theatre seems to have cracked one of the most
difficult nuts in the dramatic repertory'.

The 1970s saw a second RADA production directed
by Geoffrey Bullen with Nicholas Le Prevost doubling the
parts of the French Ambassador and the Physician. In
1975, Richard Eyre produced his second *White Devil* at
the Nottingham Playhouse, with the Irish actor Stephen
Rea as Flamineo, Patti Love as Vittoria and Tom Wilkinson
as Brachiano. But for the true 1970s' stamp on the piece,
it was to return for its third visit to the Old Vic, now free
from National Theatre subsidies and ideas, for another kind
of airing, this time involving the interventions of a contemporary dramatist: Edward Bond.

By 1976, Bond had already courted controversy with his
early Royal Court play *Saved* (1965), his once altogether
banned satire *Early Morning* (1968), his take on *Lear*
(1971) and his perspective on Shakespeare in *Bingo: Scenes
of Money and Death* (1973). There had also been at least
one 'adaptation' before 1976 of a seventeenth-century play:
Thomas Middleton's *A Chaste Maid in Cheapside*.[63] Now,
for Bullfinch productions, which slotted into the Vic after

the National Theatre left, Bond wrote his 'Acting Edition' for Michael Lindsay-Hogg's production of the Webster play.[64] From the programme pictures, the design theme was again exotic in feel, but very '70s' in perspective, with stripes, flares and flowing kaftans the order of the day for Deirdre Clancy, the costume designer. There were, however, mixed feelings about this production. Irving Wardle began his review thus:

> Pleasure that this theatre is reopening before the moths have got at it, is somewhat qualified by the first sight of Jonathan Pryce as Lodovico striding on in slacks and blazer and hurling a piece of airline baggage downstage on the opening line: 'Banished!' [...] The scene (from which the figure of Antonelli has been cut) runs its brief course, and Lodovico then makes his exit through the swing doors of what appears to be the deserted foyer of a grand hotel.[65]

Remembering the previous production at the Vic when Wardle believed Dunlop had converted it 'into an Italianate fashion show, full of delicately poisonous creatures defying place and time in their billowing draperies and effeminate high boots', he puzzled over motivations, by inference, in this case:

> the mighty Dukes of Rome and Florence come on in casual modern clothes, sometimes ceremoniously topped off with dressing gowns. The poetry voice is avoided like the plague. And when it comes to crimes of violence, Edward Bond is on hand to add the kind of precise antiseptic demonstrations which link up the act of murder with a surgical operation.

The murder team in Act 5, Scene 3 apparently administered poison to Brachiano's beaver with a hypodermic syringe and, when he started to scream, oxygen cylinders came 'whizzing through'. Wardle's critical review disliked Jackson's performance, too. John Barber, conversely, liked Jackson, but had similar misgivings to Wardle in other directions:

> though it dazzles the eye, Michael Lindsay-Hogg's production starves the ear. The charnel-house verse, justification of the whole enterprise, is often badly spoken, when audible [...] The horrific garottings and shootings-up rival 'Bonnie and Clyde.' The appalling power of the poetry is forgotten.[66]

Such ambivalence aside, productions all over the country and beyond began to emerge.[67] In May 1978, the Oxford Playhouse played host to a staging of *The White Devil* from Newcastle University, directed by Loraine Monk. In 1980, a Questors Theatre production was mounted, directed by Alan Chambers, and the Contact Theatre in Manchester saw a production directed by Richard Williams. In 1981, there were two productions recorded: one at the Cockpit in Marylebone, directed by John Wiles; and then another at the Oxford Playhouse again, Gordon McDougall. The Bristol Old Vic at the Theatre Royal mounted a staging in 1983, with Anna Nygh, an early *Rocky Horror Show* cast member, as Vittoria; it was directed by Celia Bannerman.[68] On the heels of all of this was another mainstream London production directed by Philip Prowse, who had tackled the play at least twice before and would go on to direct it at the National Theatre after this.

Prowse had been an art student at Slade School of Fine Art and designed a production of Webster's play for the Citizens Theatre, Glasgow in 1971. He was to think about the play's aesthetic qualities again for an amalgamation, again at the Citizens, of Ford's *'Tis Pity She's A Whore,* Webster's *The Duchess of Malfi* and *The White Devil* in 1978 called *Painter's Palace of Pleasure.*[69] In 1984, he designed and directed the entire play for the first time at Greenwich Theatre, with a cast including Ciaran Hinds as Lodovico, Gerard Murphy as Brachiano and Rupert Everett as Flamineo.[70] From the production photographs and the critical comments, this was a thickly gothic production, with white makeup and dark clothes predominating at a punky new-wave period in London. The *Sunday Telegraph* dubbed it a 'magnificently theatrical production', with Julie Legrand, as Vittoria, the only character not dressed in black. The set consisted of 'towering, labyrinthine walls already splashed with blood' and Prowse included sound effects such as thunder rumbles 'in the distance'.[71] The production was also noted for being heavily cut (a dumb show and young Giovanni disappearing altogether) and for Brachiano's throwing up over the dinner table from his first entrance. Michael Billington, in a comment redolent of the overall disappointment about the verse speaking, claimed that nearly 'all the characters look[ed] better than they sound' with only a few actors 'working through the poetry rather than against it'.[72] Feelings about Everett's performance were divided: at one moment he was the chief culprit when it came to the verse speaking, at another, he was someone who was clearly a star. Perhaps Irving Wardle put his finger on the overall difficulties of the production when he saw what had been achieved as an atmosphere 'of a terrible dream' that 'certainly grips the stage', but this should not have been caused by 'stage management or camp-baroque costume' alone, but also by 'Webster's verse rhythms or intended climaxes'.[73]

Undeterred, in 1991, the same year in which the Liverpool Everyman produced the play, Prowse took it on again, this time for the National Theatre. This time, he had to adapt his vision to fill the large auditorium of the Olivier with his design perspective. To put this second production in context, Prowse had gone all but straight from his Greenwich attempt to the National to direct an acclaimed adaptation of the *Duchess of Malfi*, with Ian McKellen and Eleanor Bron, in 1985. With this successful Webster under his belt, and *The White Devil* a text he must have felt he knew well, he set about casting an all-black Corombona family for his new play. It featured Josette Simon as Vittoria, Dhobi Oparei as Flamineo and Claire Benedict as Cornelia. Prowse managed the Olivier challenge by creating a cavernous church-like space – a 'basilica' as the *Evening Standard* called it – with a 'high altar' and 'funerary monuments' set upon it.[74] The critics again and again quoted T. S. Eliot's musings on Webster as 'much possessed by death', seeing, at the same time, the decision to make the Corombona family black as less than wonderful. 'Trite' was the word used by Paul Taylor of the *Independent*. Taylor surmised: 'while a theatre director who cannot think in visual terms is a non-starter, one who can only think in them may also be a liability'.[75]

Traverse and thrust: 1990s to New Millenium productions

After the 1994 Ursa Major Theatre company production mounted at the Southwark Playhouse in a converted warehouse with pillars and church pews, the next major production was something of a game-changer for new approaches to the play. It was the first time, for instance, that Webster's play was produced by the RSC and, even though it was not the first time a woman had directed it, the decision to attach Gale Edwards to the task proved an intelligent one. Previously, the Australian Edwards had produced Shaw's *Saint Joan* and Shakespeare's *The Taming of the Shrew*, so she was no doubt trusted with the feminocentrism of the project. Discussing her decision to direct the play, she described how much she adored 'the language and the imagery', but most of all she loved 'its flamboyant recklessness [...] It feels like a roller-coaster ride or a ghost-train – you go for the thrills and spills along the way'.[76]

It aired in Stratford-upon-Avon at the RSC's Swan Theatre – favoured for non-Shakespeare Jacobean plays and perfectly adaptable for the close-up trial scene and any play's more claustrophobic moments. The cast was approved of by critics, with one performer set forth as 'consistently effective': Richard McCabe as Flamineo. Charles Spencer of the *Telegraph* appreciated Edwards's 'fine new production', recognizing the 'full-blooded melodrama' which the director appeared to 'relish'.[77] Jane Gurnett gave 'a commandingly sexy performance as Vittoria' and Stephen Boxer and Philip Voss 'capture[d] the coldness of the "good" characters who behave[d] just as badly as the villains'. But it was McCabe who was said to have performed 'with an air of corruption you can almost smell':

> Pallid, pudgy and with a sly insinuating smile, he lets the audience into his confidence with conspiratorial panache.

The *Independent*'s Robert Hanks told of the 'humour and pathos' from McCabe who gave 'a startling depth to the central figure of Flamineo [...] he's not simply a pander[...] and a fawn, but also a jester'. Hanks further noted:

> It's a superbly *louche*, funny performance, which finds a degree of cynical humour in the role that reminds you we're not so far removed in time from Restoration comedy.[78]

For the new century, London's Lyric Hammersmith's artistic director, Neil Bartlett, wanted to mount a 'big Jacobean play' and so put on a production of *The White Devil* directed by the actor–director Philip Franks.[79] Like Prowse, Franks had directed Webster before at Greenwich Theatre: a production of *The Duchess of Malfi* with Juliet Stevenson and Simon Russell Beale. Franks stated that for his *White Devil* he 'wanted a vibrant world, one that's lit by fire and neon, one that's hot and dangerous'. It was in this way that he alighted on the idea of a 1950s' *La Dolce Vita*-inspired production, coupled with an Italian *Godfather* theme, complete with a machine gun-toting cast. The production cut down and changed Lodovico's part, making him Isabella's chauffeur, instead, so that the play lost the first scene and opened with Act 1, Scene 2 – thus, emphasizing 'the debauched world of

Bracciano and Vittoria'. The cuts made Vittoria more of the protagonist of the story according to Stephen Purcell.[80]

In 2008, the Menier Chocolate Factory production was a sell-out hit in London. Starring Claire Price as Vittoria, the success of the production showed eagerness, on the part of playgoers, to experience Webster's horror, if nothing else. The play was performed in traverse (i.e. with the audience split in two on either side of the stage). As with the Edwards' production at the Swan and the Pit, this proved to be a good instinct, with Philip Whitcomb, the designer, wanting to create 'a parallel universe', where an audience's sense of safety was destabilized by the staging. It took them 'inside the drama and inside the room with the characters' and during the trial scene, for instance, the audience was taking in one another as well the action.[81]

The most recent *White Devil* played intriguing games with both ideas of misogyny and of family. The style and energy of Maria Aberg's 2014 production reworked Italy along recognizably Berlusconi-esque lines, cutting the whole intelligently. But for this RSC production, Flamineo was performed by a woman actor, Laura Elphinstone. In an interview for *WhatsOnStage*, Aberg discussed how her gender-blind casting of this role hoped to address woman-hating infrastructures in society by analyzing 'how a female character might have taken on that oppressive system and internalised it'.[82] She went on to explain how 'trying to play the man's game' is a 'really dangerous trap' for women believing that doing this 'is going to change things'. As a dangerous, yet thought-provoking effect, therefore, audiences watched a female Flamineo pimping her own sister. Furthermore, Elphinstone performed the part with a north-east English accent, alienating her from the more 'received pronunciation' of brother Marcello and sister Vittoria. Marcello (played by Peter Bray) represented mixed-heritage casting, the entire family effect having the interesting outcome of not isolating the Corombonas because they were the same in a world of difference (as in Prowse's NT production), but of indicating a multi-fathered 'extended' family with divisive upbringings in the Corombona household. Within this powder keg set-up, the casting also gave visceral emphasis to the killing of Marcello when he became angry with Flamineo over the relationship with Zanche. With the casting of Elphinstone, we see this relationship not just as that between a man and woman of different ethnic backgrounds, as in Webster's text, but as a same-sex relationship. Directorial decisions here certainly succeeded in emulating the impact of the seventeenth-century killing on stage. The murder of Marcello can often come across as puzzling now, perhaps because the effect was reliant, in Webster's day, on shocked responses to a European man coupling with a Moorish woman. Today, we do not feel the same sense of shock at this, so arguably Aberg's casting and direction reclaimed a similarly alienating and provocative Websterian effect.[83]

Conclusion

At the beginning of this survey of the history of the play's staging, I quoted Webster quoting Euripides and his prophecy to Alcestides that his work would continue to be read for 'three ages' rather than 'three days'. That *The White Devil*, which struggled to be acceptable from its first performance, disappeared from our stages for some 230 years, but found itself reappearing in the early twentieth century – and is well-known today – bears witness to its durability and power to survive despite controversy, which can be considered as strong as Vittoria Corombona's survival instinct itself. Webster's extraordinary language and macabre mind was always the draw towards attempts to produce him. The playwright's outlook on actors, alongside his criticisms of the playing space and its audience, are unsurprising, as the subjects of actors, venue and context are all now lenses through which we still situate responses to performed texts. In the light of Webster's observations about the play's inadequate first audience, and to answer the introductory questions, we are probably not any more deserving, or even capable of understanding his play, than the people attending its first performance in Clerkenwell in 1612. When we reach for our credit cards in order to see a violent tragedy played out by fellow human beings, as we do with *The White Devil*, we are probably reaching, in fact, for something grisly in nature, challenging and morally overwhelming, hopefully spoken beautifully by well-rehearsed performers who will make us think. This is something the economically driven prompting of successful stage presentations must have proved to be, from venue to venue, company to company, and concept to concept in each succeeding age. Trying to change or censor the play also proves this, as it must always be, in the end, Webster's play, to succeed. The reason to produce it is risked if overly cut or softened. Somewhere among the puzzling truths that a play like this represents lies – in my opinion – the answers to the question of why we go to the theatre at all.

3

The White Devil: The State of the Art

Brett D. Hirsch

Twenty-first century criticism of *The White Devil* has drawn attention to the material and economic conditions of the play's first publication in 1612, as well as its engagement with contemporary debates about race and nation, feminine sexuality and 'the nature of woman', legal jurisdictions and abuses of power and the tenuous boundary between social reality and performance. In addition to a striking variety of topical readings of the play, Webster's macabre fascination and metatheatrical treatment of death remain scholarly staples. Editorial work on *The White Devil* stands at the crossroads between an earlier bibliographical tradition in print and the new possibilities afforded by the emerging technologies of digital publication. These and other technologies, now ubiquitous, suggest the possibility of addressing critical lacunae in adaptation, source, and stylistic studies of *The White Devil*. I explore each of these recurring themes and areas of critical concentration in turn.

Textual studies and editions

The preface to *The White Devil* is more than an opportunity for its author to justify his delay and to complain that the play's failure on stage is because 'it wanted [...] a full and understanding auditory' at the Red Bull playhouse ('To the Reader', 4–6). It also offers tantalizing insights into the relationship between playhouse and printing house and the status of the 'author' in the early modern period. As Douglas A. Brooks argues, Webster turned to publication not only in an effort to 'legitimize the printed text of *The White Devil* by discounting the reception his play received in the theatre as the consequence of an inadequate performance venue and an inept audience', but also to engage in literary self-fashioning.[1] Webster seeks refuge from the ephemerality of the theatre in print and, by delivering his manuscript to Nicholas Okes, 'a printer who is beginning to rely on a set of typographic conventions' associated with works of 'high art' and literature, to appeal to an educated readership better equipped to 'accord it the kind of respect and appreciation its writer thinks it deserves'.[2] The 'distinctly literary features' of the 1612 quarto edition of *The White Devil* include 'singular authorial attribution' and a 'Latin epigram' on the title page,[3] a preface written by Webster (and not his publisher) in which the *sententiae* are consistently marked from the text, and in the use of continuous printing, 'a compositional technique [...] in which verse lines broken between two speakers are set on one line to create a full metrical unit'.[4]

Zachary Lesser has since extended Brooks's analysis of the 1612 quarto, focusing instead on the playbook's publisher Thomas Archer, and its relationship to other titles in his catalogue. For Lesser, Archer's decision to publish *The White Devil* had nothing to do with Webster's literary aspirations and desire to recover the play from its failed theatrical debut: 'Archer chose the play for the same reason he chose his other plays [...] *The White Devil* is about a woman and the "woman question"'.[5] Thorough examination of Archer's output reveals that he engaged in what Lesser terms 'dialogic publishing', configuring his business to capitalize on 'the *querelle des femmes*, the long-running debate over the nature of woman that had a resurgence in England during the second decade of the seventeenth century' and agnostically publishing works on all sides.[6] Archer's selection of plays, including *Sir Thomas Wyatt* (or *Lady Jane*; 1607), *Every Woman in Her Humour* (1609), *The Two Maids of Mortlake* (1609), *The Roaring Girl* (1611), and *The Insatiate Countess* (1613, 1616), shared 'a formal resemblance to the dialogic mode of the *querelle* itself and of Archer's publishing strategy'.[7] Lesser's sophisticated reading of *The White Devil* in the context of Archer's publishing career begins with a consideration of Vittoria's doubleness as she 'shifts from the lustful adulteress of the first act to the powerfully persuasive defender of women and doting wife' of the later scenes, 'encoding […] both sides of the *querelle des femmes* in a single character' who, at various points of the play, exemplifies 'both the vicious and the virtuous woman'.[8] However, for Lesser, it is the trial scene that most clearly invokes the language and dialogic structure of the *querelle*, rendering it 'a trial of all women, or of the nature of woman'.[9]

Twenty-first century publishers have altogether different motivations for publishing *The White Devil*. Since the market for print editions of early modern plays continues for the most part to be driven by students, and not by scholars, twenty-first century editorial work on *The White Devil* has been motivated by the demand for student-friendly set texts. Some of these editions capitalize on particular curriculum requirements: Jackie Moore's 2011 edition in the Oxford Student Texts series, for example, is designed to meet the needs of high school students in England, Wales and Northern Ireland taking the OCR GCE (General Certificate of Education) Advanced Level English Literature specification.[10] As with her edition of *The Duchess of Malfi* in the same series, Moore's edition of the play includes contextual information about Webster and Jacobean England, discussion of major themes and interpretative strategies, and sample essay questions.[11] Other editions, such as David Bevington's for the Norton Anthology, cater more broadly to the needs of undergraduate readers.[12] Of these, Christina Luckyj's 2008 revised third edition for the New Mermaids series provides the most generous introduction to the play, notable also for its attention to modern productions and issues of staging in both the introduction and commentary.[13]

With Benedict S. Robinson's forthcoming edition for the Arden Early Modern Drama series excepted, *The White Devil* has yet to attract the comprehensive editorial treatment it received in the previous century.[14] John Russell Brown's 1960 edition for the Revels Plays remains the most significant critical edition of *The White Devil* to appear in a single play volume, justly praised for its substantial introductory essay, thorough collation of textual variants and extensive commentary.[15] Reprinted frequently, but only revised once, Brown's edition offers a wealth of information about the play and its critical reception, Webster's sources and imitations and editorial treatment of the text since the seventeenth century. However, Brown's coverage of stage productions is limited to a handful of professional productions staged in London and New York between 1925 and 1955. Twenty-first century students are also likely to find the critical framework underpinning Brown's edition rather old fashioned, given that it predates the advent of several critical movements that came to dominate literary and cultural studies, such as new historicism, cultural materialism, feminist and postcolonial literary criticism. As later sections of this survey and other chapters in this collection demonstrate, these and other theoretical approaches have shaped and continue to reshape critical and theatrical treatment of *The White Devil*.

Brown's text is also a product of its time and of the New Bibliography, a twentieth-century bibliographical approach that privileged an author's intentions and sought by analytical methods to establish the text of the underlying manuscript.

Since these manuscripts are, for the most part, no longer extant, the New Bibliographers reconstructed them by examining the printed playbooks and attempting to scrape away the multiple intervening layers of mediation by other hands in the playhouse and print-shop.[16] As the intellectual authority of the New Bibliography and the veracity of its methods received intense criticism in the 1980s and 1990s, new models for textual studies and editing emerged, including the sociological and materialist bibliographies championed by D. F. McKenzie and Jerome J. McGann.[17] The publication of the Oxford Shakespeare *Complete Works* in 1986 marked an important (and no less controversial) shift in editorial approaches to early modern drama, moving away from the New Bibliographical ideal of establishing a text as an author 'originally wrote' it in favour of 'a text presenting the play as it appeared when performed by the company of which Shakespeare was a principal shareholder in the theatres that he helped to control and on whose success his livelihood depended'.[18]

Prepared while the New Bibliography still held sway, Brown's edition of *The White Devil* is more conservative textually than other editions of the play – and, indeed, other works by Webster and his contemporaries – produced towards the end of the twentieth century. In this respect, the 1995 first volume of *The Works of John Webster* for Cambridge University Press is an anomaly, insofar as it exceeded the conservatism of Brown's edition in both form and content.[19] 'Because this edition is directed in the main towards the sophisticated reader of seventeenth-century texts', the textual editors announced, 'it generally follows Greg's and Bowers's principles of copy-text', that is, the chief proponents of the New Bibliography, 'and presents the works in old spelling'.[20] When work on the *Works* began in the 1970s, such 'old spelling' critical editions were commonplace; however, by the end of the twentieth century, they had become something of an editorial oddity. The decision to prepare an old-spelling text severely limited the utility of this edition for classroom use. The expense of the volumes, even when reissued later in paperback, rendered them library-only editions, priced out of the hands of most individual researchers, available primarily to the 'sophisticated reader' of seventeenth-century texts with access to dedicated research libraries.

Limited readership aside, the *Works* presents a monumental contribution to Webster scholarship, offering the most thorough historical collations to date, extensive commentary, and detailed critical, theatrical, and textual introductions. David Carnegie's theatrical introduction to *The White Devil* deserves further praise for its meticulous treatment of the play's stage history and attention to issues in performance, enriched with several contemporary illustrations. David Gunby's critical introduction, however, assiduously avoids engaging in contemporary debates about *The White Devil*, instead focusing exclusively on long-standing issues of character, plot, and structure. In light of the project's aim to establish an authoritative edition of enduring scholarly value, such exclusions are perhaps understandable. Nonetheless, these critical lacunae, along with the decision to prepare old-spelling texts, have denied the edition the scholarly impact it otherwise deserves.

On the question of why we need new editions of Shakespeare, R. A. Foakes responded, 'We can only understand Shakespeare in relation to our own time; his works are constantly being reinterpreted in relation to the concerns of our society, so that new insights demand new editions with new critical introductions'.[21] The same is true for Webster: new editions of *The White Devil* will be required to situate the play in relation to shifting critical trends, cultural tastes and societal concerns. Of all the changes ushered in by the twenty-first century, perhaps the most radical has been the rise of ubiquitous computing. Ours is an increasingly digital culture and, although print remains the dominant medium for the publication of editions, early modern plays are already available in a variety of digital formats. An electronic critical edition of *The White Devil* has yet to appear, but given the ways digital interfaces can support multiple texts and layers of annotation, integrate multimedia content, facilitate user interaction and customization, and incorporate new materials – contextual, critical, performance, user-generated – as they become available, it may only be a matter of time.[22]

Race, cosmetics and colour

Racial studies in early modern literature has 'grown from a subtopic to a *sui generis* field' since the late 1960s.[23] The field has been sustained by critical interest in contemporary English perceptions of and contact with Islam and the New World[24] and invigorated, in recent years, by fresh archival research into the presence of black Africans in Tudor and Stuart England.[25] A number of post-2000 studies have explored constructions of race in *The White Devil*, paying particular attention to the ideological, as well as material performances of blackness in the play. Race, these studies suggest, is not a discrete category but a complex construct that intersects with other, often contradictory, discourses. For example, Francesca Royster considers the 'intersections between African and animal' in the play, arguing that Webster's depiction of Moors is framed by contemporary discourse about 'the ownership and domes-tication of animals'. Dogs, Royster contends, are 'protectors of the domestic space', 'faithful servants' and 'guards of the margins of civilization and the outside', but this privileged access to intimate spaces and bond of trust with their owners renders them all the more dangerous should they revert to their native state of wildness. Royster's reading of *The White Devil* connects these contrasting images of dogs with 'the Moor as a silent object' (as in the case of 'little' Jacques) and 'the Moor as a dangerous ally' (Zanche), to explore 'the tension around potential domestication of black people', and contemporary debates about their 'capacity for humanity, rationality, and social control'.[26]

In her 2005 study, *Performing Blackness on English Stages, 1500–1800*, Virginia Mason Vaughan situates *The White Devil* within a longer theatrical history of blackface. Supposing that 'a young black boy had been available to Queen Anne's Company', Vaughan identifies three levels of 'mimesis and exhibition' in the play's portrayal of Moors: Jacques, 'a black boy being a black boy' who, without any dialogue and agency simply functions as exotic decoration; Zanche, 'an English boy actor impersonating a black woman'; and Mulinassar, 'an adult English male actor impersonating a powerful European male who disguises himself as a black Moor'. The audience's knowledge that white actors are underneath the artificial black skins of these Moorish characters, Vaughan argues, gives rise to a 'double consciousness', in much the same way that impersonation of women on the early modern stage invokes tensions about the social construction of gender and sexuality.[27] In this instance, the underlying anxieties exposed both literally and figuratively are miscegenation and racial pollution – aspects of the play explored more fully in Celia R. Daileader's study of interracialism. Daileader posits three generalizations about the theatrical treatment of interracial relationships: interracial sex 'is a prospect to be avoided by all means'; when one party is English, the possibility of interracial sex is 'rarely raised as a possibility' and, if so, it is 'emphatically thwarted'; and 'interracial sex never involves a consenting and a sympathetic white woman'. The first and last of these apply to *The White Devil*, and Daileader characterizes Flamineo's affair with Zanche as another instance in which 'inter-racial sex is non-consensual' and 'the sexual aggressor is female'.[28]

Vaughan's suggestion that an actual black boy may have played the character of Jacques anticipates more recent studies in the wake of new archival research on the presence of Africans in early modern England. For example, Matthew Steggle has argued that this archival evidence not only 'challenges assumptions about the all-white audience', however, given the 'fragmentariness of the theatre history' and 'racial history', must also allow for the prospect of greater 'black involvement in early modern theatre' itself.[29] Although Steggle is writing with Shakespeare's *Othello* and *Titus Andronicus* in mind, with the tantalizing possibility that Henry Peacham's famous drawing of the latter play depicts an actual black actor at work as Aaron, the implications for *The White Devil* are clear and future work on the play is certain to develop this line of inquiry further. Whether impersonated by white actors or acted by black ones, the Moorish characters in *The White Devil* are not the only racial figurations in the play. In a sophisticated reading, Lara Bovilsky analyses how 'female sexual license is coded within the monochromatic antitheses of light and dark that attend and signal processes of racialization', and how 'stereotypes of Italian moral darkness combine with notions of Italian physical darkness' to establish national differences as 'constitutively racialized'.[30] By way of 'involuted disguise plots and fluid transnational and crossracial labeling', the play stages 'fluctuating racial difference' through 'tropes of gender and national otherness', intersecting notions of 'English', 'Italian', and 'Moorish' and fracturing 'any proposed contrast between Europeans and others'.[31]

Twenty-first century critics have also drawn attention to the material and metaphorical function of cosmetics in the play's representation of gender, nation and race as impermanent, performative and socially constructed. In her study of skin colour in early modern England, Sujata Iyengar explores how practices of 'blacking, blanching and blushing' – that is, the use of cosmetics to darken, lighten and redden the skin, especially the face – break down 'as signs of moral conduct, poetic power and national origin' in *The White Devil*.[32] For Iyengar, the play's consistent linking of cosmetics with deception invokes the fears that 'the white devil is *indistinguishable* from the black' and that 'truth is indistinguishable from fiction, painted color from permanent complexion'. But cosmetics also operate as a form of social control, such as when male characters in the play employ 'paint and metaphors of cosmetic deception' as a means of reasserting their 'authority over women and their complexions'. Thus, the various men who seek to control Vittoria's sexuality 'paint [her] blushes out of existence'.[33] By contrast, Farah Karim-Cooper argues that 'Webster constructs female characters as heroic within an atmosphere of misogynistic condemnation', that 'bold women' such as Vittoria 'wear cosmetics and fashion not only their physical appearances, but also their own lives'. In this way, the otherwise 'anti-cosmetic and misogynistic tenor' of the play 'is subverted by Webster's construction of femininity'.[34] Iyengar's and Karim-Cooper's studies were published a year apart, unaware of each other's divergent readings of the play, and may usefully be read as complementary. Like Iyengar, Karim-Cooper attends to the language of cosmetics permeating *The White Devil*, frequently glossing references otherwise missed by editors. Monticelso's description of whores as 'Shipwrecks in calmest weather' (3.2.83), for example, while 'not a terribly obvious cosmetic image' is nonetheless identified by Karim-Cooper as 'one often used by anti-cosmetic moralists to describe the attention and time spent on the "rigging" up of a woman's body'.[35] However, Karim-Cooper's study of the play is more than a glossary of its cosmetic terms. Hers is a project to demonstrate that images of 'art, Catholicism, witchcraft, traps, food, death, disease, medicine, skin, the body, colour, ships, tombs and effigies, nature, and animals', so pervasive throughout Webster's drama: all 'in some way speak to the contemporary discourse on cosmetics'. To re-evaluate Webster's 'indulgence in cosmetic metaphors' and 'references to cosmetic materials' is therefore to acknowledge how central they are 'to the verbal, visual and theatrical structure' of his tragedies.[36]

As befits the play's title, moreover, a series of recent studies have explored colour symbolism in *The White Devil*. With the confrontation between Vittoria and Monticelso as her focus, Armelle Sabatier attempts to examine the role of colour in Webster's 'highly chromatic play'; but her treatment is invariably limited to the trial scene.[37] The topic receives fuller treatment in Natascha Wanninger's 'Theatrical Colours', in which *The White Devil* is read as participating in contemporary debates linking colour with the visual deception of cosmetics and 'painting', the aural deception of 'painted rhetoric' and the theatre that routinely brought these elements together.[38] Apparently, unbeknownst to Wanninger, an earlier study by Subha Mukherji covers much of the same ground but with greater focus on the law and its processes, examining 'colour' in its 'legal, rhetorical, theatrical, theological and physiognomical senses' and in relation to notions of evidence during Vittoria's arraignment.[39] In 'A Darker Shade of Pale', the fourth and final of these studies, Annaliese Connolly and Lisa Hopkins offer compelling topical readings of whiteness in *The White Devil* and *The Duchess of Malfi*. Pervasive images of winter and white-furred animals implicate Webster's tragedies in the social and geopolitical context of 'the first attempted land-grab of the Arctic' during the first half of James I's reign, 'desired not for its mineral resources but because of the hope that it would offer access to a north-east passage' to the Far East, 'and also for its wildlife, which was predominantly white' and prized as exotic commodities.[40] First mooted in 1612, this 'improbable' proposal to annex Russia was sufficiently advanced by 1613 when James hoped to send Sir Thomas Overbury as an embassy – a hope that died with Overbury in the Tower of London later that year. Given that both *The White Devil* and *The Duchess of Malfi* were 'being written and/or acted at the time that the aborted embassy to Russia was being discussed', and that Webster had known Overbury since their days at the Middle Temple (and perhaps even acted as Overbury's literary executor after his death), Connolly and Hopkins remark, it is 'not surprising that the plays should be haunted by thoughts of the white world of Russia'.[41]

James I's 1612 reburial of his mother, Mary, Queen of Scots, in a magnificent marble tomb in Westminster Abbey to mark the twenty-fifth anniversary of her death, provides another topical context for the plays. In addition to the marble tombs, alabaster funerary sculptures and other conventional symbols of mourning it employs, *The White Devil* 'deliberately alludes to a range of images of Stuart iconography' and contains 'strong parallels between the story of Vittoria, Brachiano and Camillo and that of Mary Stuart, Henry, Lord Darnley and Bothwell'.[42] Drawing on Carol Blessing's article (discussed in the next section), Connolly and Hopkins persuasively argue that Webster's depiction of Vittoria – the titular 'white' devil – is informed by a well-established 'tradition of associating Mary [Queen of Scots] with the colour white', drawing on her figuration as the 'white rose of York' and the white mourning veil customary of the French court that became a well-publicized trademark. For the Jacobeans, whiteness was, therefore, associated with mourning and death, on the one hand, and with wealth and power, on the other – this, Connolly and Hopkins conclude, 'is why there is a general fear and refusal of whiteness in both *The Duchess of Malfi* and *The White Devil*'.[43] As these studies suggest, there is more to colour in *The White Devil* than a simple juxtaposition between black and white: Webster's language and imagery spans a wide spectrum, vividly evoking a complex network of cultural, social, and topical associations.

The law and analogous cases

Webster's fascination with the law and its processes, perhaps betraying his formal legal study undertaken while at the Middle Temple, remains a staple of twenty-first scholarship on *The White Devil*. In particular, the arraignment scene (3.2) has fuelled considerable critical discussion. Luke Wilson's '*The White Devil* and the Law' poses fundamental questions about the scene's structure and usefully teases out its various jurisdictional ambiguities: Is the court or theatre the place of judgement? Is the legal system represented Italian or English? Is the language of authority Latin or vernacular, and who is authorized to judge? Is the jurisdiction ecclesiastical, common law, or equity? Wilson works through these questions in turn, demonstrating how Webster's depiction of the trial scene is informed by contemporary attacks on English ecclesiastical courts that were levelled on two fronts: by Puritans concerned that they were 'too lax on serious sins' and retained vestiges of the 'trans-national Catholic ecclesiastical apparatus' from which they originated, and by common lawyers who took issue with overlapping jurisdictional boundaries.[44]

One of the recurring debates in legal readings of *The White Devil* concerns the play's relationship to notions of equity – a body of English legal principles that developed alongside the common law, characterized by 'painstaking inquiry and fair judgment in consideration of the particular circumstances of a case'. For example, Ina Habermann argues that *The White Devil* (alongside *The Duchess of Malfi* and *The Devil's Law-Case*) exemplifies 'a type of forensic drama which foregrounds equity by placing the issues of female characters at the centre of the action', such that 'as the law interrogates femininity, femininity interrogates the law'.[45] Central to Habermann's argument is Vittoria's petitioning of the audience, both on- and off-stage, to pity her and support her cause, since this invokes equitable principles and 'the practice of equity is relegated to the audience'. Vittoria's strategy fails, although it gains her a 'moral victory' and exposes her trial as 'a travesty of justice'. However, Habermann interprets this failure 'as evidence of Webster's nationalist and anti-Catholic stance' and not reflective of his position on competing legal principles and jurisdictions: 'legal proceedings in *The White Devil* are flawed because they lack the right kind of equity'.[46] Such an equitable reading of *The White Devil*, Wilson argues, is frustrated on two grounds. First, although the play 'may appear to reflect women's recourse' in the seventeenth century 'to the prerogative courts, especially the equitable jurisdiction of the Chancery', in practice 'the advantages were technical' and 'theatrical equity does not much resemble equity in its institutionalized forms'. Second, and more importantly, 'Vittoria's arguments in the arraignment scene are not distinctly equitable at all'. The 'revelation of interiority as exculpatory', one of the hallmarks of equity, 'is almost entirely absent' and, arguably, 'knowing more about Vittoria would make her behavior seem less understandable and less forgivable'. If anything, Wilson concludes, *The White Devil* is 'an anti-equitable play, one that refuses to stand as a humanizing supplement to the law'.[47]

Twenty-first century critics have also identified parallels between the dramatization of Vittoria's trial and those of other prominent aristocratic women. One of these figures is Lady Frances Howard, Countess of Somerset, who in 1616, along with her husband Robert Carr, Lord Rochester, and a favourite of James I, pleaded guilty to the murder of Sir Thomas Overbury, while he was a prisoner in the Tower of London three years earlier. Attributed to natural causes at the time, Overbury's death was reinvestigated when allegations of poisoning surfaced 'in the midst of a bitter court struggle' between Carr and James I's new court favourite. Alastair Bellany succinctly summarizes the lurid and widely publicized details that emerged in the trials that followed:

> The crowds who packed the murder trials and gathered to witness the executions of the condemned heard fantastic stories of lust, betrayal, and murder; of ambitious men and ungoverned women; of witchcraft and poison; of pride and dissimulation; of popery, treason, and political assassination.[48]

Stevie Simkin reads the portrayal of Vittoria in *The White Devil* as a theatrical antecedent to the construction of Frances Howard in the wake of the Overbury scandal. In addition to her function as 'the mainspring of the revenge plot', Vittoria's beauty, sexuality, inscrutability and duplicity – traits also attributed to Frances – firmly establish her as 'an early modern example of the *femme fatale* mythotype'.[49] The timing of the play's composition and performance extinguish the possibility that Webster drew inspiration for *The White Devil* directly from Frances's divorce from Robert Devereux, 3rd Earl of

Essex, or the Overbury affair that followed.[50] Nonetheless, Simkin outlines a range of parallels between Vittoria and Frances, including their grounds for divorce, refusal to be silenced, and determination to outface their accusers at court.[51]

Another figure whose 'famous trials became the stuff of legend, providing ripe material for Webster's law scenes' is Mary Stuart, Queen of Scots.[52] Mary's first husband, François II of France, died in 1560 and her second marriage to Henry Stuart, Lord Darnley, came to an abrupt end in 1567 when Darnley was murdered. Although the identities of those responsible remain hotly contested, Mary's involvement in the conspiracy was strongly suspected at the time, fuelled by rumours that she was involved in an illicit affair with James Hepburn, 4th Earl of Bothwell, who she married in equally questionable circumstances later that year.[53] In a provocative reading, Carol Blessing traces Marian echoes in *The White Devil*, beginning with the play's title. 'Le Deuil Blanc', François Clouet's 1567 portrait of Mary wearing the customary mourning attire of the French court – 'a white veil flowing down from a headpiece' over a black mourning dress – suggests a possible influence: 'Although "deuil" in French means "mourning", in the context of mourning attire, its resemblance in print to the English word "devil" may have incited Webster to wordplay'.[54]

Whether Webster saw this particular portrait or others in the same style is immaterial to Blessing's argument: Mary inaugurated a 'new style of mourning head-dress' in England, importing and adapting the *deuil blanc* 'French hood' in a form that would become iconographically synonymous with her.[55] In fact, as Blessing notes, Mary was 'essentially dressed in mourning from the age of seventeen onward', famously 'appearing in widow's weeds at her second and third marriages'. In addition to the possible wordplay of the title, Blessing identifies further parallels between the depiction of Vittoria and the life of Mary Stuart, 'whose infamous affairs mirror Webster's provocative heroine'.[56] Both women married two men in quick succession, and were accused of murdering the first. Both are 'described overwhelmingly' in terms of their appearance, whose 'beautiful exteriors' deceitfully mask their deviant sexuality and inclination to murder exemplifying the contemporary proverb, 'the white devil is worse than the black'. A casket of letters was introduced as evidence in Mary's trial for adultery and murder to establish her affair with Bothwell; likewise, Monticelso produces a letter as evidence of Vittoria's unchastity at her arraignment, although she refutes it: 'Temptation to lust proves not the act' (3.2.199). Webster's identification of Vittoria with Mary, Blessing suggests, allows an opportunity for the on- and off-stage audiences to evaluate the actions and words of both figures.

Death and the dumb show

'Plenty of blood', says a young mouse-dangling John Webster in the 1998 film *Shakespeare in Love*, 'That's the only writing'.[57] This caricature exemplifies the popular perception of Webster as a macabre figure obsessed with images of decay, torture and madness, despite his acknowledged authorship of at least three comedies. Critics, too, have been drawn to Webster's fascination with death and his ability, in T. S. Eliot's words, to see 'the skull beneath the skin'.[58] In particular, recent scholarship has explored the metatheatricality of *The White Devil* in relation to the performance of violence and death.

The sequence of dumb shows in Act 2, Scene 2, through which Brachiano witnesses the intricate murders of Isabella and Camillo, has occasioned detailed critical interpretation and debate. Julie Sanders argues that Webster's use of the device 'to depict some of the most extravagantly engineered deaths of the play' allows 'what might have stretched the imagination if staged for real' to be 'both naturalised and heightened in its horror'. For Sanders, the effect of the dumb show to condense stage action and to render death 'pictorial and spectacular' explains the 'particular taste' for the device's re-emergence in Jacobean tragedy.[59] In his study of theatrical representations of death in the context of Renaissance memory arts, William E. Engel suggests that these dumb shows' 'effect of emblematically collapsing time and space' renders them 'all the more memorable', since they are 'accorded a separate (and, as it were, impossible) space within which to transpire'.[60] Engel's likening of the scene's 'staging of double perspective' to 'a concealed closed-circuit television camera' in modern terms is adopted, but not acknowledged, in Zoltán Márkus's article on 'Violence in Jacobean Drama'. Márkus argues that the audience's shared viewing of the dumb shows gives rise to a temporary identification with Brachiano, broken only when he is turned 'from a fellow audience member into the object of their attention'. For Márkus, the dumb shows both enable and exemplify a larger theatrical and ideological focus of the play: '*The White Devil* is more interested in theatrical representations of its modes of dying than its modes of killing', betraying a greater fascination with the 'victims of revenge than the revengers'.[61]

Critics are divided, however, on the function of the dumb shows and the question of the audience's identification and/or complicity with Brachiano during this scene. Drawing on media theory, Katherine M. Carey argues that the dumb shows in *The White Devil* are instances of 'hypermediacy', allowing the audience to watch both murders occur while, at the same time, observing Brachiano's reactions: 'two frames within one theatrical frame'. The effect, according to Carey, is one of distancing and alienation: although the immediacy of the dumb shows 'evoke an even greater visual horror', their artificiality also serves as a 'very present reminder that the play is just a play'.[62] For David Coleman, who approves Carey's analysis, this feature of the dumb shows demonstrates Webster's mastery of different theatrical techniques 'to effect audience engagement or detachment' as appropriate.[63] By contrast, David K. Anderson suggests that, rather than detachment, the dumb shows emphasize Brachiano's – and, therefore, also the audience's – 'complicit spectatorship', thereby problematizing 'the ethical distance between the staged bloodshed and the customers who view it'.[64]

The metatheatrical qualities of other deaths in the play give rise to similar questions about the slippages between fiction and reality. 'Death scenes' in Webster's tragedies, Roberta Barker argues, 'exposed the tenuous boundaries between character, actor and spectator in a society whose subjects were all performers'.[65] Barker quotes John Dryden as suggesting that short of *actually* dying on stage, the action of death is one that cannot be represented or 'imitated to a just height'. Barker suggests that Webster overtly acknowledges this theatrical impossibility in his depictions of death, but nonetheless 'raises the question of its potential in a world where unstable identities are grounded in ceaseless social change', while simultaneously underlining 'the familiar anti-theatrical trope that conflates acting with socially and spiritually destructive hypocrisy'.[66] Central to these arguments is Flamineo's 'double death' in the final scene (5.6), in which his feigned death at the hands of Vittoria to test her loyalty is followed by a 'real' death when Gasparo and Lodovico exact their revenge. Lisa Dickson has persuasively argued that this 'doubling of death scenes' is not only a 'confusion of the boundary between the real and the theater', but is also 'linked to the play's central epistemological crisis', namely, 'the instability of knowledge based on visible signs'.[67] It is not that the white devil is worse than the black, but rather that the two are indistinguishable. So, too, with 'mock death and real': the 'signs for both look the same' and 'Flamineo playing dead is indistinguishable from an actor playing a dead Flamineo'. As a result, Dickson suggests, 'Flamineo's status at the moment of his death – both of them – is tantalizingly unclear'.[68]

Adaptation, source study and style

An interlude sketch in an episode of *The Young Ones*, first aired in 1984, depicts two Victorian prisoners conversing as they wait to board a prison ship:

> FIRST PRISONER Transported for life in the colonies.
> And for what? Scum I was to that beak,
> Nothing but scum. 'Tis for my accent and
> My situation that I am condemned.
> 'Tis for the want of better graces and
> The influence they bring that I am to
> Board this prison hulk.
> SECOND PRISONER And for all 'em murders you done.[69]

When I first watched this exchange, I was struck by its similarity to the opening scene of *The White Devil*, in which Antonelli and Gasparo rehearse a litany of offences justifying Lodovico's banishment, culminating with 'certain murders here in Rome, / Bloody and full of horror' (1.1.31–2). Lodovico's dispassionate and dismissive response to this – 'they were flea-bitings' (32) – and the other charges betrays the same black humour at work: eloquent as they may be, both Lodovico and the first prisoner are seemingly oblivious to the full extent of their crimes. As Ceri Sullivan elsewhere remarks, this aspect of Webster's drama may explain the play's continued popularity with modern audiences 'versed in the filmmaker Quentin Tarantino's formal pleasures', namely, 'mordant wit, grotesque caricatures of the human body, and cheery good humor at (other people's) torture', conceived 'as revenge comedies, perhaps, more than revenge tragedies'.[70]

Adaptation studies have gained significant critical ground in recent years. As might be expected, much of the fruits of this critical labour have attended to the multiple adaptations of Shakespeare's works across an equally staggering array of media formats, although so-called 'screen adaptations' on film and television continue to dominate discussion.[71] By contrast, adaptations of *The White Devil*, even at the fundamental level of allusion, have received scant critical attention. Scholars have identified allusions to *The White Devil* in the poetry of T. S. Eliot, Herman Melville and Allen Tate and also the prose of Margaret Drabble, Thomas Hardy and Virginia Woolf, among others.[72] Beyond allusion-hunting, two articles exploring inter-textual, structural and thematic echoes of *The White Devil* in Amiri Baraka's 1964 political satire *Dutchman* and also in Anthony Trollope's 1861–2 serialized novel *Orley Farm*, signalled a brief twenty-first century spike in more detailed adaptation study of the play.[73]

Perhaps the limited number of adaptation studies of *The White Devil* may simply reflect a paucity of materials to examine. This is certainly true in the case of film: although the script for Alex Cox's proposed 2006 screen adaptation of *The White Devil* is available and has occasioned some discussion,[74] a film of the play has yet to appear.[75] However, no detailed study of Nahum Tate's (apparently unperformed) theatrical adaptation of 1707, *Injured Love, or The Cruel Husband*, has appeared since Hazelton Spencer's primarily textual description of the play in 1934, and no account has yet been made of late twentieth- and twenty-first century adaptations and echoes.[76] For example, Justin Evans's 2011 novel *The White Devil* owes not only its title to Webster, but also elements of plot (including a vengeful ghost rehearsing lines for a school production of the play).[77] In an episode of the period drama series *Boardwalk Empire*, also first aired in 2011, the mob enforcer Jimmy Darmody (played by Michael Pitt) reminisces about his time at Princeton, with flashbacks to a classroom discussion about *The White Devil*.[78] With so little existing scholarship and an ever-expanding selection of derivative materials to consider, opportunities abound for adaptation studies of *The White Devil*.

Source study is another area that promises to offer fresh critical insights into a play that, according to James Shapiro, 'owes so much to Shakespeare' – and, we might add, other authors – 'that it often hovers between plagiarism and parody'.[79] Critics have long recognized Webster's predilection for imitation: he has a 'tendency to recycle the same common-places frequently' and, at times, the dialogue of his plays simply devolves into an exchange of *sententiae*.[80] Generations ago, Gunnar Boklund and R. W. Dent published extensive studies of such 'borrowings' in *The White Devil* and Webster's other plays.[81] In 1960, Dent remarked that 'more than three-fourths of Webster' could be traced to other sources, 'if only we had access to all the works he employed'.[82] With the prolif-eration of large-scale full-text databases in the 1990s and 2000s, such as *Literature Online* and the *Early English Books Online Text Creation Partnership*, Dent's dream is much closer to becoming a reality than ever before. New theoretical models and computational methods for source study have also emerged, enabled by these digital resources and informed by critical turns in literary studies to book history and materi-alism.[83] Thus, only recently has a systematic study of sources, parallels, and other inter-textual echoes in *The White Devil* become a possibility, and with it, an opportunity to completely re-evaluate Webster's reading and writing practices.

By the same token, wider availability of machine-readable texts of Webster's works and those of his contemporaries, together with the development of increasingly sophisticated software tools for their analysis, provides twenty-first century scholars with the means to investigate elements of Webster's style – his lexical and grammatical habits, recurring images, and use of rhetorical devices – with greater precision than ever before. To date, scholarly efforts in this area have focused entirely on authorship attribution studies, such as MacDonald P. Jackson's thorough analysis to establish Webster's canon for the Cambridge *Works*, work that continues now that the editors have decided to include Webster's collaborative plays as an additional fourth volume.[84] While computational studies of Shakespeare's language beyond questions of authorship have begun to appear, similar analysis of Webster and *The White Devil* remains to be written.[85]

Coda

Asked from where inspiration came for the song 'My White Devil', lyricist Ian McCulloch of British post-punk outfit Echo and the Bunnymen replied that, in desperation, he turned to his girlfriend's exercise book only to find a single page with writing on it:

> It was about this bloke John Webster who I hadn't heard of – not being that great an English student – and the first line was 'John Webster was' and it all fitted like that![86]

Reviewers of the album were just as desperate to discern Webster's presence in the song, much to McCulloch's amusement: 'they imagined I was some great literary freak or something'.[87] The obtuse lyrics perhaps better reflect prejudicial accounts of Webster's writing than the writing itself. Henry Fitzgeffrey, for example, scorned Webster's laboured and slow composition in a satire of 1617, confident that any retort would 'be so obscure / That none shall understand'.[88] Even so, it is possible to strain glimpses of Webster between the wandering lines and distorted guitar noises. The chord progression in a major key is at odds with the dark psychedelia of the lyrics, a dissonance mirrored in the juxtaposition of grotesque imagery: love 'upside down' and 'monkey brains' laughing, for example. Although the lack of erudition and *sententiae* would certainly have irked him, this is not necessarily that far removed from Webster's art. The alternating lyrics of the chorus – 'change in the never' and 'chancing forever' becoming 'changing the never' and 'chance in forever' – are instances of the homophonic wordplay that Webster frequently revelled in.[89] Vittoria's reference to Monticelso's 'pistol' (3.2.211), a homophone for 'pizzle' (penis), provides a bawdy example.

Such artificial parallels aside, if McCulloch did not find inspiration in *The White Devil*, he, nonetheless, found in

'John Webster' a name to conjure with. Not to belabour an already overwrought reading, the shift in title between the play and the song, between 'the' and 'my' *White Devil*, oscillating from the abstract to the individual, neatly encapsulates how Webster's tragedy continually resists universal interpretation. If Shakespeare's works could be characterized as they are in the 1623 First Folio as 'not of an age, but for all time', Webster is the opposite. As the twenty-first century criticism surveyed in this chapter suggests, it is only ever 'the' or 'my' – and never 'our' – *White Devil*.

4

New Directions: Ritual Dissonance in *The White Devil*

David Coleman

Discord, dissonance and the uncanny

How might we understand the religious, legal and cultural ceremonies and rituals in *The White Devil*? Do they bring or represent order or disorder? Although undoubtedly familiar with the Renaissance celebration of balance and harmony as a guiding principle of artistic production, the drama of John Webster generally rejects this aesthetic standard in favour of an emphasis on discord and dissonance. The experimental theatrical techniques of *The White Devil* demonstrate this more clearly than any of Webster's other dramatic works, especially through Webster's focus on rituals. Discord has a key structural function in this play, from the implied oxymoron of the title (devils are conventionally black in Renaissance culture, rather than white, albeit the phrase was in relatively wide circulation in the period), through to the frequent accusations of hypocrisy levelled at Vittoria's appearance and behaviour (as, for example, in Monticelso's comment that 'She comes not like a widow; she comes armed / With scorn and impudence' (3.2.121–2)).[1] Yet, for all its emphasis on discord, *The White Devil*, nevertheless, is a play which can at times seem preoccupied with considering the 'correct' observance of ritual form. For example, the English Ambassador can, without any intended irony, outline to the audience his understanding of the appropriate manner in which a papal conclave should take place:

> when first they enter
> 'Tis lawful for the ambassadors of princes
> To enter with them, and to make their suit
> For any man their prince affecteth best;
> But after, till a general election,
> No man may speak with them.   (4.3.26–32)

By this point, the audience has already seen the adaptation and inversion of a number of ceremonial forms; and this new stress on the formal observance of ceremonial possesses a discordant character of its own, as does the ritualized appearance of 'A Cardinal on the terrace' and the Latin proclamation '*Vivat Sanctus Pater Paulus Quartus*' ['Long live the Holy Father, Pope Paul IV'] (4.3.40SD; 4.3.46). Both of these dramatic moments may well have carried intense psychological meanings for some audience members: in these instances, the play's interrogation of ritual engages with the complex history of religious reform in sixteenth- and seventeenth-century England, in which reform of the rituals of the Church was accompanied by a rejection of both papal authority and Latin liturgies.

Moments such as these – where Catholic rituals are faithfully observed – form part of an ongoing oscillation in the play between ordered and disordered rituals. This, I contend, is a more accurate view of the play than Charles R. Forker's influential suggestion:

From first to last Webster's staging is organized around a series of spectacles or ceremonies that suggest a kind of public order. Yet these ritualistic effects only supply the ironic backdrop for a display of psychic and social derangement and for the essential loneliness and egoism of individuals.[2]

Forker's distinction between public order and private disorder fails to comprehend fully the relationship between public ritual and what he terms 'psychic and social derangement'. Rather than simply functioning as an ironic backdrop in the play, the rituals of *The White Devil* have significant effects on the individuals and the society presented. While much of the ceremonial form on display in *The White Devil* is superficially religious in nature, this discussion argues that Webster's interest in religious ceremony is of a piece with his broader social, cultural and psychological explorations. Martin Wiggins' reading of the public rituals of the play is valuable, as he suggests that they demonstrate 'the play's concern with the interlocking impulses of public probity and private corruption'.[3] However, I want to expand on this insight by demonstrating the pressures which adherence to ceremonial form brought to bear on both public and private identities.

Surprisingly, given the anthropological inspiration behind many recent readings of Renaissance drama, theoretically informed readings of Webster's rituals are relatively rare. The most focused reading of the rituals of *The White Devil*, James R. Hurt's essay of 1962, in fact, significantly predates literary critics' turn to theory in the last decades of the twentieth century. Although a useful compendium of ritual moments in the play, Hurt's reading of *The White Devil* is limited by his insistence on a single paradigm for the articulation of Webster's interest in ceremonial form: Webster's 'inverted rituals' are 'parodies', linked to their historical context as 'part of a complex series of witchcraft images that run throughout the play'.[4] By presenting Webster's dramatic technique as a relatively unsophisticated form of parody, and by suggesting the occult as the primary historical frame of reference for the play, Hurt fails to acknowledge both the wider role of ritual in complex societies, and the sophisticated nature of Webster's dramatic techniques. Hurt is one of the few critics to correctly identify Webster's interest in the sacramental rituals of the Catholic Church: 'Amid the somber atmosphere of the play [...] appear inverted versions of the sacred rites of marriage, confession, and extreme unction'. However, his reading of Webster's rituals is less tenable: 'the lost souls of *The White Devil* invert the ceremonies of marriage, confession, and extreme unction as symbols of their worship of the Devil'.[5]

As I have noted, rituals in the play are not always presented either in a manner which suggests public order, or in an 'inverted' fashion. Rather the play swings back and forth between correctly and incorrectly performed rituals. This tension between order and disorder contributes to the dramatic effect which I will refer to as dissonance, which is most explicitly explored through the discordant effect associated with the experience of competing ritual forms. This discord can also have a psychological effect, both on the fictitious subjects in the play, and on the audience in the theatre. I am aware that in referring to the psychological experience of the audience, this discussion may be open to charges of assuming that Renaissance selves are identical to modern identities. I do not wish to deny the significance of culture in contributing to the experience of selfhood, but nevertheless I would like to suggest that considering Sigmund Freud's notion of 'the Uncanny' may help us understand something of the psychological effect of witnessing Catholic rituals on stage. For Freud, the Uncanny – *das Unheimliche* – is a feeling that things are not right, an unsettling feeling which is caused by the perception that there is a difference between what the subject is currently seeing, and what the subject believes that he or she should be seeing. So an inanimate object which appears to be lifelike – a doll, for example, or a waxwork figure – may create a sense of the Uncanny. Freud is also clear that art and culture can give rise to an Uncanny feeling: the central example in his essay is of a short story, 'The Sandman', by the German Romantic writer E. T. A. Hoffmann. It is important for Freud's schema that this feeling of the Uncanny is understood to have deep psychological roots:

> In the unconscious mind we can recognize the dominance of a *compulsion to repeat*, which proceeds from instinctual impulses. This compulsion probably depends on the essential nature of the drives themselves. It is strong enough to override the pleasure principle and lend a demonic character to certain aspects of mental life; it is still clearly manifest in the impulses of small children and dominates part of the course taken by the psychoanalysis of victims of neurosis. The foregoing discussions have all prepared us for the fact that anything that can remind us of this inner compulsion to repeat is perceived as uncanny.[6]

Particularly important for the purposes of this discussion is the Freudian understanding of the Uncanny as related to 'doubling' and to something which is both 'homely' and 'unhomely'. As one recent reader of Freud puts it, the Uncanny is 'a peculiar commingling of the familiar and the unfamiliar. It can take the form of something familiar unexpectedly arising in a strange and unfamiliar context, or of something strange and unfamiliar unexpectedly arising in a familiar context'.[7] This gloss on the Freudian understanding of the Uncanny as that which reminds us of the inner compulsion to repeat is also, I would like to suggest, a useful way of thinking about Webster's presentation of ritual in *The White Devil*. It captures succinctly the ways in which ritual is a dissonant force in the play, and the ways in which that dissonance can create a psychological effect of alienation and discomfort which is similar to the Freudian experience of the Uncanny.

As I indicated earlier, this is in no small part due to Webster's insistence on staging rituals – marriages, trials, religious ceremonies – in a theatrical context where they are alienated both by virtue of being removed from their normal contexts, and by being performed by actors – who are necessarily insincere participants. Moreover, Webster disrupts the expectations of his audience by, in some instances, *faithfully* representing the rituals of Catholicism. Such rituals had supposedly been discredited for Webster's audience of (mainly) Protestants; and so the failure of an anticipated parody of Catholic ritual to emerge would have strengthened the play's alienating effects on its audience.

Psychological dissonance

The dissonant theatrical effects of *The White Devil* work to emphasize what should be considered as one of the animating preoccupations of the text: the destabilizing effect of culturally demanded, yet philosophically contradictory, ritual processes on both the integrity of the self and the maintenance of social relations. Lara Bovilsky notes that *The White Devil* is characterized by 'multiplicity and concomitant fluidity'; in other words, the variety of senses of selfhood available in the play leads to the possibility of subjects moving between different conceptions of the self.[8] However, this multiplicity is not an end in itself, nor is Webster straightforwardly championing such fluidity; rather, the play is primarily interested in the social and psychological tensions which are unleashed by the multiplicity on display. To approach this from a slightly different angle, one can bear in mind the long critical history which considers Webster, and many other Renaissance dramatists, as drawing emphasis from the tensions between the will of the individual and the restraints of society. Such a viewpoint has recently been restated by Andrew Strycharski, who suggests that *The White Devil* 'documents an individualism motivated by ideological decay'.[9] In this reading, the 'ideological decay' represents the downfall of one (older) system of social relations, to be replaced by a new form based on the desires and aspirations of the individual.

This is a traditional view of Renaissance drama, and indeed of Renaissance culture as a whole. But by positing 'decay' as the motivating force behind the disintegration of social structures, Strycharski implies an inevitability about the process by which the individual will triumphs over the structures of social obligation. I would suggest, however, that instead of ideological decay, one might more profitably consider ideological dissonance: that is, that there are tensions and contradictions within the structure of society in *The White Devil*, and that Webster's focus on ritual calls attention to these very contradictions. Whereas Strycharski suggests that Vittoria's 'characterological drift expresses the dislocations implicit in creating a self unavailable within the fund of society's prefabricated egos', I would argue that the widespread significance of ritual dissonance in the play must qualify the assertion: Vittoria is the only character significantly affected by this unavailability of a ready-made identity.[10] Strycharski is perhaps guilty of a certain romanticism in his claim that 'Brachiano is not so much trapped by oppressively rigid social structures overdetermining his identity as unbearably free from them, losing any communal confirmation of self in the contingency of Vittoria's love'.[11] Rather, it is the competing rigidity of incompatible structures of ideas which are largely responsible for 'the sense of interiority, whose depth comes from fragmentation, doubt, and self-division', which Strycharski correctly identifies in Flamineo.[12]

It may be worth clarifying in more detail how my view of the play differs from this recent reading. Strycharski's view of competing ideologies in the play – 'both an exhausted traditional value system and an emerging ethos of individualism'[13] – appears to be influenced by the distinction between residual and emergent cultural forms made by the Marxist theorist Raymond Williams.[14] Williams influentially argued that any particular society is composed of relationships, often tensions, between dominant, residual and emergent forms of culture. The relationship between these forms is complex and dynamic at any given moment. Strycharski's analysis focuses on residual and emergent forms of culture, with less focus on the dominant ideology; but if *The White Devil* is to be used as a means of interpreting cultural change, attention must be paid to the dominant ideology, and the ways in which it is represented in the text. I argue that Webster's dramatization of ritual draws attention to some of the contradictions inherent in the dominant cultural forms of his moment, particularly those of religion and the law.

To take one specific example, the play's emphasis on a ritually conditioned psychological dissonance is intimated through its dumbshows, which function as condensed presentations of the play's vision of ritual effects on individuals. Thus, Isabella, for example, '*kneels down as to prayers, then draws the curtain of the picture, does three reverences to it, and kisses it thrice. She faints, and will not suffer them to come near it; dies*' (2.2.23SD). The emphasis here on repeating the action three times physically calls attention to the Trinitarian aspects of Christian theology and ritual, where actions repeated three times often have a theological reference to the three persons of the Trinity (for example, in the division of the host into three sections in the Catholic Eucharist); the fainting and death, meanwhile, visually enunciate the irreversible psychological damage which, in the play's vision, can be inflicted through ritual performance.

Therefore, there is an implicit challenge to Christian ritual here, a challenge which may also have a counterpart in the play's representation of a crucifix. Elizabeth Williamson has recently explored the relevance of Cornelia's familiar crucifix in the play, alongside the implications of Flamineo's infantile vandalism of the object, as related by Marcello: 'I have heard you say, giving my brother suck, / He took the crucifix between his hands, / And broke a limb off' (5.2.11–13). It is, of course, Marcello himself who identifies this act of destruction as both theologically and materially efficacious:

Oh mother now remember what I told
Of breaking off the crucifix: farewell –

> There are some sins which heaven doth duly punish
> In a whole family.   (5.2.18–21)

Williamson's reading of this moment, however, emphasizes the way in which the broken crucifix is removed from a ritual context: 'Webster's play deftly skirts the problem of idolatry by distancing Cornelia's crucifix from any kind of religious ceremony and focusing its audience's attention instead on the tragedy of a family's disintegration'.[15] On one level, this is true, but on another, the broken body of Christ is a powerful image, which cannot be extricated from the discourses of idolatry, iconoclasm and sacramental reform.[16] The latter point is almost admitted by Williamson when she notes that there is a 'second crucifix' in the play, 'a counterfeit liturgical object' used in the torture of Brachiano.[17] Williamson's concern that this should be seen as a 'false crucifix' is puzzling: what is a 'false' crucifix? And while she is right to stress the differences between the two objects, it is nevertheless important to acknowledge that, in the dramatic construction of the play, Brachiano's crucifix illuminates Cornelia's, and vice versa; moreover, the 'doubling' of the crucifix, and the appearance of a familiar or similar stage property in strange or different contexts, contributes to the Uncanny effect of the play as a whole. Thus, Williamson's assertion that Cornelia's crucifix possesses its 'affective value' purely 'as part of [a] secular inheritance system' fails to capture the full significance of the Catholic devotional object.[18]

Gentle penance (1.1.36)

In *The White Devil*, the destabilizing effect of conflicting ritual processes is sometimes presented as a discordant clash of the legal and the theological, made visible through their ritual forms: the main ceremonies staged in the play are either legal (as in Vittoria's trial) or religious (as in the installation of Monticelso, or Brachiano's last rites). While theoretically Christian and secular law are compatible in the society of the play, in practice the relationship is one of tension. Vittoria suggests as much when she wishes to 'appeal then from this Christian court / To the uncivil Tartar' (3.2.128–9). Similarly, the location of 'lawyers' and 'divines' beside each other in Monticelso's 'general catalogue of knaves' is not coincidental, but rather forms another instance of the play's insistence on juxtaposing religion and the law, in order to point out the shortcomings of both (4.1.59–62). In the play's opening scene, for example, Gasparo's sense that the banishment of Lodovico is a 'gentle penance' is just the first instance of the language of sin, penitence and reparation which is found throughout the play in both legal and theological registers (1.1.36).

While Webster occasionally draws on the populist practice of presenting Catholicism as exotically corrupt, as when Lodovico reveals his murderous plans under the cover of the confessional, religious ritual is more generally displayed as making demands of its subjects which are incompatible with the requirements of other such culturally mandated ritual forms. While it has recently been argued that early modern English juries were too numerous and complicated to represent realistically on stage, and thus that the drama of the period does not present an accurate reflection of legal reality, what matters more in the case of *The White Devil* is that Webster's drama concerns itself with the social and psychological effects of living under competing and contradictory forms of law.[19] This is by design.

Religious rituals, which often involved fewer participants, may have been more straightforward to represent realistically on stage. Indeed, the Catholic sacrament of penance and its ritual form of confession to a priest is frequently represented and interrogated in the play, much as the sacrament of marriage is in Webster's slightly later *Duchess of Malfi*. Brachiano urges Monticelso to use the confessional as a means of gathering knowledge: 'Will you urge that, my good lord cardinal, / As part of her confession at next shrift[?]' (2.1.56–7). Confession is also on the mind of Francisco, as when he tells Brachiano that 'Thy ghostly father with all's absolution / Shall ne'er do so by thee' (2.1.68–9). A form of the sacrament, internalized as a bodily process of excretion and purgation, also structures the conversation between Brachiano and Isabella later in the same scene:

BRACHIANO	Devotion?
	Is your soul charged with any grievous sin?
ISABELLA	'Tis burdened with too many, and I think
	The oft'ner that we cast our reckonings up,
	Our sleeps will be the sounder. (2.1.150–4)

The idea that confession of sins can result in a calmer conscience is a common conception of traditional devotional writings of the period, although it was of course denied by many Protestant and reformist writers.[20] Certainly Webster's audience would have tended towards the latter viewpoint, associating the former with Catholicism; yet, it was a view of interiority which was influential for many dramatists, including Marlowe and Shakespeare.[21] Isabella's recasting of confession as a physical rather than a spiritual process is broadly in line with the preoccupations of the play as a whole, which has little interest in the spiritual efficacy of ritual forms (significant examples notwithstanding, as discussed below). Isabella's sense that the purgation of sins will have a physical effect, which may in turn have a psychological benefit, is, however, more optimistic than the play as a whole, which traces the conflicting physical and psychological effects of clashing and discordant ritual forms.

Penance re-appears later in the play too when, as Hurt has previously noted, Lodovico pre-empts Monticelso's plans by insisting upon the secrecy of the confessional:

> Holy Father,
> I come not to you as an intelligencer,
> But as a penitent sinner. What I utter

Is in confession merely; which you know
Must never be revealed.   (4.3.107–11)

As with Isabella's earlier submission to the rite of penance,
the ritual bears witness to a tension in the play between the
view of Catholicism as a religion that facilitates Machiavellian
scheming (because of the possibility of acquiring and putting
into circulation clandestine knowledge), and a more positive
view of sacramentality. This view suggests that submission to
the ritual can have a significant psychological benefit for the
penitent.[22] It is important to note that Lodovico's confession
to Monticelso explicitly follows the prescribed form of the
sacrament. Thus, for example, as Lodovico is not displaying
the correct signs of contrition, Pope Monticelso is unable to
provide absolution:

And so I leave thee
With all the Furies hanging 'bout thy neck,
Till by thy penitence thou remove this evil,
In conjuring from thy breast that cruel devil. (4.3.124–7)

Webster's play here draws on a tradition of dramatizing
penance in English Protestant drama that dates back at least
to the work of John Bale in the 1530s, whose *King Johan*
(1538) mounted a ferocious polemic against the Catholic
understanding of the sacrament. *The White Devil*, however,
explores the ritual in the context of what Lara Bovilsky refers
to as 'a dense combination of dis- and cross-identification,
English and Italian, nation and race'; that is, in a much
more complex manner than the proto-nationalism of Bale's
drama.[23]

Penance also reappears in muted form towards the end
of the play, as part of the parodic last rites administered to
Brachiano (examined in more detail below). It is also staged
in a dramatically unexpected yet theologically informed
moment, in which Zanche confesses to Francisco/Mulinassar
and Lodovico:

[ZANCHE]   I sadly do confess I had a hand
              In the black deed.
FRANCISCO   Thou kept'st their counsel.
[ZANCHE]   Right.
              For which, urged with contrition, I intend
              This night to rob Vittoria.
LODOVICO   Excellent penitence!
              Usurers dream on't while they sleep out
              sermons.   (5.3.247–52)

Traditional Catholic understandings of the sacrament of penance stressed the tripartite nature of the rite: contrition (on the part of the penitent), confession (from the penitent to the confessor), and absolution (granted by the confessor, on behalf of God, to the penitent). Some early modern understandings of the sacrament also stressed the importance of reparation, from the penitent to the wronged party, especially when economic sins (like usury) were concerned.[24] With the necessary exception of absolution, all the core elements of the sacrament are present here, albeit reparation (and to some extent, given the nature of the figures involved: confession) is presented parodically. Penance, then, is an example of a ritual form which is both taken seriously by the play, and subjected to a radical interrogation. This approach to ritual – an evacuation of meaning contrasted with a reinforcement of ritual significance, thus establishing an Uncanny dislocation of meaning – is not confined to one specific religious form, but rather is characteristic of the play's approach to ceremony more generally.

Sophistic tricks (2.2.7)

This interrogation of ceremonial form in the play necessarily leads the audience towards scepticism concerning the validity of such ritualized practices. If the trial of Vittoria is unlikely to instil a sense of the outworkings of justice in culturally codified forms, then the play's frequent religious references might encourage audiences to view the play's bloody end as a perversion of religious ritual. (This includes the breaking of the crucifix.) Brian Chalk's recent observation that *The White Devil* 'establishes a dramatic context that makes questions regarding the afterlife both central to the play's thematic concerns and subject to derision' may be worth considering here.[25] In the wider context of the play's stance on religious matters, Flamineo's attitude to his proposed marriage to Zanche should be placed among such interrogatory instances: 'Faith, I made to her some such dark promise and in seeking to fly from't I run on, like a frighted dog with a bottle at's tail that fain would bite it off and yet dares not look behind him' (5.1.150–2). In this regard, Marcello's racially inflected opposition to the proposed marriage might also be relevant:

> I had rather she were pitched upon a stake
> In some new-seeded garden, to affright
> Her fellow crows thence.   (5.1.184–6)

Although the logic of Marcello's racial insult is convoluted and insecure, nevertheless, it does call attention to the play's preoccupation with colour as an inherently unstable marker of social identity.

The scepticism towards religion and ritual is arguably enhanced by the play's sophisticated awareness of its own contingent and constructed nature: that is, the play is aware of itself as a play, and often calls attention to the nature of its dramatic fiction. In so doing, it obliquely suggests something of the 'fictional' nature of ritual at the same time. This dramatic self-referentiality is clear from the play's opening moments, with both Vittoria – 'more lights' – and Flamineo – 'put out all your torches and depart' – directing action and effects in the roles of playwright and spectator (1.2.2, 1.2.9). Similarly, Webster allows characters to explicitly dress the stage in preparation for set pieces, as when '*ZANCHE brings out a carpet, spreads it and lays on it two fair cushions*' (1.2.202SD). In this instance, Zanche, Flamineo and Cornelia form an onstage 'audience', comparable to the audience in the theatre. If this self-conscious theatricality calls attention to the fictional nature of drama, the potentially fictional nature of ritual is also emphasized by the play's awareness that some ritual practices are inauthentic: the Conjuror contrasts his (nominally authentic) rituals with the inauthentic and inefficacious performances of impostors and mountebanks: such people use 'sophistic tricks', and 'juggle upon cards, / Seeming to conjure when indeed they cheat … speaking fustian Latin' (2.2.7–20). The impetus behind the Conjuror's speech is to reinforce the validity of his magical ceremonies, but it necessarily casts at least a measure of doubt on such practices in general.

Similarly, the display of confused ritual moments, when the form of the ceremony presented seems at odds with either the impetus towards, or the anticipated effect of, the action, supports the notion that the play as a whole is sceptical of the truth-claims of ritual practices. Isabella's superstitious appropriation of a ritual intended to test the validity of powdered unicorn's horn to her 'arms', which will 'charm [the] poison' of Brachiano, and 'force it to obeying' (2.1.15–17) is an example of the idea of ritual as a compelling force: Brachiano will not be able to resist the impetus of ritual, regardless of his own urges or desires. But in this instance as in others, the idea that ritual is automatically efficacious is a view which the play insistently works to undercut and problematize. Of significance here is Francisco's deliberate juxtaposition of the rituals surrounding marriage and death:

> Thou hast a wife, our sister; would I had given
> Both her white hands to death, bound and locked fast
> In her last winding-sheet, when I gave thee
> But one.   (2.1.64–7)

In developing this particular example, Francisco is drawing on a connection between death, marriage and birth/rebirth which is deeply engrained in Webster's culture, and evident in a number of cultural discourses and practices. A good example, which may have been known to Webster, is the link between marriage-sheets and winding-sheets in Shakespeare's *Othello* (in 4.3). This linkage is also important in the Freudian schema of the Uncanny, where the fear 'of being buried alive by mistake' is closely linked to 'the phantasy [...] of intra-uterine existence'.[26] In other words, the fear of being buried alive, which is simultaneously a fear of the awareness of death, is psychologically linked to the imagination of being unborn, of existence in the womb. As Nicholas Royle explains, Freud here presents us with 'a sort of micro-analysis of psychoanalysis in two sentences, the story of life from A to Z, or from Z to A, from death to birth, from the imminence of death to the timeless pleasure of womb-life'.[27] This is, then, another Uncanny 'doubling' in the play, and the conjunction is also hinted at later, in Brachiano's 'accursed be the priest / That sang the wedding mass, and even my issue' (2.1.190–1).

Indeed, the 'wedding-mass' of Brachiano and Isabella is an important context for one of the play's central explorations of discordant ritual. Brachiano's ritualized 'divorce' of Isabella is conducted in terms which link it to the marriage which it seeks to annul. As Hurt noted some time ago, this scene involves 'a fairly detailed parody of the wedding service'.[28] It involves, inter alia, a 'kiss', a 'ceremony of my love', a 'wedding ring' and a 'vow [which] is fixed' (2.1.192–205). Isabella's attempts to reinstall the spiritual import of the original wedding ceremony – 'the saints in heaven / Will knit their brows at that' (2.1.199–200) – have little effect. It is also, intriguingly, in this instance that the play's insistence on the inefficacy of rituals allows some of the characters to intimate that their interests might be best served by turning to secular, rather than spiritual, laws. Thus Isabella's reaction first of all turns to anger, and to rehearsing the link between marriage and winding-sheets, between Eros and Thanatos:

> To dig the strumpet's eyes out, let her lie
> Some twenty months a-dying, to cut off
> Her nose and lips, pull out her rotten teeth,
> Preserve her flesh like mummia, for trophies
> Of my just anger!   (2.1.245–9)

The direction of Isabella's resolve, however, then turns to the public, audible and visible form of the law:

> And this divorce shall be as truly kept
> As if in thronged court a thousand ears
> Had heard it, and a thousand lawyers' hands
> Sealed to the separation.   (2.1.255–8)

Thus Isabella's vow becomes fixed, as had Brachiano's; and she explicitly rejects the idea of physically purging mental disturbances: 'this my vow / Shall never on my soul be satisfied / With my repentance' (2.1.260–2).

A similar inversion of conventional ritual form can be found in Francisco/Mulinassar and Lodovico's verbal imaginings of the humiliation of Brachiano. This can be seen in their suggestions that it would be appropriate to have 'crowned him with a wreath of stinking garlic' in order to have 'shown the sharpness of his government / And rankness of his lust' (5.1.82–3). This is a rather straightforward parody of ceremonial form, rather than an interrogation of the assumptions of ritual language. Similarly, when Lodovico '*sprinkles BRACHIANO's beaver with a poison*' (5.2.76SD), he is here parodying a Catholic priest's blessing with holy water. Parody is among the less sophisticated techniques which Webster employs to critique ceremonial form. But parody – particularly the parody of the last rites – is nevertheless deserving of critical attention, as it is undoubtedly among the most theatrically exuberant instances of the play's interest in ritual. The Catholic last rites are a trio of sacraments administered to a dying person, to make the recipient as free from sin as possible, therefore aiding them in the afterlife (by, for example, reducing some of the time which the soul would have to spend in Purgatory before being admitted toHeaven). The last rites consist of a final confession to a priest, a final chance to receive communion and an anointing with oil known as 'extreme unction' (literally, 'final anointing'). Hurt is typical of critics when he notes 'the parody of the ritual of extreme unction' as the 'climax of this strand of the revenge plot'.[29] Williamson, meanwhile, reads this scene as 'an indirect attack on Catholicism itself'.[30] The play, however, does not present Catholic ritual as simply spiritually vacant, as might be suggested by Williamson's sense that 'the falseness of the revengers [...] mirrors the falseness that Protestants perceived as being at the heart of the Catholic faith'. This is because, for Williamson, 'the revengers' crucifix is nothing more than an element of their false show'.[31] Here, a sense of Webster as an anti-Catholic writer obscures the significance of his inter-rogation of religious ritual. Williamson does make efforts to temper this viewpoint – 'the point is not that Catholicism is inherently superstitious, but rather that its outward ornaments have the potential to be abused and often accompany other signs of hypocrisy' – but the view of Webster as anti-Catholic does threaten to contaminate the reading.[32] Rather, as Bovilsky notes, 'an audience's likely pleasure in dramatic spectacle [...] complicates any reading that would imagine the English to be simply revolted by the portrayal of Italianate excess'.[33]

Similarly to Shakespeare's *Hamlet*, a play which explores related theological concerns, Webster calls attention to his interest in the Catholic last rites in a manner which is not straightforwardly contemptuous. Brachiano is prepared for death by the entrance of the Capuchins: 'They have brought the extreme unction', explains Flamineo (5.3.39). Brachiano's seeming last rites represent a perversion of Catholic ritual – where the whispered 'private meditations' (5.3.146) are in fact designed to provoke spiritual despair. Nevertheless, it would be a mistake to perceive such perversion simply as a result of a Websterian anti-Catholicism, or of what one critic has referred to as this play's 'weakly delimited and overlapping notions of foreignness'.[34] Rather, the presentation of the last rites is consistent with Webster's dramatic strategy of presenting rituals in dissonant forms, as a means of exploring the contradictions of legal and religious imperatives.

'Full executor / to all my sins' (4.2.122–3)

Thus, the sense of discord presented by the play is not just a result of the tension between the competing discourses of religion and the law. Discord is also provoked through the dissonance between ideals enunciated in the discourses of mercy and justice, and how the social and psychological effects of the rituals conducted in their name are experienced and understood. The ineffectuality of religion is outlined early in the play by Flamineo, when he compares religious pronouncements to 'politic enclosures for paltry mutton': they fail because they lead to 'rebellion in the flesh' (1.2.90–1). The incongruity between religious ritual and the illicit licence it affords is also demonstrated in Flamineo's declaration that there is 'no time fitter than this night' of the papal conclave, for smuggling Vittoria away from the city (4.2.203). Similarly, Monticelso imagines Vittoria in a scene which fails both in its imitation of social aspiration and, through the ironic language employed, the Christian reversal of social judgment:

> Who knows not how, when several night by night
> Her gates were choked with coaches and with rooms
> Outbraved the stars with several kinds of lights.
> When she did counterfeit a prince's court
> In music, banquet and most riotous surfeits,
> This whore, forsooth, was holy?   (3.2.73–8)

Here the 'counterfeit' nature of Vittoria's court is expressed as an inappropriate imitation of socially elevated ceremonial forms; yet the sarcastic nature of Monticelso's closing comment is undercut by the ironic similarity between a holy whore and the characteristic reversals of social and moral judgement found in theoretical Christian doctrine. After all of these instances in which religious ritual is employed to secular ends, it should come as no surprise to the audience that Monticelso uses his newly acquired papal powers in a similar manner: 'We do denounce excommunication / Against them both' (4.3.68–9). It is also against this backdrop that we might see Franciso and Lodovico's subversion of Eucharistic power – 'You have ta'en the sacrament to prosecute / Th'intended murder' (4.3.72–3). The repetition – and hence re-emphasis – of the illicit adoption of the Eucharist towards the end of the play ('You have our vows sealed with the sacrament / To second your attempts') heightens the audience's awareness of the play's deliberately discordant appropriation of religious ritual (5.1.62–3).

Characters also find themselves in moments when culturally codified responses present themselves, but are then shown to be in tension with the psychological drives and urges they should experience. So Vittoria's dream of the yew and the blackthorn presents an image of 'terror' which the characters 'know' should be subjected to the appropriate religious response; yet, as Vittoria admits, 'I could not pray' (1.2.231–2). Similarly, Brachiano retrospectively reinterprets the ceremonial set-piece of his wooing of Vittoria as a spiritually illicit ritual form:

Thou hast led me, like an heathen sacrifice,
With music and with fatal yokes of flowers
To my eternal ruin.   (4.2.85–7)

Thus, the relationship between Brachiano and Vittoria is imagined in terms of secular, legal and religious ceremonial forms (the wooing, the arraignment, the heathen sacrifice). For Bovilsky, the reference here to the 'heathen' also evidences what she sees as an audience's underlying national and aesthetic identifications: 'The heathen sin is the Italian sin: 'not just human sacrifice, but a fatal and seemingly unethical deployment of aesthetic cues, a "savage" and malign misappropriation of Eurocentric decorative (musical and floral) forms'.[35] I am less confident that Webster's stage 'Italianness' should be set in such stark opposition to the 'Englishness' of his audience because, as I have suggested earlier, the Italian Catholicism on stage is in part an Uncanny doubling of the English Catholicism of previous generations. It may also be worth considering that the relationship between the Christian and the 'heathen' is less straightforward than the relationship between truth and falsehood, which is the position that Bovilsky appears to ascribe to Webster: 'In the reference to an Irish "dissembling trade" in grief, as in the prior analogy involving deceitful "heathen" paraphernalia, flowers, and music, Brachiano presents a view of Vittoria's beauty and emotion as artificial, prosthetic, and immoral'.[36] As I have suggested throughout this chapter, Webster is somewhat sceptical of the truth claims behind any of the rituals displayed, but is instead interested in the social and psychological effects of these rituals. The inability of a particular ritual form to contain the relationship between Vittoria and Brachiano is on a par with the general instability of ritual as envisioned by the play. A related effect may be in operation when Flamineo aims to draw the 'traverse' and 'discover' to the audience the 'superstitious howling' of Marcello's mourners (5.4.59–60). What the audience actually sees is Cornelia, '*in several forms of distraction*' (5.4.89SD), but expressing her grief through the ceremonial form of a rhyming song; as Thomas Rist has noted, in this scene 'Cornelia is an old woman once again performing the rites of an older, pre-Reformation generation'.[37] This is a rare moment in the play where the cynicism expressed by Flamineo seems to be undercut by the apparent efficacy of a traditional, ritualized, form of mourning in dealing with psychological trauma.

It is possible, although I think not fully justified, to see the eloquence of Cornelia's lament as indicating that Webster is sympathetic to the rituals of Catholicism. It is also possible, as Michael Neill argues, to see Cornelia's mourning as an anti-ritual moment: 'Webster's choice of a scene of domestic grief to replace the public ostentation of funeral [...] speaks of a world where the forms of ritual display, no longer answering to any profound intimation of social order, are felt to be inadequate, or even inimical, to the intensity of private emotion'.[38] Webster's references to Irish wakes, however, indicate his understanding that rituals are not always defined by courtly pomp and circumstance, but can be located and experienced in more domesticated settings. In part, moreover, Neill here makes a similar assumption as does Strycharski – namely, that the emergent social order of the individual will has already triumphed over the established social structures. My contention is that Webster dramatizes a society in flux. And while Cornelia's mourning presents a domesticated form of Catholic grief, it is not in keeping with Webster's worldview to privilege this form of expression over the variety of ritual and ceremonial forms in the play, regardless of the apparent efficacy of the song at this particular dramatic moment.

A clearer example of how the competing imperatives of the society on display can lead to rather than soothe psychological trauma, can be witnessed through the confused utterances of Vittoria in Act Four, including her statement that 'I do wish / That I could make you full executor / To all my sins' (4.2.120–1). Here legal and theological terminology are brought together, but instead of leading to a resolution of trauma, Vittoria's psychological difficulties are dramatized through the limits of language and physical action against which she arrives: 'for all thou art worth / I'll not shed one tear more – I'll burst first. *Throws herself [face down] upon a bed [and weeps]*' (4.2.122–4SD). And the play's insistent juxtaposition of the legal and the theological again finds expression in Brachiano's poison-induced dying vision, in which a Judas-like Flamineo, 'A money-bag in each hand, to keep him even, / For fear of breaking's neck' is joined by 'a lawyer / In a gown whipt with velvet', who 'stares and gapes / When the money will fall' (5.3.111–14). Mortal sin and legal practice are brought together in Brachiano's vision by the desire for money which motivates them both; but even if shorn of the association with base lucre, the conjunction of religion and the law is typical of the play as a whole.

Conclusion

What, then, to make of the presentation of ritual in *The White Devil*? Strycharski's recent attempt to reinvigorate traditional ways of reading tragedy is subtle and sophisticated, but ultimately it should be resisted. 'To feel the moral value of a play such as *The White Devil*', he claims, 'we need to revisit the idea of catharsis, the arousal and purging of deeply disturbing effects, and how catharsis might work as a principle of sharing among the participants, including readers of centuries remove, in dramatic ritual'.[39] Submission to a cathartic effect, however, may perhaps be unavoidable to a theatrical audience (in particular circumstances), but is inappropriate as a critical response to a dramatic work because it is the task of the critic to analyse and contextualize, rather than to submit to the psychological effects of drama.

The White Devil is a sophisticated play, with an intricate dramatic construction, which leads to complicated emotional and psychological responses from audiences. Acknowledgement of the complexity of Webster's vision of the relationship between ritual, theology, the law, and ceremonial forms, allows an elaboration of the dominant critical readings of the play's set-piece (the trial of Vittoria) and of an influential critical view that Webster's approach to ritual is one of 'desecration'.[40] Such an approach problematizes Syme's recent assertion that 'foreign scenes of [legal] judgement', of which Vittoria's trial is the example par excellence, 'lack the essential probing quality of English trials'.[41] If the implication of Syme's reading is that dramatists of the period privilege an English form of legal inquisition over its European counterparts,

Webster's play, in fact, challenges the validity of all such idealized ways of interpreting the world, regardless of their perceived national identifications. The trial is of interest, not because of what it tells us about conceptions of Englishness or Italianness, but rather because it is the dominant instance of the many examples which cumulatively demonstrate the importance of exploring ceremonial form to Webster's modes of dramatic composition in this play. That form of dramaturgy is invested with what Bovilsky refers to as 'Webster's characteristic fascination with dramaturgic paradox'.[42] In *The White Devil*, Webster's dramaturgy explores the tension between recognition and alienation, central to the Uncanny effect created by the play.

The tension between recognition and alienation also structures the play's approach to some of its dramatic forebears; most notably, as I have earlier indicated, the play has a self-conscious relationship with Shakespeare's *Hamlet*. Frequent references to Shakespeare's play make the action on stage both familiar and disorientating to the audience, a technique which Michael Cordner has described as 'the later play's Shakespearean indebtedness, but also the degree to which it chooses to wear its rue with a difference'.[43] When Monticelso chastizes Brachiano for having 'in your prime age / Neglect[ed] your awful throne, for the soft down / Of an insatiate bed' (2.1.30–2), the audience is encouraged to recall the 'insatiate' and 'enseamèd' bed of Claudius and Gertrude, but the comparison does not actually give the audience any clear moral or interpretative guidance.[44]

Another way of thinking about this moment, and by extension about the play as a whole, might be to suggest that the appropriation of Shakespeare works according to the same structures of 'Uncanny' dissonance as do the play's adaptations of ritual and ceremonial forms. As Royle notes, the Uncanny 'would appear to be indissociably bound up with a sense of repetition or "coming back" – the return of the repressed, the constant or eternal recurrence of the same thing, a compulsion to repeat'.[45] I have already noted how this structure of Uncanny doubling, and the dissonant psychological experience associated with it, informs Webster's approach to ritual. If the play 'unsettles time and space, order and sense' in this way, it also does so through its appropriation of *Hamlet*.[46] Thus, ritual in *The White Devil* is not simply inverted or parodied to demonstrate the failings of Webster's Italianate villains; nor is it represented as an outdated relic of a bygone age. Rather, the play presents several perspectives on ritual and ceremony: a sustained exploration of the psychological effects of ritual on individuals; the dissonance associated with subjection to competing ritual imperatives; and the ('Uncanny') unease which individuals and social groups may experience when trying to deal with recent social trauma (particularly, the impact of the Reformation in England). What is more, through its self-conscious theatricality and appropriations from Shakespeare, the play resists the presentation of straightforward solutions to the issues raised, instead interrogating the very capacity of drama as a vehicle to explore such urgent questions.

5

New Directions: Unbridled Selfhood in *The White Devil* – Webster's use of Calvin and Montaigne

Paul Frazer

Without knowledge of self there is no knowledge of God.[1]

And there is nothing I desire more to be informed of, than of the death of men: that is to say, what words, what countenance, and what face they show at their death.[2]

Within the kaleidoscopic patterns of Webster's intertextual writing style, critics have long since noted his extensive borrowings from the French Catholic thinker Michel de Montaigne.[3] Many studies have traced Montaigne's influence upon Jacobean drama more broadly and have identified his dynamically introspective meditations as primary source-texts for the years that followed their translation to English in 1603 by John Florio.[4] The full depths of *The White Devil*'s indebtedness to Montaigne have not yet been plumbed and deserve considered revision against the complexities of Webster's theological context. What seems to have fascinated Webster most about Montaigne's writings is their central devotion to learning about death. Montaigne held death to be a key route to learning about the self – by learning how to stop fearing death, he claimed, subjects can achieve a degree of introspective knowledge not otherwise attainable: 'let us remove her [death's] strangeness from her, let us converse, frequent, and acquaint ourselves with her, let us have nothing so much in mind as death, let us at all times and seasons, and in the ugliest manner that may be' (1.19.80–1). For Montaigne this was not knowledge for knowledge's sake, but a measure of pious learning: 'I know by myself (quoth Saint *Bernard*) how God is incomprehensible, since I am not able to comprehend the parts of mine own being' ('Apology for Raymond Sebond', 2.12.310). Introspective puzzles of selfhood are not only comparable to the mysteries of God; they are (for Montaigne) abstract routes to those mysteries. For to devote oneself to the knowledge of one's inner secrets was to seek intimacy with God's most exalted creation – the soul. This is, as you might imagine, a complicated business; but for authors like Montaigne, taking one step towards self-knowledge brought the subject that step closer to the divine substance of their creator. Issues such as these fascinated Jacobean playwrights and their audiences.[5]

Webster's *The White Devil* is steeped in the religious complexities that surrounded discussions of interiority, death and salvation in this time. The play's fixation on death, and on how the dead are remembered and commemorated, haunts its closing scenes – most overtly through Marcello's murder, and his mother Cornelia's descent into madness in Act 5 Scene 4. Important literary criticism has traced some of the ways in which *The White Devil* was intervening in contemporary debates about the nature of commemoration through its dialogue pertaining to grief and memory, and the material presence of the crucifixes.[6] But less attention has been paid to Webster's dogged obsession with the experience of death itself and the soteriological impulses and fears of Jacobean subjects. Michael Neill long ago stated that Jacobean tragedy was the chief art form 'by which the culture of early modern England reinvented death', but his inclusion of *The White Devil* in a linear 'secularizing process' is in need of revision and nuance.[7] Neill's model pitted English subjects on a neat trajectory towards secular (sceptical, non-religious) theorizations of death. Similarly, Jonathan Dollimore's *Radical Tragedy* (1984) drew Webster's play into a narrative of social evolution, where Jacobean tragedies played out a cumulative disintegration of providentialist belief – that is, they edged *progressively* away from belief in divinely ordained life, death, and passage to the afterlife.[8] My discussion disentangles *The White Devil* from these critical narratives and proposes instead, that we read Webster's investment in the theological and philosophical ideas of his day as indicative of a more complex and nuanced model of theologically rooted self-knowledge.

To do this, I begin by exploring how *The White Devil*'s world echoes and applies the writings of the radical French reformer Jean Calvin. By the time *The White Devil* was written and performed in 1612, the Church of England had been an essentially 'Calvinist' institution for over two decades. Calvin's writings and teachings saturated English devotional life, so it makes sense that the plays of the period bear their hallmarks. However, Webster's echoes of Calvin centre repeatedly upon the trope of physical mobility and the idea of the subject moving (always moving) towards either salvation or damnation. This was a conceit that Calvin borrowed from St Augustine of Hippo and my reading situates Webster's interest in Calvinist soteriology alongside the trope of the wayward, errant and perverse movement of the reprobate subject – that is, the subject who is divinely predestined to go to hell when they die.[9] As bodies jockey for position in this play, they act out their doomed spiritual destinies. Montaigne was also fascinated by the Augustine's trope of the mobile subject and, in the second half of the discussion, I explore how Webster's reading of Montaigne's essays both enlivens and complicates his play's engagement with mobility and spiritual passage. For while Webster casts his protagonists as damned and frames his play's Italian setting as a site of near if not total reprobation, he weaves a Montaignian thread through the character Flamineo; and this thread leads *The White Devil* to a remarkable retelling of two of Montaigne's essays in its final act: 'Of Exercise or Practice' and 'That to Philosophise is to Learn how to die'. From these ruminations on the nature of death, near-death, and the self, Webster appropriates Montaigne's use of equine imagery to emphasize the precarious soteriological implications of the moving subject in terms of elevation, speed, and the control of base impulses. Through *The White Devil*'s final scene, then, Webster stages a didactic dramatization of Montaigne's near-death experience. This crucial moment of colliding and trampling bodies layers and fuses dichotomies of Calvinist and Montaignian selfhood, raising vexing questions of modes of thinking and learning about what it means to die.

Reining the subject: Calvin and Augustine

Calvin instructed his followers to celebrate the knowledge that salvation was out of their own hands, exactly because humans are innately prone to think and act in sinful ways. Belief in the utter, irreversible rottenness and corruption of mankind was central to Calvinist creed: Man had lost any hope of sanctity, purity or innocence when Eve and Adam were purged from Eden. Calvin taught that Man lost the ability to achieve salvation through her/his own will and that God had predetermined every subject's spiritual fate. Because of Man's disgraced condition, knowledge of predestination – of who would be saved – was 'secret knowledge', privy only to God. Such emphasis fostered much preoccupation among Calvinist subjects, regarding whether one's soul was capable of being led triumphantly to heaven or dragged (Faustus-like) to hell. This created inevitable, crushing pressures on subjects who treated knowledge of God through devotion and doctrines of salvation as their central focus and purpose of everyday life. Calvinist Protestants were expected to devote themselves entirely to their faith, and Calvin taught that they could only do so through committed adherence to God's instructions, as set down in the Bible.

In his preface to the 1560 French version of his *Institutes of the Christian Religion*, Calvin described the Holy Scripture as containing 'a perfect doctrine, to which one can add nothing', glossing that the Christian exegete (Bible interpreter) requires 'guidance and direction, to know what he ought to look for in it, in order not to wander hither and thither, but to hold a sure path, that may always be pressing toward the end to which the Holy Spirit calls him' (1.6). Using the conceit of physical-spiritual movement, Calvin explained the subject's negotiation of scripture as a navigation – a narrow pathway (the only pathway) that could lead the elect to salvation. Drawing from passages such as Psalms 119.105–8 ('Thy word *is* a lantern unto my feet, and a light unto my path') and Acts 17.28 ('For in him we live, and move, and have our being'), Calvin explained virtuous spiritual devotion in terms of physical labour.[10] The elect subject seeks God, follows his instructions, traces his pathways, shadows his examples, and strives to reach him through the labyrinth of his scripture:

If we turn aside from the Word, as I have just now said, though we may strive with strenuous haste, yet, since we have got off the track, we shall never reach the goal. For we should so reason that the splendour of the divine countenance, which even the apostle calls 'unapproachable' [1 Tim. 6:16], is like for us an inexplicable labyrinth unless

we are conducted into it by the thread of the Word; so that
it is better to limp along this path than to dash with all
speed outside it. (1.3)

In this respect, Calvin uses the conceit of measured and
determined, straight and obedient passage (against all obstacles,
conditions, and barriers) to describe the internalizing 'mobility'
expected of the elect. Often able only to blindly shuffle and
limp, the elect must endure labyrinthine trials of movement,
where biblical reading and interpretation is the only possible
guide. So not only is existence perceived as a passage from
conception to afterlife, but the Christian subject's reading of
scripture becomes the central (internal: intellectual, emotional
and spiritual) navigation. Calvin teaches that scripture should
be life's map – *the* co-ordinating principle that makes salvation
possible for the few subjects predestined to be saved.

This trope of the onward moving Christian was a
conventional one, and in giving it such prominence in his
writings Calvin was echoing one of the cornerstone influ-
ences of Christian history: the writings of Saint Augustine
(354–430 AD). Augustine lived and wrote from the fourth to
fifth centuries and, though his writings were crucial to the
development of Christianity, their emphasis on the subject's
personal relationship with God assumed an unprecedented
importance for early modern reformers like Calvin. In
Augustine's *Confessions,* an autobiographical of its author's
sinful youth and eventual conversion, he emphasized the
personal challenges of faith in bridling the unruly passions
of the corrupt self. For in his lustful youth, Augustine claims
to have 'ran wild in the shadowy jungle of erotic adventures'
(2.1), consigning his adolescent self 'a wandering spirit' who
feared traversing 'the twisted path along which walk those
who turn their backs and not their face towards' God (2.6).[11]
Only through divine intervention could Augustine correct
his transgressions: 'As an adolescent I went astray from you
(Ps. 118.76), my God, far from your unmoved stability. I
became to myself a region of destitution' (2.18); 'God, from

far off you saw me falling about on slippery ground and in the midst of such smoke (Isa. 42.3) discerned the spark of my integrity' (4.2); 'You direct my eyes towards you and "rescue my feet from the trap" (Ps. 24.15)' (4.11). Augustine recollects his sinful condition as wayward and in exile, unmoored and untamed, awaiting correction and discipline. For Calvin, Augustine was led to the right path *only* because God willed it. Though Calvin disagreed with Augustine's conception of free will, wherein humans enjoy freedom to choose between good and evil actions, his adoption of the walking/wandering conceit is constant in the *Institutes*.[12] And because of Calvin's influence over English devotion in the Jacobean years, ideas of movement became important to contemporary soteriological discourses. Issued twenty-five times by 1640, vastly popular tracts such as Arthur Dent's *Plain Man's Pathway to Heaven* (1601) – 'wherein every man may clearly see whether he shall be saved or damned' – used physical movement referents as narrative crutches to expound the complexities of Augustine-influenced Calvinist teaching, paving the way for works like John Bunyan's *Map of Salvation* (1644) and *The Pilgrim's Progress* (1678).[13]

The White Devil's obsession with paradigms of reprobation and damnation centre repeatedly upon notions of agency and movement, chiming with the phrasing of contemporary Calvinist dogma. In line with their *de facto* reprobate (because Catholic) settings of Rome and Padua, almost every major character is referred to as hell-bound. In the opening act, Cornelia interrupts her daughter and Brachiano's rendezvous by warning, 'Woe to light hearts, they still fore-run our fall' (1.2.251–2). The idolatrous Isabella, who perishes by kissing a poisoned portrait of her erstwhile husband, wails that, 'Hell to my affliction / Is mere snow water' (2.1.249–50). In the trial scene, the corrupt Cardinal Monticelso (soon to be Pope Paul IV) frames Vittoria's guilt as postlapsarian, when he scathes, 'Were there a second paradise to lose / This devil would betray it' (3.2.70–1), and condemns whores as 'the true material fire of Hell' (86); this before Vittoria rebukes

Francisco as somehow privy to his fate: 'I fain would know if you have your salvation / By patent, that you proceed thus' (270–3). Brachiano claims to have been led to his 'eternal ruin' (4.2.87), is imagined by Lodovico as striking 'His soul into the hazard!' (5.1.72), and is condemned by his assassins as 'damned / Perpetually' (5.3.147). Similarly, Vittoria's resolve to go 'Weeping to heaven on crutches' (4.2.118) rebounds obliquely against her realization that 'This place is hell' (5.3.177), before forsaking 'that which was made for man, / The world, to sink that was made for devils, / Eternal darkness' (5.4.60–2). Perhaps the only major character in the play who might transcend reprobation is young Giovanni, who not only rejects Flamineo's manipulations in 5.4 ('Study your prayers, sir, and be penitent' [19]), but also closes the play with his pious warnings: 'All that have hands in this shall taste our justice / As I hope heaven' and 'Let guilty men remember their black deeds / Do lean on crutches, made of slender reeds' (5.6. 288–97). In this sense, if in no other, Giovanni represents a mere glimmer of hope in a setting encircled by the deviant trajectories of reprobation.

The fallen reprobate condition is most unambiguously embodied by the malefactor and murderer Lodovico, 'an Italian Count, but decayed' (*Dramatis Personae*). Always significant to the wider themes of its play, the opening utterance of this tragedy is spoken by Lodovico as he contemplates his lapsarian-exiled state: 'Banished?' (1.1.1). His comrades then ruminate upon how he is 'justly doomed' (13), has 'staggered' through 'All the damnable degrees / Of drinking' (18–19), and reflect scathingly on the nobles who 'fore-deeming you / An idle meteor' jest 'you were begotten in an earthquake' (24, 27). Lodovico's deviant trajectory is also instanced when Francisco terms him 'chief engine of my business' (4.2.132) and elsewhere the prying Monticelso scorns him 'a foul black cloud', 'fashioned for all ill', 'Wretched creature!' and 'Miserable creature!' (4.3.101–16) – echoing one of Calvin's favourite phrases of Man as the blind, wandering wretch.[14] Such associations with physical transience were, moreover, voiced by a 1651 critic, who reflected on 'Lodovico weltering in his gore'.[15] Monticelso, too, condemns Lodovico, referring to his plan for revenge as 'damnable', and asking: 'Dost thou imagine thou canst slide on blood, / And not be tainted with a shameful fall?' (117–19).[16] Elsewhere, Lodovico himself uses the idiom 'There's but three Furies found in spacious hell; / But in a great man's breast three thousand dwell' (4.3.151–2), before reflecting upon how he has repaid 'All my debts, so if I should chance to fall / My creditors fall not with me' (5.5.4–5), and is later labelled 'my death's man' (5.6.205) by Vittoria. Lodovico's symbolically exiled, decayed, and damned status seems to wholly symbolize Calvin's conception of Fallen Man.

Much of this harks back to Augustine. When, for instance, he recalls his wild years' sexual misdemeanours, Augustine emphasizes his deviation from God's way using this important equestrian conceit:

> The reins were relaxed to allow me to amuse myself. There was no strict discipline to keep me in check, which led to an unbridled dissoluteness in many different directions. In all of this there was a thick mist shutting me off from the brightness of your face. (*Confessions*, 2.8)

Augustine's model of the bridled subject echoes Plato's conception of the soul from *Phaedrus*, whereby the soul is likened to a chariot leading two winged horses: one is 'beautiful and of good stock', while the other 'is the opposite and has the opposite sort of bloodline'; every human soul has, for Plato, 'a mixture' of the pure and corrupt equestrian breeds (246a–b).[17] Thus, the soul's direction requires mastery and control of the chariot's competing engines. When Augustine describes his wayward self as the *unbridled* equine, he captures themes of utter depravation: voracious sexuality, untamed mobility, and blindness, making use of a conceit Calvin would make central in his writings of the dissolute.

Webster emphasizes reprobate trajectories in similar ways, drawing particular emphasis upon themes of sexual

debauchery in the scene in which Monticelso (the new Pope
Paul IV) demands knowledge of Francisco de Medici's plot
with Lodovico:

LODOVICO   Why, my lord,
            He told me of a resty Barbary horse
            Which he would fain have brought to the
                career,
            The 'sault, and the ring-galliard. Now, my lord,
            I have a rare French rider.
MONTICELSO   Take you heed:
            Lest the jade break your neck. Do you put
                me off
            With your wild horse-tricks?   (4.3.92–8)

As with Iago's use of the Barbary horse image to depict the
frenzied passion of the Moor (*Othello* 1.1.113), Lodovico
invokes the dialectics of Otherness inherent to Webster's
play's title.[18] This tragedy is concentrated with 'devils', and
Monticelso's reversion to the African mare implicates Lodovico
(alongside Vittoria, Zanche the Moor, and Francisco's
performance as Mulinassar) in the white–black thematic
dichotomy.[19] Though he articulates a wildness of movement
commensurate with the acrobatics of ''sault' ('leaps and
vaults') and 'ring-galliard' ('a mixture of bounding forward
and lashing out with the heels': Luckyj 106n.), the adjective
'resty' means a refusal to go forward and resistance to control
(*OED adj.*2.Ia.).

According to Elizabeth Anne Socolow, to 'be astride a horse
meant that passion and discipline, restraint and speed, height
and skill, judgement, learning and wisdom, as well as *active*
agency, were in one's *armamentarium*'.[20] Good horsemanship
reflected the rider's control and discipline, but here Lodovico
abandons any notion of restraint and his actions assume an
unbridled, irregular and 'black' trajectory – replete with the
erotic connotations surrounding the Moorish bodies elsewhere
in this and other texts.[21] Given that the horse can also figure

'both a disturbing propensity for baseness (especially sexual baseness) and an equally disturbing sense of that baseness as somehow intrinsic to human behaviour', Monticelso reverts immediately to sodomitical fantasy, placing Lodovico as an unruly, thrashing, sexual object.[22] His reprobation is such that he is beyond control, however, embodying Calvin's warning of how 'we rush headlong, without thinking what he requires, but so raging in our unbridled lust that we deliberately strive against him [God]' (1.17.5). Monticelso moves at too slow a pace to bridle him, and his admission that 'You have o'erta'en me' (4.3.110) is signified by Lodovico's deft rhetorical shift from denial into his aural 'confession' of the revenge plot as this scene continues.

In contrast to the subservient positions that Lodovico assumes as Francisco's engine of revenge, fellow malefactor Flamineo claims to move of his own accord, and in defiance of any overarching notions of providence.[23] He addresses 'fate' and 'Misfortune' as rushing on 'like the crowner's business, / Huddle upon huddle' (3.3.67–9). Since 'crowner' also means 'coroner' here, Flamineo enjoys a snapshot of the play's rising body count – his role in which, of course, marks his most certain reprobation.[24] And when Flamineo visits Vittoria and demands reward for his machinations, she underscores his fate by instancing the archetypal Christian exile and fratricide: 'I give that portion to thee and no other / Which Cain groaned under having slain his brother' (5.6.13–15). Murderer of his brother Marcello, Flamineo embodies the crime of 'vagabond and runagate' (Gen. 4.12) Cain, compounding his sister's rhyming allusion later in the scene with 'my hand is stained with blood already' (93).

These allusions to movement form a core aspect of how Calvin theorized the soul. Comprised of two 'faculties', understanding and will, the prelapsarian (pre-exile from Eden) soul had the capacity to make free choices between good or evil, both of which Calvin conceives as forms of motion. This is why Adam's failure becomes a matter of agency and constancy: 'Adam could have stood if he wished

[...] But it was because his will was capable of being bent from one side or the other, and was not given the constancy to persevere, that he fell so easily' (1.15.8). So because Adam's will proved too weak and corruptible, the postlapsarian soul's capacity for free will was stripped away, and resultantly 'all events are governed by God's secret plan' (1.16.2). It makes sense for theologically minded English subjects, like Webster, to try to capture the complexities of Calvinist denial of free will using metaphors of physical movement; because when they turned to scripture that is inevitably what they found. In 1598, for instance, perhaps England's most famed and influential Calvinist, William Perkins, claimed 'that in human actions, man's will is weak and feeble, and his understanding dim and dark; and thereupon he often fails in them [...] the will of man is under the will of God, and therefore to be ordered by it; as Jeremiah saith, chap. 10. v. 23. *O Lord I know that the way of man is not in himself: neither is it in man to walk or direct his steppes*'.[25] So Flamineo's attempts to direct his own steps serve to further exaggerate his reprobate symptoms. He states, for instance: to have 'made a kind of path / To her [Vittoria] and mine own preferment' (3.1.33–4); he later challenges providence itself: 'I do dare my fate / To do its worst' (5.4.136–7); and he refuses Gasparo's 'Recommend yourself to heaven' with 'No, I will carry mine own commendations thither' (5.6.192–3). Flamineo comes to realize these attempts as futile, as the final scene sees him acknowledge 'my infected blood' (5.6.103), and his sister rail that 'thy sins / Do run before thee to fetch fire from hell / To light thee thither' (136–8). He is ultimately forced to concede that

> Fate's a spaniel,
We cannot beat it from us: what remains now?
Let all that do ill take this precedent:
'Man may his fate foresee, but not prevent'.
And of all axioms this shall win the prize:
''Tis better to be fortunate than wise'.   (173–8)

That the malefactor finds himself subject to a predetermined fate is hardly noteworthy, but the nature of Flamineo's attempts to out-manoeuvre that fate may well be. For the precedent that Flamineo arrives at may be Calvinist in substance, but his methodology in reaching it points to a more complex and nuanced model of subjectivity.

Flamineo is the only character in the play who is reflective and enquiring about his own providence. And when he claims, 'This night I'll know the utmost of my fate' (5.4.110), his assertion anticipates the entrance of Brachiano's Ghost by just eight lines. In this moment, the Ghost prompts an introspective impulse which brings Flamineo to reflect upon his existence beyond the grave:

> *Enter Brachia[no's] Ghost. In his leather cassock and breeches, boots, a cowl [and in his hand] a pot of lily-flowers with a skull in't*
>
> Ha! I can stand thee. [*The Ghost approaches*] Nearer, nearer yet.
> What a mockery hath death made of thee? Thou look'st sad.
> In what place art thou? In yon starry gallery
> Or in the cursed dungeon? No? Not speak?
> Pray, sir, resolve me, what religion's best
> For a man to die in?   (5.4.118–23)

Set against the grieving lunacy of Cornelia and vengeful agonies of Francisco, Flamineo's detached curiosity amplifies his perverse and deviant persona. That the spirit appears replete with Catholic funereai flower (lily) and *memento mori* exaggerates the ties between Catholicism and superstitious commemoration. Because Calvinist belief in predestination 'made enactments of prayer befitting the dead redundant', Jacobean Protestants were prohibited from practising traditionalist funereal and memorial practices, and impelled by the Church to commemorate their dead in 'moderation'.[26] It is on these grounds that young Giovanni accosts Flamineo in Act 5, Scene 4 for his sentimental anecdote about the loss of his father (Brachiano): 'be penitent. / 'Twere fit you'd think on what hath former bin, / I have heard grief named the eldest child of sin' (19–21). Giovanni terms grief the offspring of wickedness, snubbing Flamineo's manipulative attempts to feign bereavement. In overcoming *his* grief, Giovanni transcends the Catholic reprobation of the narrative.

Similarly, Flamineo's detached amusement sets him apart from traditionalist superstition and prompts an unprecedented soteriological impulse. Something that has often escaped critical attention here is the importance of the Ghost's attire. Despite meeting his death by strangulation (presumably) in his bedclothes, Brachiano appears in full riding gear – a detail that can be read in dialogue with the play's wider fixation with themes of movement, death, and soteriology. His revenant is, however, purgatorial – and, therefore, inert.[27] And when Flamineo muses at how the ghost 'look'st sad', he uses an adjective that carried (early modern) meanings of being firm, stiff and heavy (*OED* III.8a; 8b); he sees the ghost as both emotionally dejected and physically motionless.[28] Its riding gear emphasizes this stationary spiritual dislocation, adrift from 'yon starry gallery' in the Catholic middle-space of Purgatory. That Flamineo observes the spirit as a 'mockery' relates to the risible nature of Catholic superstitious belief for the reformed. Yet despite its ludicrousness to Flamineo, it does prompt an important, and theologically hybrid, soteriological impulse that stays with him for the remainder of the play. In pursuing Flamineo's inward compulsion in the final scene of this play, Webster reaches beyond Calvin and immerses his audience quite deliberately in the philosophical maze of Montaigne.[29]

Loosened bonds: Montaigne and the liberty of death

In his meandering pursuit of selfhood, Montaigne refers to the 'strange and vagabond' ('Of Exercise or Practice', 2.6.66) pathway of self-description and -analysis. And this emphasis upon not only mobility, but the lure of the winding, vexing, and perverse directionality of the wandering vagrant constantly shadows his inquiries throughout. Montaigne asserts that the study of 'Each motion' of the self 'showeth and discovereth what we are', and that (similarly to Calvin) the enquiring subject's autonomy is comparable with ambulation: 'I must' he states 'walk with my pen, as I go with my feet' ('Of Vanity', 1:50.295–6). Unlike Calvin, however, Montaigne advocates deviation, stating that this 'common high way must have conference with other ways', and that while 'Reason doth appoint us ever to walk in one path', he advises his reader 'not always to keep one [pace]' ('Of Sleeping', 1.44.371). Montaigne also argues that while 'a wise man should not permit humane passions to stray from the right carrier', he must duly govern whether 'to hasten or to slow his pace, and not place himself as an immoveable and impassible *Colossus*' ('Of Sleeping', 1.44). Mapping a reactive, agile, and omnidirectional pursuit, his *Essais* formulate an aesthetics of self-exploration through metaphors of fluid mobility: wandering, following, straying, turning and swerving.[30] So, when writing of his younger self, Montaigne reverses the Augustinian conceit of wayward adolescence: 'in my youth I have ever accustomed myself to tread a plain beaten path, and have ever hated to entermeddle any manner of deceit of cousoning-craft, even in my childish sports' ('Of Custom' 1.22.116). In other words, as an adult Montaigne finds he must venture from beaten ways to the irregular and prohibited and become lost: 'to penetrate the shady, and enter the thick-covered depths of these infernal winding cranks' ('Exercise or Practice', 2.6.66), to sate his fascination with his inner regions. Montaigne turns the Augustinian insistence on unfaltering, unquestioned obedience on its head, prioritizing the process and outcome of veering from known ways into an unknowable inner wilderness.

The White Devil is riddled with Montaignian moments, where characters describe themselves as physically astray. Brachiano introduces Flamineo to the play as 'Quite lost Flamineo' (1.2.3), and courts Vittoria by stating 'if you forgo me / I am lost eternally' (1.2.189–90) – anticipating her later wailing utterance: 'I am lost for ever' (5.3.36). The Conjuror later instructs Brachiano to 'turn another way' (2.1.35); upon Brachiano and Vittoria's embrace, Flamineo marvels at Brachiano's pliability: 'So now the tide's turned the vessel's come about' (4.2.189). Furthermore, Francisco instructs Lodovico to 'Divert me not' (4.3.75), and Lodovico later scorns 'You would not take my way' (5.1.66); Marcello provokes Flamineo with the insult: 'The very flames of our affection / Shall turn two ways (5.1.196–7); Vittoria shrieks 'Turn this horror from me!' (5.6.27); Flamineo wonders 'Whither shall I go now?' (5.6.105); and in an unusual stage direction, refusing to turn his back to Brachiano, Flamineo actually '*walks backwards*' (4.2.63).[31]

The play's obsession with wayward physical impulses and its aversion to obedient passage is sharpened when Webster uses equine imagery to draw upon themes of linearity and control. When, for instance, Vittoria makes her spectacular exit from the stage in 1.2 she 'passes over the stage in a blaze of light' (0–10SD) – foreshadowing her preordained Fall – and Flamineo instructs 'Let the caroche [carriage] go on' (1.2.8).[32] Monticelso later levels the accusation that 'Her gates were full of coaches' (3.2.74). As the coach-making Webster family knew well, the carriage was a horse-drawn place of concealment whose mobility (and association with prostitution) wrought a transgressive association with deviant movement and subterfuge.[33] In Act 3, Flamineo is termed Brachiano's 'engine, and his stalking horse / To undo my sister' (3.1.31–3) by Marcello. The stalking horse was a horse trained to allow a hunter to conceal himself behind it – hence also a 'person whose agency or participation in a proceeding is made use of to prevent its real design from being suspected' (*OED*; *n.*1a1b).[34] Elsewhere, Flamineo adopts the sexualized equine retort that 'none are judges at tilting, but those that have been old tilters' (3.1.15–16), before ridiculing the French Ambassador as inactive and impotent: 'A lame one in his lofty tricks; he sleeps o'horseback like a poulter' (3.1.62–9). As he plots with Brachiano, moreover, Flamineo also alludes to that famously duplicitous equine vehicle – 'the Grecians in their wooden horse' (4.2.195) – in an echo and verbal parody of Camillo's bizarre murder: tripped and thrust head-first into a vaulting horse in the second dumb show of 2.2. Furthermore, Lodovico considers the merits of poisoning the 'pommel' of Brachiano's saddle (5.1.68); and at the close of her arraignment, Vittoria challenges Monticelso to 'Instruct me some good horse leech to speak treason' (3.2.281), in reference to the duplicity of cunning rhetoricians (Luckyj, 70n.).[35] Throughout this play, the capacity of the horse for controlled forward motion is underwritten by a potential for perverse, unexpected motion, and violent death.

The Paduan context of the play's final act is also associated with equestrianism. One of many Italian regions famed for horse breeding, Padua's connection to the hagiographic legacy of Saint Anthony (of Padua) renders a noteworthy link between the play's context and its interest in Catholicism and false memory. Patron saint of horses, travellers and shipwrecks, Anthony of Padua reportedly 'caused his horse to kneel down and worship the holy host, by which strange sight, a stout Heretic was converted', according to Thomas Beard's 1616 anti-Catholic invective against 'their miraculous transubstantiation'.[36] The saint's reputation in reformist England seems to have been associated with Romish duplicity and confidence trickery and Webster's audiences might well have connected Brachiano's 'O Saint Anthony's fire!' (2.1.301) with this Paduan equestrian context. The play makes reference to the Catholic sacrament of the Eucharist several times which,

David Coleman claims, 'draws an ironic parallel between the sacrifice of Christ's blood in the sacrament, and the spiritually empty bloodletting which is to follow'.[37] Reformed opposition to Catholic belief in the Eucharist as a living, carnal presence of Christ encapsulated Protestant emphasis upon the utter separation between worldly and divine, and the anathema of remembering the dead as if they still lived.[38]

Webster almost certainly derives the equestrian-doubleness theme in part from Montaigne. For throughout the French thinker's writing, he uses the conceit of equine movement and agency to discuss the relationship between the subject and the self. For example, in an early essay in which Montaigne explains his decision to 'solitarily and quietly' devote his life to his introspective process, he explains his hope that inactivity might render the self to 'become more settled and ripe'. However, he found 'him' to be,

> contrariwise playing the skittish and loose-broken jade, he takes a hundred times more career and liberty unto himself, than he did for others; and begets in me so many extravagant *Chimeras*, and fantastical monsters, so orderless, and without any reason, one huddling upon another, that at leisure to view the foolishness and monstrous strangeness of them, I have begun to keep a register of them, hoping, if I live, one day to make him ashamed, and blush at himself. ('Of Idleness', 1.2.35)

The irregular and unbridled force of Montaigne's 'loose-broken jade' assumes an important discursive function here, and subsequently throughout his essays: it signifies impulses, motions, and instincts that function beyond human reason and constraint – a rebellious, incompliant monster that rushes beyond any means Montaigne can muster to control it.

Such natural imagery is not incidental; it performs a central role in Montaigne's spiritual investment of tracing the self. When Montaigne translated Raymond Sebond's *Natural Theology* (the same author he would later honour in his

longest essay, 3.12.151–403), he foregrounded the soteriological importance of learning about the natural world: 'to
make your way towards the Holy Scriptures you will do well
to acquire this science as the rudiments of all sciences; in order
the better to reach conclusions, learn it before everything else
[…] for this is the root, the origin and the tiny foundations
of the doctrine proper to Man and his salvation'.[39] In nature
Montaigne finds divine design, and zoomorphic traits often
embody and literalize the spiritual workings of Man. And of all
the natural imagery employed in Montaigne's own writing, the
horse provides the most prominent, recurring, and semantically
proximate to issues of will and mastery of the self.[40] According
to Juliana Schiesari, this symbol of rider on horseback has
Aristotelian roots, emanating 'from the idea of the equestrian
and warrior class' whereby 'the horse's ability to run fast, carry
its rider, and await an enemy' marks an important symbol
of masculine agency, mastery, and force.[41] The horse's chief
metaphorical traits are its mobility and will; and in order to
elevate and mobilize, it must be tamed and controlled.

The spiritual connotations of Montaigne's equine conceit
manifest most powerfully when it comes to his favourite
subject: death. In 'Of Exercise or Practice' Montaigne recounts
how, riding at speed towards his estate, a servant 'mounted
upon a young strong-headed horse' careered towards him and,

> as a *Colossus* with his weight riding over me and my nag,
> that were both very little, he overthrew us both, and made
> us fall with our heels upward: so that the nag lay along
> astonied in one place, and I in a trance grovelling on the
> ground ten or twelve paces wide of him. (2.6.58–9)

His face 'all torn and bruised', Montaigne's injuries were so
severe that his men supposed him dead and carried him back
to his home. Recalling his semi-conscious stupor, Montaigne
describes a weak 'imagination swimming superficially in my
mind', through which he became alienated from any sense of
himself: 'only sprinkled by the soft impression of the senses

[...] It was a slumbering, languishing and extreme weakness, without any pain at all. I saw mine own house and knew it not'. Nor could he remember anything about the accident, until several days later:

> when I perceived the horse riding over me (for being at my heels, I chanced to espy him, and held my self for dead; yet was the conceit so sudden, that fear had no leisure to enter my thoughts) me seemed it was a flashing or lightning, that smote my soul with shaking, and that I came from another world. (2.6.65)

This description is so important because it triggers his assertion that 'truly, for a man to acquaint himself with death, I find no better way than to approach unto it' (66). His remembered detachment from all senses and consciousness brought him closest to the realization he points to in 'That to Philosophise is to Learn how to die': 'To know how to die, doth free us from all subjection and restraint' (1.19.81). Montaigne instructs his reader that proximity to death can illuminate aspects of the self (and therefore God), that could otherwise not be attained. In the danger of horseriding, Montaigne finds an alterity that becomes comparable to handling the wild jade within: 'his hurts, his stumbling, his death, draws your life and fortune into consequence, if he chance to startle or be afraid, then are you induced to doubt or fear' ('Of Steeds', 1.48.397). Not only does he liken the self to a 'loose broken jade', he figures the subject's conscious, and often helpless, relationship with it as a rider to a horse.

In the final scene of *The White Devil*, Webster does more than borrow Montaigne's conceit, he attempts to dramatize it. Scene 5.5 is just fifteen lines long and serves no major narrative function until Hortensio speaks the closing couplet: 'These strong court factions that do brook no checks / In the career oft break the riders' necks' (14–15). Scene 5.6 then opens with Flamineo's pseudo death pact with his 'best loved Moor', Zanche, and sister, Vittoria. In this exchange Flamineo instructs the pleading Vittoria to 'not trouble me / With this vain worldly business' (31–2), and then Zanche twice alludes to him as a teacher of death ('persuade him teach / The way to death'; 'teach her how to die' [5.6.71–2; 91]). The moment that the pair shoot him is accompanied by peculiarly violent stage directions:

FLAMINEO   Shoot, shoot,
              Of all deaths the violent death is best,
              For from ourselves it steals ourselves so fast
              The pain once apprehended is quite past.

              *They shoot and run to him and tread upon
              him.* (113–17)

We have already seen how both Zanche and Vittoria's bodies have been related to horses – Barbary mare and Venetian hobbyhorse – and in *trampling* the body of Flamineo (just as he apes Montaigne's 'If it be a short and violent death wee have no leisure to fear it' [1.19.86]), Flamineo is *trodden underfoot*. Thinking him at the brink of death, Zanche and Vittoria instruct Flamineo to 'Think whither thou art going. / And remember / What villanies thou has acted' (127–8). This remarkable moment actually positions Flamineo as 'Montaigne', building up to his dying utterances: 'There's nothing of so infinite vexation / As man's own thoughts' (201–2), and 'I do not look / Who went before, nor who shall follow me; / No, at myself I will begin and end' (253–5).[42] Flamineo finds momentary solace in the vagabond pathways that Montaigne wrote of pursuing, overcoming his fear of mortality through the perverse motions that, elsewhere in the play, encapsulate his reprobation. He resolves to escape typical Catholic obsessions with the past and Calvinist anxieties of the future by not looking to those before or after, finding momentary solace in the introspective gaze. This focus on the self is still deeply Calvinist, but through Montaigne he finds a way of tempering the crushing certitude of predestination with self-focus of the now. Flamineo's grapple with his own mortality brings him to a subjective precipice, and Webster uses Montaigne to actualize the subjective value of overcoming fear of death, and the soteriological uncertainties that follow.

In the final lines of *The White Devil*'s prefatory message 'To the Reader', after Webster praises the chief dramatists of his age (Chapman, Jonson, Beaumont, Fletcher, Shakespeare, Dekker and Heywood), he uses the codicil: '*non norunt, haec monumenta mori*' ('These monuments do not know death': Luckyj, 6n.). Away from the stage, Webster's equestrian family business was, among other things, a purveyor of funereal and theatrical trappings. He almost certainly knew the business of death and loss quite intimately.[43] And from his preface to this play, he clearly envisaged his dramatic identity as linked to notions of death and loss to a greater extent than his rivals and collaborators. This macabre reputation is of course evident in both of his two great tragedies; but *The White Devil* betrays a distinctive philosophical investment in portraying the randomness and happenstance nature of death. Read against Montaigne's fixation on death, *The White Devil*'s cadaverous narrative and dialogue are marked by a sophisticated incorporation of the radical introspective ethos of Montaigne into a Calvinist world of utter reprobation. This raises important questions about the role of the stage at this time, and the spiritually and intellectually didactic design of Jacobean tragedies. Through metaphors of unbridled and perverse movement, Webster appropriated the Augustinian conceit of the moving subject by fusing and clashing the distant ideals of Calvinist and Montaignian creeds. In so doing, *The White Devil* is suggestive of the troubling inadequacy of Calvinist providentialism for many English subjects, and the perceived role of the early modern dramatist to address and mediate theologies and philosophies of life, death and deliverance.

6

New Directions: Boy Prince and Venetian Courtesan – Political Critique in *The White Devil*

Christina Luckyj

It is now two decades since *The White Devil* has been read as an early modern text charged with contemporary political meaning. Beginning with J. W. Lever (1971) and Jonathan Dollimore (1984),[1] this historicist strain of modern criticism culminated in John Russell Brown's contention in 1996 that Webster's Italian setting functions as 'a pretense that allowed Webster to evade the strict censorship that had landed Ben Jonson and other dramatists in prison for showing too clearly their criticism of King James I'.[2] Even if the exact nature of Webster's political critique often remained vague, the play's apparent moral dissolution could now be explained as Webster's principled repugnance (like Vittoria's) for 'the court' (5.6.257).[3] More recently, however, critics of *The White Devil* have veered away from this interpretation of the play as a displaced image of contemporary English political affairs, treating it instead as a lurid portrait of the vices of Italy. For Lara Bovilsky, for example, Webster's 'view of Italy as steeped in religious, sexual and criminal license' informs Vittoria's 'Italianate alterity'[4] while for Emma Rhatigan this 'Italianate stage world [...] would have remained unambiguously "other" for the members of the Red Bull audience'.[5] Consistent with this approach is a reading of Vittoria as the eponymous white devil, an 'anti-heroine', guilty of 'indulged sexuality and the trail of dead men and women she leaves in her wake', a 'diabolical' schemer, 'a paradigm of [Joseph] Swetnam's covetous and evil women', whose trial confirms her 'public sexuality, like that of a prostitute'.[6] Contemporary critics begin to sound a great deal like the Cardinal in the trial scene – or like early critics of *The Duchess of Malfi* who identified Webster's heroine with the 'bestial sensualitie' of which she is accused in Webster's source.[7] Gone is the admiration for Vittoria expressed by the play's English ambassador (3.2.140) and by critics such as Brown, who asserts that 'her "brave spirit" and the bitterness of her adversaries [...] take confidence and force out of any ready-made moral judgments a member of the audience might have brought to the play'. Even Brown, however, fails to explain Vittoria's place in Webster's political critique as more than an elaborate subterfuge to avoid censorship: 'for who would dare to say that a "notorious strumpet" heralded a play that was an attack upon the centre of political power?'[8] However, recent work on early modern political and print cultures and on Webster's hot Protestant and common law allegiances may help to illuminate both Vittoria and *The White Devil*.[9] In his first solo play, I argue, Webster develops an ultra-Protestant critique of authority by highlighting the dual heroic figures of militant boy prince (Giovanni) and oppressed and defiant woman (Isabella / Vittoria). The former was probably indebted to the chivalric Protestant ideal embodied in Prince Henry, whose untimely death in 1612 at the age of eighteen Webster mourned in print shortly after the first performance of *The*

White Devil. The latter conflates contemporary resistance theory in which woman represents the political subject of tyranny with notions of Venice as a site of political liberty and challenge to popery.[10]

Vittoria, Venice and the *querelle des femmes*

Webster's engagement with the topical *querelle des femmes* – the controversy about the nature of women that generated both attacks on and defences of women – has often been noted, yet underexplored.[11] Webster writes the very terms of the debate into *The White Devil*: beginning with Lodovico's cynical commentary on Fortune as a 'right whore' (1.1.4), the play features a continual stream of misogynist remarks, often directed at Vittoria as a representative of her sex. Examples in the text abound: to Brachiano, Flamineo describes women like Vittoria as 'cursed dogs […] let loose at midnight' (1.2.180); in the trial scene, Monticelso associates Vittoria not only with his 'character' of a 'whore' (3.2.79–80) but also with Eve: 'Were there a second paradise to lose / This devil would betray it' (3.2.70–1); in the house of convertites Brachiano accuses Vittoria of being a 'stately and advanced whore', and a 'devil in crystal' (4.2.72, 84); after Brachiano's death Flamineo remarks of Vittoria's distress, 'There's nothing sooner dry than women's tears' (5.3.184); in the final scene, after he laments her feminine betrayal – 'Trust a woman? Never, never' – he cries: 'we lay our souls to pawn to the devil for a little pleasure and a woman makes the bill of sale' (5.6.157–9); and elsewhere, Brachiano complains that 'Woman to man / Is either a god or a wolf' (4.2.87–8). In this play, men usually identify her with the latter. In each case, however, the speaker is either corrupt and self-interested (as in Flamineo's case, or the Cardinal's) or just plain wrong (as in Brachiano's). Furthermore, as Martin Orkin observes, women's crimes 'hardly compare in the play with

the extent to which Webster explores throughout episodes of
male violence: the plots they hatch, their verbal assaults, their
repeated resort to poison, cruelty and murderous kinds of
verbal as well as physical violence'.[12] In *The White Devil*, as
Orkin contends, misogyny is shown to be a frequent form of
masculine displacement – or, to borrow from the words of Jane
Anger's *Protection for Women* (1589), the play often presents
woman as a construction of man, 'through whose desire in
estimation of conceit we [women] are made ill'.[13]

In Webster's play, this pervasive misogyny is effectively
countered by dramatic strategies also employed by contemporary defences of women. 'No woman is bad except she
be abused', writes Esther Sowernam in 1617;[14] in *Othello*,
Emilia remarks, 'The ills we do, their ills instruct us so'
(4.3.98). Even as the male characters in the play condemn
Vittoria, Webster is careful to suggest that they are the instruments of her corruption. The first time she is mentioned,
Lodovico represents her as a principled woman holding
out against Brachiano, who 'by close panderism seeks to
prostitute / The honour of Vittoria Corombona' (1.1.41–2).
Her agonized response to her mother's intervention in the
next scene suggests that she has suffered not only her social
superior's coercion but also his threats. 'I do protest if any
chaste denial, / If anything but blood could have allayed /
His long suit to me', she cries on her knees (1.2.273–4), with
'blood' possibly meaning sex, or hinting at the bloodshed
her submission to Brachiano was designed to forestall.[15] At
their first meeting, it is by no means clear that 'Vittoria may
immediately initiate sexual advances' or that 'her silence
implies acquiescence at the very least'.[16] Brachiano's opening
line, 'Give credit', followed by his Petrarchan compliment,
'You are a sweet physician', elicits from her not sensual acquiescence but the dry and witty rejoinder: 'Sir, a loathed cruelty
in ladies / Is as to doctors many funerals: / It takes away
their credit' (1.2.184, 193–5). Comparing her position with
that of a doctor whose livelihood depends on saving lives,
Vittoria intimates that she simply cannot afford the chaste

disdain of the Petrarchan mistress. Petrarchan compliment masks economic relations: while Brachiano figures himself as 'lost' (1.2.3, 190) and appears to assign Vittoria the power to determine his fate, he in fact rapidly takes control of the action, asserting his social and economic power. Fingering her jewel, he asks after its value; she retorts, 'Tis the ornament / Of a weak fortune' (204–5). He then seizes it (playing vulgarly on 'jewel' as pudendum) and gives her his jewel, urging her to wear it 'lower', with Flamineo reinforcing the sexual implications. Unlike his source, Webster portrays Vittoria's husband not as a 'young man of comely stature and personage', but as a foolish, impotent ass and menial dependant in the Duke's household (1.2.119–21).[17] Both Camillo's insufficiency and Brachiano's predation appear to be designed to diminish Vittoria's guilt. And while neither fully accounts for Vittoria's dream, interpreted by Flamineo as instigation of the double murder (1.2.239–40), even here Webster works to mitigate Vittoria's responsibility. The dream contains enough vivid detail to suggest that it may be more than a contrived fiction, representing instead Vittoria's sense of her own victimization and possibly even her demonic temptation.[18] Brachiano interprets the dream allegorically, as a plea for his protection; but she is never directly linked to the murders. By contrast, Brachiano's adulterous passion leads him not only to treat his virtuous wife with extraordinary cruelty, but also to commission and oversee her murder. Indeed, the pathos of Isabella's plea ('You have oft for these two lips / Neglected cassia or the natural sweets / Of the spring violet' (2.1.165–7)), recalls William Heale's *Apologie for women* (1609), a text that proscribes wife-beating: 'Who could violate those eyes the spears of light and loadstars of affection? Who could wrong those lips such rubies of value, and rivers of delight?'[19] In the play's dramatic construction, Vittoria and Isabella are situated not as rivals or enemies but as parallel victims of Brachiano.[20] Lever rightly notes that 'Brachiano occupies the position of the traditional tyrant, the unscrupulous slave of passion';[21] not only does he succumb to his lust, but he also violates both his own marriage and Vittoria's.[22] In *The White Devil*, Webster works to situate female sexual transgression in a world of masculine economic and social injustice. 'These politic enclosures for paltry mutton makes more rebellion in the flesh', observes Flamineo (1.2.90–1), drawing a suggestive analogy between women's supposed 'lust' as a response to masculine oppression and the 1607 Midlands uprisings against the land enclosures that created such economic hardship in England.[23]

The principal generic marker of *The White Devil* as a 'just defence' (3.2.126) of women comes, of course, in 'The Arraignment of Vittoria' – a scene carefully marked out as a set-piece by the printer. This oft-discussed exchange, traditionally heralded as 'one of the great moments of the English stage', has just as often been viewed as an ethical and aesthetic failure on Webster's part or as an illustration of the discontinuous position of woman in early modern England.[24] More recently, it has been read as simple confirmation of the play's misogyny.[25] For Alison Shell, this misogyny is also virulently anti-Catholic as Vittoria is identified with the Whore of Babylon.[26] Yet, because in his 'whore' diatribe, the Cardinal unwittingly describes *his own* allegiances as a scarlet-robed Catholic churchman, as Vittoria says, the 'filth returns in's face' (3.2.151).[27] Her observation that 'It doth not suit a reverend cardinal / To play the lawyer thus' (3.2.60–1) anticipates Webster's own Character of a Jesuit: 'His vows seem heavenly, but in meddling with state business he seems to mix heaven and earth together'.[28] If the Cardinal and his rhetoric are clearly associated with Catholicism, Vittoria's rejection of his arguments, coupled with her ridicule of the lawyer's Latinity and ornate rhetorical figures (3.2.12–42) evoke hot Protestant defiance of detested Latinate papist traditions. This may – surprisingly – put her discursively in the company of female martyrs such as the subject of John Bale's *Examinations of Anne Askew* (1547).[29] Jennifer Summit remarks that, in '[p]ositing a timeless enmity between women and the agents of Rome, Bale envisions in the lost history of women a narrative of dissent that prefigures and grounds the history of English Protestantism'.[30] In the trial scene, Vittoria's 'modesty / And womanhood' (3.2.132–3) are similarly associated with the frank, bold, anti-Papist speech of reformed tradition; in her repeated appeals to 'this auditory' and 'all this assembly' (3.2.15–19), Vittoria openly aligns herself with the Protestant theatre audience.[31] What Franklin terms her 'Attic style' – characterized by 'extreme brevity [and] plain language' – was associated with reform Protestantism.[32] Indeed, Vittoria's final speech before sweeping off the stage openly repudiates Catholicism for a distinctly Protestant, neo-Stoic interiority:

> My mind shall make it honester to me
> Than the Pope's palace, and more peaceable
> Than thy soul, though thou art a Cardinal. (3.2.290–2)[33]

The anti-papist rhetoric with which she is associated might well have appealed to Protestants shaken by the recent assassination of France's King Henry IV by a fanatical Catholic, and appalled by James's conciliatory stance on religious matters. Webster daringly requires his audience to identify this 'famous Venetian Curtizan' with the familiar Protestant rhetoric of bold resistance to corrupt papist traditions.[34]

Indeed, it is in the trial scene that the Cardinal specifies Vittoria's birthplace as Venice (3.2.235), unlike Webster's sources which place her origins in either Rome or Gubbio.[35] Recent critics associate Vittoria with Italianate corruption and specifically with Venice as 'the pleasure-seeking centre of Europe, the sink of sensual excesses', yet they overlook contemporary associations of Venice with republicanism and defiance of popery.[36] While Webster was writing *The White Devil*, the longstanding conflict between republican Venice and ecclesiastical Rome reached crisis point.[37] After Rome issued an interdict against Venice in 1606, Venice not only retaliated by expelling the Jesuits, but according to James Doelman, it 'proved a ripe field for conversions to Protestantism', with implications beyond Venice:

The English saw the quarrel between Venice and Rome as the counterpart to their own struggle: in both cases the civil government was challenging what they saw as the intrusion of the pope into matters of secular authority.[38]

As a Venetian, Vittoria not only defies a Cardinal who later uses his papal power to excommunicate her (4.3.68), but also insists on the principles of justice he violates (3.2.125–9; 225–8; 274–5). Famed for its equitable justice system, Venice, as Edmund Spenser declares, 'far exceeds in policy of right'.[39] Lewis Lewkenor's 1599 translation of Contarini's *Commonwealth and Government of Venice* portrayed Venice as the ideal government, a mixed monarchy in which the ruler, wholly subject to the laws, deferred to the decision-making powers of both Senate and Council.[40] Such a model had considerable appeal for those resisting James's growing absolutism; Mark Matheson observes that 'Members of these […] aristocratic circles were interested in the mixed government of the Venetian republic, and as Protestants they approved of its steadfast opposition to the authoritarianism of the Counter-Reformation'.[41] Venice was clearly on the minds of English king and commons during the parliamentary sessions of 1610: if the King accused his MPs of attempting to reduce his powers to those of the Duke of Venice, MPs themselves proposed 'to deliver their voices by lot, as in Venice'.[42] Though Vittoria is far from simply innocent – she has, she later laments, been Brachiano's 'whore' (4.2.140) – she is, nonetheless, deployed by Webster to proclaim the emerging discourse of the liberties of the subject in the face of an autocratic regime.[43] Webster trades on the political values of Venice to represent this contest between Roman prelate and Venetian woman as a contest between tyranny and liberty.[44]

Thomas Archer and the Queen's Men

Webster's ultra-Protestant politics and his engagement with the *querelle des femmes* are also suggested by his association with printer Thomas Archer. Building on Zachary Lesser's claim that publishers catered to partisan readers, I have argued elsewhere that Archer's involvement (with Nathaniel Butter and Nicholas Bourne) in publishing English news-books (or corantos) in the early 1620s marked him as a 'hotter' Protestant keen to offer indirect encouragement to those who, unlike King James, favoured England's involvement in the Thirty Years War.[45] Webster may have shared this view, putting it in the mouth of Mulinassar, who comments on 'the misery of peace' (5.1.113). Chris Kyle notes that 'Thomas Archer had been imprisoned in summer 1621, and Butter and Bourne frequently ran afoul of the authorities. James I, worried that the impact of news about war on the Continent might inflame public opinion toward a more interventionist stance, asked the Dutch government to ban the export of corantos'.[46] Archer's business in publishing works related to the *querelle des femmes* in the second decade of the seventeenth century should be seen in this light.[47] If in woman as the 'quintessential political subject […] many men saw reflected aspects of their own social situations', defences of women could take on highly politicized overtones.[48] As Julie Crawford points out, 'those who took the side of women […] were associated with the rights of the subject and, crucially, with limitations on the monarch's power'.[49] By associating the Cardinal's misogyny with his tyranny and Vittoria's self-defence with anti-authoritarianism, Webster aligns himself with the latter – a position that would also have put him at odds with the increasingly autocratic rule of King James.

In Jacobean England, works that suggested covert criticism of the King and his court might nonetheless win royal favour by appealing to the rival courts of Queen Anne and Prince Henry.[50] *The White Devil* was acted by the Queen's Servants, a company 'set up to please the consort Queen' by staging woman-centred plays.[51] At the centre of Webster's play, Vittoria kneels before the ambassadors and cries:

> Humbly thus,
> Thus low, to the most worthy and respected
> Lieger ambassadors, my modesty
> And womanhood I tender; but withal
> So entangled in a cursed accusation
> That my defence, of force, like Perseus
> Must personate masculine virtue to the point. (3.2.130–6)

This speech alludes to Jonson's 1609 *Masque of Queens* – a masque inspired, organized and performed by the Queen and her ladies.[52] As the Queen's own company thus pays her a compliment, it also links Vittoria and her just defence to the Amazonian queens in the masque. These are figures that, as Kathryn Schwartz points out, suggest both 'the potency of Elizabethan nostalgia' and 'a direct challenge to the terms of male sovereignty'.[53] If, moreover, as Knowles points out, 'many of [Queen Anne's] courtiers were displaced associates of the Leicester-Essex faction, with its interests in militant Protestantism', their political engagements may well have coincided with those of publisher Thomas Archer and Webster himself.[54] Vittoria's speech aligns her specifically with Perseus, the figure in the masque who 'embodies a power derived from women'.[55] Moreover, this was a figure who, Roberta Barker suggests, may have been intended to represent Prince Henry, for whom Jonson provided an extensively annotated copy.[56] As Alastair Bellany claims, the entourage of the Prince 'was threatening to become a court within a court, a haven for discontented men inclined towards a militantly Protestant and expansionist foreign policy'.[57] Webster showed more than merely conventional interest in the Prince when he published the verse elegy *A Monumentall column* (1613) shortly after Henry's unexpected death, and then reanimated him as a political ideal a dozen years later, in his Lord Mayor's Show

(1624). Heralded as the revitalized leader of British chivalry and the warrior-hero of a militant Protestant faction, Henry represented ideals openly at odds both with his father's public goal of international peace and with James's debauched private habits. Building on previous critics, I shall argue that Webster's portrait of Giovanni in *The White Devil*, as a tribute to Prince Henry, further advertises the dramatist's political allegiances.[58]

Boy Princes: Giovanni and Prince Henry

Unlike the boy actors whose fluid and ambiguous gender identities have attracted extensive scholarly discussion, boys who played *boys* on the early modern stage teetered at the threshold of adult masculinity and had the potential to suggest alternative models of manhood-in-process. As apprentices and hence subordinates in the adult theatrical companies in which they served, boy players ranged in age from twelve to twenty-two 'with a median age of around sixteen or seventeen'.[59] Their median age thus mirrored that of Prince Henry, whose investiture as Prince of Wales, in 1610, at age sixteen, was celebrated in a series of magnificent festivals. Perhaps influenced by the cultural 'text' of the Stuart royal family in which similar dynamics were being played out on the 'stage' of England, Webster expands the role of Brachiano's young son into a full-blown portrait of a model warrior-prince who, much like Prince Henry, functions as a powerful critique of the adult males in *The White Devil*.[60] Webster's representation of this boy prince taps into larger cultural discourses surrounding competing models of masculinity that, Robin Headlam Wells has argued, came into prominence between 1608 and the year of Henry's death (1612).[61]

In a short scene near the end of *The White Devil*, Giovanni (son of the recently murdered Duke of Brachiano) runs into his father's servant and court malcontent Flamineo. '[W]hat said the little boy that rode behind his father on horseback?' Flamineo asks before continuing: '"When you are dead, father" (said he) "I hope then I shall ride in the saddle". O, 'tis a brave thing for a man to sit by himself: he may stretch himself in the stirrups, look about, and see the whole compass of the hemisphere. You're now, my lord, i'th'saddle' (5.4.12–19). In Flamineo's version of the transition from son to father, the boy simply replaces and replicates the man; as Flamineo later says cynically of Giovanni, 'he hath his uncle's villainous look already / In *decimo-sexto*' (29–30). Yet here he is plainly wrong. Indeed Giovanni rebukes him, precipitating Flamineo's anguished self-awareness: 'Study your prayers, sir, and be penitent. / 'Twere fit you'd think on what hath former bin, / I have heard grief named the eldest child of sin' (20–2). If sin produces a child quite unlike its progenitor, so Webster's anti-hero Brachiano produces a young son who differentiates himself from the adult males and holds the potential to bring moral justice to their corrupt and chaotic world.[62] While 'young Giovanni' (2.1.0SD) does exist in the various sources Webster is believed to have used for *The White Devil*, there 'he is merely a name' – the incidental product of the ill-fated union of Brachiano and Isabella.[63] In the Fugger newsletter (whose lost Italian original is considered an undisputed source), his uncle Francisco (de Medici) takes charge of 'the young forsaken Prince Giovanni' after his father's murder, and the Government is credited with executing justice on the criminals.[64] By contrast, in Webster's play Giovanni becomes the new Duke, a powerful independent agent who offers effective political action, condemning all the assassins (including his uncle) 'to prison and to torture' at the end of the play (5.6.289). Indeed, Giovanni's powerful moral *sententiae* are the final notes heard in the play: 'Let guilty men remember their black deeds / Do lean on crutches, made of slender reeds' (5.6.298–9). Critics who have seen this final statement as 'unintentionally ironic or as naive' have to ignore much of the authority Webster bestows on this boy who grows into an entirely different kind of man before our eyes.[65]

Giovanni quickly comes into theatrical prominence in the play's second act. Taking centre stage clad in the suit of armour furnished by his uncle Francisco (2.1.95), he is heralded by Monticelso as a living object lesson for both Brachiano and Francisco:

> Your son the prince Giovanni. This is a casket
> For both your crowns, and should be held like dear.
> Now is he apt for knowledge; therefore know
> It is a more direct and even way
> To train to virtue those of princely blood
> By examples than by precepts: if by examples
> Whom should he rather strive to imitate
> Than his own father: be his pattern then,
> Leave him a stock of virtue that may last,
> Should fortune rend his sails and split his mast. (2.1.97–107)

Here, Giovanni is an emblem of chivalric virtue for whom Brachiano is (ironically) being urged to set a pattern. As he proceeds to brandish a pike, much like Prince Henry in Simon van de Passe's engraving, his uncle's attempts to reduce him to a puerile object of fun backfire so that (to quote Vittoria again) 'the filth returns in's face' (3.2.151).[66] 'Might not a child of good discretion / Be leader to an army?' asks Giovanni of Francisco (2.1.113–14). If Giovanni understands 'discretion' here to mean 'judgment' (*OED* II.2), demonstrating his own good judgment, Francisco immediately shifts its meaning to something closer to 'circumspection' (*OED* III.6) with his typically sardonic reply: 'Yes cousin, a young prince / Of good *discretion* might' (114–15, my emphasis). The lines immediately recall Falstaff's famous defence of his own cowardice in battle: 'the better part of valour is discretion' (*1 Henry IV* 5.4.117–18). Giovanni's ironic riposte unpacks Francisco's anti-chivalric implications: 'Indeed I have heard 'tis fit a general / Should not endanger his own person oft

[...] O 'tis excellent, / He need not fight; methinks his horse as well / Might lead an army for him'. He then carefully distinguishes his own heroic ideals from Francisco's: 'If I live / I'll charge the French foe, in the very front / Of all my troops, the foremost man [...] And will not bid my soldiers up and follow / But bid them follow me' (2.1.114–25).[67] Brachiano may patronizingly praise his son as a 'forward lapwing' who 'flies with the shell on's head' (2.1.125–6), but we may already hear strains of Webster's elegy for Prince Henry, whose 'star / Had markt him for a just and glorious war', and who emulated Edward the Black Prince, 'Hee that like lightning did his force advance / And shook to th'Center the whole Realm of France'.[68] The scene is moralized by Francisco with 'See, a good habit makes a child a man, / Whereas a bad one makes a man a beast' (2.1.137–8). Yet, as well as referring to Brachiano, the comment is self-reflexive: the kind of manly *virtù* represented in embryo by Giovanni is contrasted not only with his father's debauchery but also with his uncle Francisco's Machiavellianism. The difference between the son as a 'champion' (2.1.95) 'soldier' (108) and the father who has sacrificed his public duties 'for the soft down / Of an insatiate bed' (2.1.31–2) is patently obvious. For when Brachiano is named Vittoria's 'champion' by Monticelso (3.2.180) at the moment he abandons her in the trial scene, we hear an ironic echo of Giovanni's appearance. Webster uses Giovanni as an implicit critique of Brachiano's unmanly behaviour most notably in the dumb show of Isabella's murder, in which Giovanni's mute 'sorrow' is juxtaposed with Brachiano's exultant comment, 'Excellent, then she's dead' (2.2.24).

Furthermore, Giovanni's idealized portrait as child soldier in 2.1 stands in marked contrast to the degeneration of chivalry in the rest of the play world. Camillo, once 'turned soldier' (2.1.368), is 'o'th'captain's humour right; / [...] resolved to be drunk this night' (372–3), and Flamineo offers extended commentary on his soldier-brother Marcello's dependent poverty (3.1.36–50). Francisco rejects war as a means of punishing Brachiano for Isabella's murder: 'Shall I defy him, and impose a war / Most burdensome on my poor subjects' necks, / Which at my will I have not power to end?' he says (4.1.5–7). While he longs in passing 'To have ta'en him [Brachiano] by the casque in a pitched field' (5.1.78) what he opts for instead is poison. And if he appears to echo Giovanni's insistence on direct princely engagement in risky actions by assuring Lodovico that their 'danger shall be like in this design' (4.3.79), Gasparo reveals the truth in the final scene: 'Princes give rewards with their own hands / But death or punishment by the hands of others' (5.6.184–5). In the last act, Francisco further debases heroic values by adopting the disguise of a 'brave soldier' who claims to have served the Venetians in wars against the Turk (5.1.5–45) merely to further his criminal designs.

But the best illustration of the decline of honour in this world depends on the Red Bull audience's awareness of a crucial intertext for 5.3. This, the scene of Brachiano's death by poison, begins with '*fighting at barriers; first single pairs, then three to three*'. Critics have recognized Webster's debt here to *Prince Henry's Barriers*, an elaborately ceremonial tournament performed on Twelfth Night 1610 in the Whitehall Banqueting House. As Roy Strong observes, there the 'theme is war, not peace, and it is aggressive not passive. It overtly casts the Prince into a revival of Elizabethan chivalry that in its wildest fantasies could see England at the head of a pan-Protestant, European, anti-Catholic and anti-Spanish crusade'.[69] David Carnegie asserts that, in this scene (5.3), 'one of the most spectacular sequences in the play', Webster was clearly drawing on this 'immediate courtly context of political display and entertainment'.[70] Given this intertext, the opening becomes highly ironic, as the chivalric occasion rapidly gives way to chaos, with Brachiano's Lear-like ravings taking centre stage before he is strangled in private. Although Giovanni himself is reduced here to an anguished observer, the barriers evoke a similar chivalric ideal against which the corrupt court world is measured and found wanting.

Yet Giovanni is not merely an emblem for the chivalric manliness that is in such short supply in the adult males of this play. In his first appearance, Giovanni interrupts his powerful uncle Francisco with 'Lord uncle, you did promise me a horse / And armour' (2.1.6–7) before exiting abruptly. His eruption into public space only to disappear from view is paradigmatic of the play as a whole. Later, in response to Giovanni's anguish for his mother's death, Francisco cries 'Take him away for God's sake' (3.2.339), and upon Giovanni's pained cry at his father's imminent death, Brachiano commands, 'Remove the boy away' (5.3.17). Giovanni is often cut in modern productions, but such small moments signal Webster's canny use of the boy to illuminate in a brief flash a field of action and experience that the play's male characters are attempting to suppress. As David Carnegie observes, 'his brief scenes and few lines have a powerful impact on audiences'.[71] And, apart from his warlike valour, Giovanni expresses a deep anguish coupled with compassion that only Flamineo of all the other men achieves – albeit fleetingly at 5.4.112. Immediately after the trial scene, Giovanni enters Hamlet-like, in black mourning garments for the death of his 'sweet mother' (3.2.314) and poignantly reveals his deep bond with her. If he himself 'has not slept these six nights', he has 'known her wake an hundred nights / When all the pillow, where she laid her head / Was brine-wet with her tears' (3.2.327–31). His final words in the scene not only implicitly indict the men responsible for her murder, but also identify Isabella's maternal love as a source of sustenance that male princes cannot provide: 'I have heard her say she gave me suck, / And it should seem by that she dearly loved me, / Since princes seldom do it' (335–6). While it may not be irrelevant that Queen Anne and Henry shared a similarly close bond (to James's infinite irritation), the crucial point here is that Giovanni's liminal masculinity – with its close connection to the maternal sphere – allows him access to genuine emotions that seem to be short-circuited in most of the men.[72] By representing a successful boy prince whose proximity to the maternal co-exists with his masculine valour,

Webster incorporates his defence of women into his paean to chivalric masculinity.

The White Devil is far from a transparent political allegory in which Giovanni 'represents' Prince Henry, Brachiano, his father, King James, and the Cardinal and Monticelso, the Catholic powers that threatened the small Protestant nation from without. Such a reading would reduce the play's complexity and fail to account for its unpredictable, dangerously attractive characters, who shift and change under the pressure of events. If the liaison between Brachiano and Vittoria initially seems exploitative, it later looks more like a love match ratified by marriage; if Brachiano moves from seducer and murderer to tragic hero confronting death, so Vittoria shifts from adulterous woman to defiant victim of misogyny. Yet close examination of the play's material and cultural contexts suggests that the boy prince Giovanni and the Venetian courtesan Vittoria together activate a rich web of contemporary political allusions – allusions that would not have been lost on the 'full and understanding auditory' Webster desired for his play.[73]

7

New Directions: The Look of Love? – Pornography and *The White Devil*'s 'terrible vision'

Adam Hansen

Pornography is men telling lies about women.[1]

What harm is there in seeing a man mount a woman?[2]

Introduction

As early as 1617, people thought John Webster had a dirty, even monstrous mind, and commented on 'his brain's coitus'.[3] More recently, others have elaborated on this, linking Webster and pornography. A review of *The White Devil* at London's National Theatre in 1969 asserted: 'Of all the dramatists of this period, Webster was the supreme pornographer.'[4] Almost forty years later, a director of the play commented that Webster's 'stage violence' was 'almost pornographic. It's extremely voyeuristic.'[5] If Webster was obsessed with 'the skull beneath the skin', he was also fascinated by the body beneath the costume and the disgusting or desirable things that might be done to it.[6] Intrusive, violating voyeurism intensified in Maria Aberg's 2014 production for the RSC, which was full of projections, screens and photography, leaving audiences in no doubt they were watching watchers being watched. Aberg's production exposed how women have to perform in sexual ways and the sexual violence of pornography, too, in the repeated scenes of inverted striptease, where Vittoria dresses herself and also in the moment when Vittoria's first husband, Camillo, meets his end not on a vaulting horse, but as a punter strangled in a sadomasochistic brothel, peopled by faceless figures in white PVC bodysuits, bound with red cord. Moreover, as Erin Sullivan has shown in an online visual essay, this production's scenery referenced a music video notorious for featuring topless female dancers next to fully clothed male singers.[7] Yet the sexualized aesthetic of this production did more than titillate men, or objectify women. Aberg affirms: 'I'm a feminist and I think that affects everything I do and it's important to me that it does.'[8] The production was marketed as part of a 'Roaring Girls' season of plays. These stagings sought to unsettle and challenge assumptions about gender. Kat Banyard's contribution to the programmes for the season argued for gender equality, while discussing the ways pornography makes achieving such equality harder:

> today, one in four young people have viewed pornography by the time they hit their teens. Yet this is an industry fundamentally built on the objectification of women. [...] The sex industry offers men the chance to opt out of the twenty-first century, providing online and offline spaces where 'men can be men' and where women's role is to sexually service them.[9]

From this perspective, because heterosexual pornography so often involves men telling lies about women, as noted in the first epigraph, the answer to the question posed by the early modern erotic writer Pietro Aretino (1492–1556) in the second epigraph is: *a lot*. So, the more space given to championing equality the better: the fact that Banyard does not actually refer to any plays in the season (including *The White Devil*) hardly matters. However, are the connections so clear between producing early modern drama representing powerful women and tackling contemporary issues of gender inequality and sexual exploitation? Or might attending productions of seventeenth-century plays involve opting out of the twenty-first century, in ways comparable to Banyard's analysis of the sex industry? We can answer such questions in different ways, but Banyard's contribution and the assumptions behind it suggest that concerns like pornography were a live issue (or should have been) for the production, and its audiences. This raises another question, which this chapter tries to address, if not resolve: what does it mean to call Webster a 'pornographer'?

We might answer that question by noting that picturing Webster in these ways develops his own sense of the significance of his and our 'terrible vision' (5.4.141). In this play, people love to look, but hate what they look on, because what they look on disturbs their sense of who they are. People cannot control their desire to look at what disgusts them, and are disgusted by their desire to look. People look on things they feel they cannot control in order to control them better, but find that the more they look and try to control, the less control they have. This afflicted Webster himself: he complained that *The White Devil* 'wanted […] a full and understanding auditory', but perhaps the issue was he lacked spectators who would see the play in the ways he hoped it would be seen ('To the Reader', 5–6). Moreover, the play may resonate with what the Conjuror calls a 'tragic sound' (2.2.37), but it staged scenes that required – and repaid – intensive scrutiny, especially in what Webster termed 'so open and black a theatre' ('To the Reader', 4). Clearly, Webster self-consciously conceived of 'the visual as well as the verbal impact of his art'.[10]

Characters in *The White Devil* repeatedly discuss sight, and how it is experienced and manipulated, in terms that go far beyond an 'interest in the motif of portraiture' Webster may have cultivated through his associations with painters.[11] For example, Flamineo describes 'a pair of spectacles fashioned [...] with perspective art' which multiply the 'hands [...] taking up' Vittoria's clothes, and which might, in turn, incite 'horrible causeless fury' in Camillo. Camillo maintains the 'fault' lies 'not in the eyesight' of the perceiver of such beguiling, appalling scenes, but in the figure perceived. Before Camillo can make this explicit, Flamineo cuts him off, suggesting that jealousy is a disease like 'the yellow jaundice', which makes the seer see yellow (1.2.94–105). Both Flamineo and Camillo are right as they articulate this ambiguous, sexualized double-vision (at least): perception *is* subjective, limited, partial, open to corruption, manipulation and bias; but adultery *is* happening, and the husband rightly suspects his wife.

Webster's critics emphasize and contextualize this visuality. Dena Goldberg influentially explicated how 'voyeurism' and eavesdropping are 'pervasive' in the play. Espionage queries 'the demarcation between public and private' on stage, while implicating the audience off-stage: as we navigate the plot's (and plots') complexities, we 'participate', 'eavesdrop' and 'spy'. Goldberg's survey of meta-dramatic scenes of seeing others see and hearing others hear concludes that Webster was feeding his audience's 'hunger for court gossip', thereby allowing that audience to 'purge itself of fascination with life at court': watching others access privy places in such reflexive ways encouraged a cathartic scepticism towards Jacobean authority.[12] Since critiques of James I's court, not least one just a year before *The White Devil*, focused on the money lavished on 'shews, sights' and such like, there is much strength in this argument.[13] But are there other ways to contextualize the play's links between looking, hearing, hating and hurting, this 'terrible vision'? As Sarah Toulalan suggests: 'Voyeurism is an integral part of the pornographic'.[14] To explore the relevance of this claim for *The White Devil*, defining terms matters.

This involves the vexed issue of defining pornography, which, at best, can seem a glaringly ahistorical or anachronistic term. Nevertheless, as Aberg's production indicated, we see the past, including the past encapsulated in Webster's play, or in earlier forms of pornography, through the present. Indeed, present readings of pornography are informed by its past forms: 'the attitudes and practices of this century [the twentieth] as well as those that intervened between the renaissance and our own time have greatly influenced our study of the subject'.[15] Clearly, it is not always easy or desirable to use modern definitions of pornography to talk about early modern incarnations of it; but we can do little else if we want to understand Webster's world, and our own. So this chapter does try to be mindful of historical distance and discontinuity as well as parallels and connections between then and now. Equally, this chapter is not trying to offer a definitive reading of the play, but explore some of its more troubling and engaging features; this may make both the play, and this reading of it, more suggestively fragmentary than conclusively coherent.

Defining and discriminating

Mary Joe Frug notes that 'what constitutes pornography is usually a charged and unexplored question in any discussion involving pornography.'[16] This is because in the past and present, pornography means and involves many things, and represents a 'moving target'.[17] Not all pornography is made or used in the same ways, even when, as in this chapter, the focus is on representations of 'heterosexual' relations. As Ian Frederick Moulton suggests, 'pornography is not an essential category but rather an historical one.'[18] There are lots of definitions of the term and the practice, and these change through time, complicating any linking of Webster and pornography. For example, Diana E. H. Russell defines pornography as 'material that combines sex and / or the exposure of genitals with abuse or degradation in a manner that appears to endorse, condone, or encourage such behavior.'[19] Even the worst production of *The White Devil* hardly does that. In terms of definitions, too, there are some other very obvious ways it does not make much sense to call Webster a 'pornographer'. He did not write 'pornography' because that was a word, a way of representing people, and an idea, not available or current when he wrote:

> Pornography did not constitute a wholly separate and distinct category of written or visual representation before the early nineteenth century.[20]

Dictionary definitions reinforce this point. The term 'pornographie' occurs in a French 'treatise on prostitution' from 1800, but we can go further back: Restif de la Bretonne published *Le Pornographe* in 1769, 'in which details are given of a grand scheme to institutionalize brothels, so that they run on a more humane, healthy and discreet basis'.[21] The *Oxford English Dictionary* identifies the use of 'pornography' in *English*, in a work from 1842 discussing 'the lower classes of art', and pornography as 'a description of prostitutes or of prostitution, as a matter of public hygiene' was recurrent from the mid-nineteenth century. Some scholars, such as David Foxon, suggest an even earlier date for the emergence of pornography, which, he says, 'seems to have been born and grown to maturity in a brief period in the middle of the seventeenth century'.[22] Other discussions of the development of the term 'pornography' tell other stories. One is that it was generated by nineteenth-century historians describing some of the sexual imagery and artefacts discovered in Pompeii, citing 'a unique instance in classical Greek of the word *pornographoi* ("whore-painters")'.[23]

Bringing these stories and histories together, we might surmise that 'pornography' is a term associated with writings about and representations of prostitutes, that stimulate disgust or desire in readers (a distinction which is not always clear cut, as we will see). Whatever dating or definition we decide, Webster seemingly missed the boat.

We might add that Webster is a serious, canonical, literary dramatist, deeply concerned with ethical, social and ideological issues (as the ideas and arguments in this collection attest). He is this because his texts exploit and generate troubling ambiguities in his context; as the diverse critical and conflicting theatrical interpretations of Webster's works show, we can never quite be sure what to make of him. Pornography, in contrast, is not renowned for its profundity or ambiguity. Quite the opposite:

> What porn does is to take [...] cultural messages about women [and about men, we might add] and present them in a succinct way that leaves little room for multiple interpretations.[24]

This is doubtless true, and worth stating. However, perhaps a critical reading of pornography, if not pornography itself, can be used to consider the sorts of ethical, social and ideological issues some more comfortably locate in literature? Moreover, perhaps literature can invoke devices from pornography to do the same? If we discriminate between them, what assumptions do we make about definitions of pornography and literature?[25] Discriminations are easy to make, and worth making, not least because literary texts and pornography can be seen to try to do different things: arguably, in pornography intent on stimulating men (of whatever sexual orientation), 'The pornographer aims for erection (at least)'.[26]

Yet as Angela Carter notes 'pornographic writing retains this in common with all literature – that it turns the flesh into word'.[27] Furthermore, she suggests that as it tries to condition desires, pornography is 'always art with work to do.'[28] But all art is trying to do something. In this regard, 'pornography is the most political form of fiction, dealing with how we use and exploit each other'.[29]

These questions, issues and indistinctions become even more complicated when things are done in fictions *on stage*, underwritten by a playwright's words. David Mura suggests: 'In contemporary capitalism, pornography has become primarily visual rather than written.'[30] Equally, 'people are concerned about pictures' and 'make no reference to text' in contemporary debates about internet pornography.[31] But a play is more than a visual tableau, text or a scene – it is also bodies, sometimes speaking, sometimes moving, always doing. Moreover, plays are very good at stimulating 'scopophilia (pleasure in looking)'.[32] They have to be, because their commercial success depends on it: in the early modern period, part of what people loved to pay to look at was people 'making love', if not having sex. Having sex on the early modern stage would have been tricky, not to say impossible: '[T]here would have been little realistic heterosexual action on the stage with an audience always aware that boys were playing the parts of women'.[33] Nonetheless, theatre past and present is adept at stimulating fantasies where the imagination fills in the blanks:

> It seems bizarre to think of a play, performed on a stage, as a sexual fantasy: the one is overtly public, the other essentially private. But [...] fantasies, like plays, are typically visualized; they are enacted in a scene.[34]

Precisely because the early modern stage stimulated and depended upon scopophilia, it also attracted and generated an intense anxiety about looking – or 'ocularophobia' – keying into a context where the eyes 'gave access to all manner of physical horrors and moral evils which corrupted the seer and destroyed his or her moral and psychological stability.'[35] Stuart Clark finds this ocularophobia exemplified in a text called *The*

Vanitie of the Eye by the cleric George Hakewill. Published in different editions in 1608 and 1615 – either side of the first performance of *The White Devil* – this clearly depicted the problems of seeing, in ways that resonate with the play. Eyes are forever 'prying always into other men's business', not least their intimate affairs: 'we see the very chair and throne of adultery, to be seated in the eye'. Hakewill counsels 'gaze not on a maid, lest thou fall by that that is precious in her'. He affirms: 'lusting for the most part follows looking'. Hakewill contends these urges are so dangerous because they are so insatiable: 'The ear being never filled with hearing, nor the eye satisfied with seeing.' Proverbial wisdom rules, then: 'out of sight, out of mind'. This is one of the reasons why Vittoria must be removed to the house of convertites. If she is not, chaos ensues:

> How many have we seen and heard of who after the sight of women have grown peevish? And some stark mad, others have raised armies, and razed whole cities and towns to make away their competitors, and at length have laid violent hands on themselves?[36]

The love of looking (especially at women), what Saint Augustine would assert 'the divine word' calls '"the lust of the eyes" (1 Jn 2.16)', destroys societies and selves.[37] To Hakewill, many stimuli foment this destructive voyeurism, from 'the lewd masking which the Papists use in their Carnivals' to what the Jesuits put 'upon their stages', and including 'the beholding of vain and wanton pictures, such as Aretine's'.[38] Aretino himself may have dismissed the harm caused by seeing a man mount a woman, but Hakewill is far from convinced. Likewise, for Anthony Munday, 'much evil' could come 'in at the ears' at the theatre, but much more 'at the eyes': 'by these two open windows death breaketh into the soul'.[39] For William Prynne, the 'lively action and representation' of players 'make them pierce more deeply into the Spectators eyes, their ears and lewde affections'.[40] By assaulting eyes and ears, the stage shattered souls and disturbed bodies; the 'antitheatricalists' anxiety about theatre as idolatry' was also a horror at pornographic representations.[41]

Yet even the most contemptuous observers of the early modern stage based their contempt on the assumed power of the fantasies enacted in the theatre: 'such wanton gestures, such bawdie speeches: such laughing and fleering: such kissing and bussing: such clipping and culling'.[42] As Peter Stallybrass suggests, what such commentators 'gazed at' was 'a theatre imagined as a *bedroom*, a bedroom which spills off the stage and into the lives of players and audience alike.'[43] The early modern stage thereby afforded Webster plenty of models of dramatic, erotically charged action set on doing something. In this context, Webster got more from a play like *Othello* than a model for a blacked-up Francisco acting as the respected Moorish tactician Mulinassar, who is, like Othello, 'experienced [...] in rudiments of war', and who 'served the Venetian', being 'chief / In many a bold design', and quick with a 'lofty phrase' (5.1.7–33). For Shakespeare's play offers its fair share of 'scopophile excitements of erotic encounters'.[44] As numerous critics have shown, *Othello* is a study in obsessive observation. Othello says 'I'll see before I doubt' (3.3.185); he demands 'ocular proof' of Desdemona's infidelity from Iago (3.3.363), petitioning him: 'Make me to see't' (3.3.367).[45] Yet obsessive observation is animated by Iago too, through whom Shakespeare 'dramatizes a pornographic imagination', intent on stimulating and simulating copulation in Othello's and the audience's minds' eyes.[46]

As Lynda Boose has suggested: 'men are the lookers and women are objects to be looked at, trapped within and constructed by the pornographic images transmitted inside of an increasingly lethal circuitry of male discourse'.[47] This was augmented in the 'quasi-pornographic explicitness' of later graphic depictions of Desdemona's death scene, often featuring a 'voyeuristic manipulation of the parted curtains' around her bed.[48] Whether in an image or on a stage, that scene 'announces ocular proof of all that the audience have most desired and feared to look on, exposing to cruel light the obscure erotic fantasies that the play both explores and disturbingly excites'.[49] Though *The White Devil* does not feature in Michael Neill's list of 'Sensationalized bedchamber scenes that seem indebted to *Othello*', Webster learns from this play about how to use depictions of sexuality to make people confront what both disturbed and excited.[50]

Salacious scenes

We can see this in 1.2, when Vittoria and Brachiano 'come together in delight' in a scene that has been described as evoking the 'salaciousness of the brothel':[51]

> ZANCHE *brings out a carpet, spreads it and lays on it two fair cushions*
>
> *Enter* CORNELIA [*listening*]
>
> BRACHIANO   Let me into your bosom, happy lady,
> Pour out instead of eloquence my vows;
> Loose me not madam, for if you forgo me
> I am lost eternally. …   [*They embrace*]
> ZANCHE   See now they close.
> FLAMINEO   Most happy union. …
> BRACHIANO   What value is this jewel?
> VITTORIA   'Tis the ornament
> Of a weak fortune.
> BRACHIANO   In sooth I'll have it; nay I will but change
> My jewel for your jewel.
> FLAMINEO   Excellent,
> His jewel for her jewel; well put in Duke.
> BRACHIANO   Nay let me see you wear it.
> VITTORIA   Here sir.
> BRACHIANO   Nay lower, you shall wear my jewel lower.
> FLAMINEO   That's better; she must wear his jewel lower.
>   (1.2.187–211)

Luckyj asserts that because the stage direction was 'squeezed' in by the compositor 'we cannot [...] be certain' of when exactly Zanche does what she does; what is beyond doubt, however, is the 'overtly sexual nature of the lovers' encounter' in a pornographic tableau, consciously stimulating and depicting voyeurism, 'with Vice (Flamineo and Zanche) and Virtue (Cornelia) present as observers, probably framing the lovers on either side' (1.2.186, note). This 'stage picture' bears 'an erotic charge', with 'connotations of illicit sex'.[52] Several productions have realized this: 'by the end of the scene' in Gale Edwards' 1996 RSC staging, Vittoria and Brachiano 'had kissed and groped one another, and she had sunk orgasmically to the floor'.[53]

But *is* this pornography?

Later, Monticelso berates Brachiano for neglecting the 'awful throne' befitting his social standing, 'for the soft down / Of an insatiate bed', thereby indulging in a 'lascivious dream' (2.1.31–5). He recollects but hardly celebrates their coupling. Consequently, just because Vittoria and Brachiano are observed by audiences on- and off-stage, this does not mean people in those audiences are aroused or approving, or meant to be. The scene is 'highly meta-theatrical and aware of its own artifice'.[54] This alienation effect can 'distance audience reaction' rather than implicate us more deeply, as this scene generates multiple, contradictory on-stage commentary on the cunning, moral depravity, or success of the enterprise.[55] With this, Webster complicates any possible reactions we might have to this 'salacious' moment. Later, similar, moments in the play have comparable effects:

[ZANCHE]	I knew last night by a sad dream I had
	Some mischief would ensue, yet to say truth
	My dream most concerned you.
LODOVICO	Shall's fall a-dreaming?
FRANCISCO	Yes, and for fashion sake I'll dream with her.
[ZANCHE]	Methought, sir, you came stealing to my bed.
FRANCISCO	Wilt thou believe me sweeting? By this light

                  I was a-dreamt on thee too, for methought
                  I saw thee naked.
[ZANCHE]   Fie, sir! As I told you,
                  Methought you lay down by me.
FRANCISCO   So dreamt I,
                  And lest thou shouldst take cold, I covered thee
                  With this Irish mantle.
[ZANCHE]   Verily I did dream
                  You were somewhat bold with me; but to come
                  to't.
LODOVICO   How? How? I hope you will not go to't here.
FRANCISCO   Nay, you must hear my dream out.
[ZANCHE]   Well, sir, forth.
                  When I threw the mantle o'er thee, thou didst
                  laugh
                  Exceedingly methought.
[ZANCHE]   Laugh?
FRANCISCO   And cried'st out,
                  The hair did tickle thee.
[ZANCHE]   There was a dream indeed.
LODOVICO   Mark her, I prithee: she simpers like the suds
                  A collier hath been washed in.
[ZANCHE]   Come, sir; good fortune tends you; I did tell you
                  I would reveal a secret – Isabella
                  The Duke of Florence' sister was empoisoned
                  By a fumed picture and Camillo's neck
                  Was broke by damned Flamineo, the mischance
                  Laid on a vaulting-horse.
FRANCISCO   Most strange!
[ZANCHE]   Most true.
LODOVICO   The bed of snakes is broke.   (5.3. 221–46)

There may be several reasons why Lodovico does not want
Zanche and Francisco to 'go to't here', if we take the pronoun
''t [it] to be a sexual act, truncated to fit the metre, but
also to contain and diminish it even further. By this point,
Cornelia has already beaten Zanche and ordered her to 'Fly

to th'stews' with the prostitutes; while kicking her moments later, Marcello calls Zanche a 'strumpet', and an 'impudent' one at that, saying she should be set 'upon a stake', like a witch, 'to affright / Her fellow crows' (5.1.179–85), which may mean other women tainted by or embodying black arts, including prostitutes, especially Moorish ones. Maybe these prejudices inform Lodovico: he might not want to see two 'Moors' copulate. Alternatively, he may not want to see what he knows to be a blackface white Italian copulate with a Moorish woman of seemingly ill repute. Lodovico himself terms Zanche 'the infernal' (5.3.214). That description suggests that as a mocked-up Capuchin priest he is clearly too pious to witness such things as ''t', and may not want to see any man with any woman, given the way the period so often figured female genitals as hellish. On the other hand, he may simply be suggesting that the bedchamber of a man who has just been murdered (Brachiano) is not the best place for these kinds of relations; or this may be a metatheatrical comment, a wink to the audience, that they may dream what they like, but they cannot enact those dreams on stage: they can 'go to't' anywhere but 'here'. Another reason why they cannot, and should not, 'go to't here' is because Zanche is a male performer. Staging this sex scene would be to stage sodomy. Lodovico, thus, hints at the limits of what can and should be shown on stage, acting as an internal censor.

Yet just as the exchange generates multiple readings and interpretations, Lodovico's breathless 'How? How?' suggests our censor is himself obsessing about other forms of speculation and fantasy. Mimicking Iago, wondering aloud to himself and his audience about the best way to fabricate fornication in Othello's mind – 'How? How? Let's see' (1.3.393) – Lodovico muses: how will they do what they are talking about? Lodovico's lewd pun, playing on Zanche's words and the polysemy and ambiguity of a sexualized 'it' (as Marlowe had done in *Hero and Leander*) is what makes all these improper associations possible.[56] For herself, Zanche could simply mean 'come to the point'; it is Lodovico who makes that point sex. Furthermore, the punning prohibition makes Zanche and Francisco's dream enter the audience's heads too: in telling them not to do it 'here', we are invited to fixate on it, and make it happen here. What the characters say so often, echoing each other – 'methought' – becomes what '*we* thought'. Rather than suppressing and censoring ''t', Lodovico uses an imperative to instruct us to observe Zanche's excitement and sexual pleasure: 'Mark her'. Covering nakedness and desire in a censorious mantle makes their contours all the more tangible and enticing.

Such passages imply that if 'Shakespeare's audience heard his plays [...] with some sense of a tradition of erotica', that audience included Webster, and in his work too we can identify that tradition.[57] One other significant aspect of that tradition was the work of Aretino. Aretino was 'infamous' in England by the 1590s; he functioned as a 'layered metaphor', like Italy itself, eliciting or symbolizing desire and disgust in Elizabethan and Jacobean drama.[58] As a byword for 'authorial success' in England, works he published while ensconced in Venice (notably, Vittoria's home city) represented autonomy in the face of pressures exerted by the authorities.[59] His explicit dialogue between two women published in England in 1584, and in English a further five times before 1660, evinces an 'endless variety of objects and actions that can be eroticized', including power relations.[60] Writing about sex could be a way to arouse and stimulate, but also to critique hypocrisy:

> I am all out of patience with their scurvy strictures and their dirty-minded laws which forbid the eyes to see the very things which delight them most.[61]

Webster's allusions to the period's pornographer-in-chief assume telling forms. In 1.2, Flamineo tricks Camillo, promising to induce Vittoria to 'go to bed' with her husband (an assignation neither Flamineo nor Vittoria desire nor intend). Flamineo suggests Camillo will give his wife 'a ring with a philosopher's stone in it', prompting Camillo to chip in,

'Indeed, I am studying alchemy'. As Flamineo woos Vittoria
on Camillo's behalf he offers this vision of conjugal bliss:

> Thou shalt lie in a bed stuffed with turtles' feathers, swoon
> in perfumed linen like the fellow was smothered in roses, so
> perfect shall be thy happiness. (1.2.132–41)

These lines, and the image of Camillo as a self-deluding,
gullible, and lascivious fool who thinks he knows something
of alchemy, owe much to the characterization of Sir Epicure
Mammon in Ben Jonson's *The Alchemist*, first acted and
entered into the Stationers' Register in 1610, but eventually
published the same year as *The White Devil*. Mammon's
fantasies prefigure the delights Flamineo dangles before
Camillo:

> I will have my beds, blown up; not stuff'd:
> Down is too hard. And then, mine oval room,
> Fill'd with such pictures, as Tiberius took
> From Elephantis, and dull Aretine
> But coldly imitated. [...]
>   My mists
> I'll have of perfume [...]
>   we will come forth,
> And roll us dry in gossamer and roses. (2.2.41–52)[62]

Webster's beds may *be* stuffed in contrast to Jonson's, and
he may not have mentioned Aretino, or Mammon (though
is he 'the fellow' hinted at?).[63] Nonetheless, does Flamineo
inflame Camillo's fantasies by triggering associations with the
hot postures of Aretino and his illustrators? If so, Webster's
imitation here suggests the submerged, even repressed,
presence of both a major dramatic contemporary *and* the
period's pre-eminent pornographer in his play.

What does all this tell us? Perhaps that when we take a
simultaneously broader historical and more detailed view, we
see that distinctions between proper and improper writing

have not always been clear. Aretino's work embodied how this was especially true in Webster's period:

Erotic writing is not confined to low genres, unsophisticated readers or marginal texts. Sexual representation of all kinds permeated literary culture in ways that were often profoundly different from what our own cultural experience of pornography might lead us to expect.[64]

Just because the term 'pornography' did not exist in Webster's period, this does not mean that texts and images doing work we would now call pornographic did not exist: 'pornography [...] was not a separate, clearly defined genre'.[65] In seventeenth-century England, pornography was 'interspersed' with 'other sorts of material, such as philosophical discussion or comic narrative, with the sexual'.[66] Furthermore, while we might accept that definitions are historical and terms change just as attitudes do, perhaps we also have to acknowledge if not endorse the idea that maybe not that much differs between periods or genres:

The pornographers, modern and ancient, visual and literary, vulgar and aristocratic, put forth one consistent proposition: erotic pleasure for men is derived from and predicated on the savage destruction of women.[67]

Sometimes, taking a longer perspective allows us to be both more and less usefully specific, that is, both closer to and further from definition:

In its widest application, pornography may be said to refer to cultural productions that depict human sexual activity in a relatively explicit manner, and that are seen by some observers as being offensive or morally reprehensible. As this formulation suggests, the fundamental problem with definitions of pornography is that the term is applied simultaneously to the content of a given product, to the manner in which that content is represented, and to the attitude of the observer toward the product.[68]

Here, Ian Moulton (necessarily and wisely) uses qualifying terms and phrases like 'may', 'relatively', and 'some' because he knows that pornography and its definitions are not static. The real strength of Moulton's historical perspective, which will inform the rest of this chapter, comes through how he can use it to explain a shift in focus in his own understanding of pornography:

> I have often thought that it might make more sense to see pornography as a way of reading rather than a mode of representation. As a way of reading, pornography would be characterized by an obsessive interest in the material read, an abstraction of the self and an abdication of critical faculties, and a sense of voyeurism – of observing without being observed in return. Pornographic reading would often be followed by a lingering sense of disgust, guilt, or sheepishness which nonetheless would not preclude an urge to repeat the experience.[69]

The case for distinguishing *The White Devil* from pornography in these terms is clear and unambiguous in some ways, yet unclear in others. Clearly, in *The White Devil*, the faculties of Vittoria's critics are nothing but critical. Moreover, the trial scene depends on Vittoria and her accusers being observed: Monticelso wants justice to be seen to be done. However, as we will see, other terms in Moulton's take on pornography are resonant in relation to *The White Devil*'s key scene: disgust, obsession, repetition. These terms and behaviours affect both men and women in the play, but revolve around Vittoria, infamously termed on the 1612 title-page, 'the famous Venetian Curtizan'.

Staging whores

Whatever the title page calls Vittoria, the play's characters are less discreet in their descriptions of her: 'the word "whore" and its associated misogynistic discourse' are 'one of the materials' Webster uses to construct his play.[70] Lodovico tells us early on that Brachiano 'seeks to prostitute' Vittoria (1.1.41): she is, in Monticelso's words, his 'whore' (3.2.78). Again, perhaps Webster learned of the dramatic power of such designations from Shakespeare:

> The word 'whore' is not the only word in the Shakespeare canon used for denigration of female sexuality […] but it is the term with the most abusive punch.[71]

If, as we have seen, pornography is a form of writing about prostitutes, it also turns women into whores, and men into whore-haters, fulfilling its function as a way for men to tell lies about women:

> The women who wander through this world are, whether they know it or not, all whores by nature, as they all have a price […] in porn the man makes hate to the woman.[72]

Such conceptions build upon the terms used by Andrea Dworkin and Catharine A. MacKinnon to define pornography, in their revisions of the Human Rights Ordinance of the City of Minneapolis in the 1980s:

> Pornography is the graphic sexually explicit subordination of women, whether in pictures or in words, that also includes one or more of the following: (i) women are presented dehumanized as sexual objects, things, or commodities; […] (v) women are presented in postures or positions of sexual submission, servility, or display; […] (vii) women are presented as whores by nature; […]

(ix) women are presented in scenarios of degradation [...] shown as filthy or inferior.[73]

In this light, and given the abuse heaped on Vittoria by Monticelso and others in the trial, *The White Devil* could absolutely be considered pornographic: hinting at pornography's etymology as 'whore painting', Monticelso promises to 'paint out' her 'follies' (3.2.51–2). However, Vittoria throws Monticelso's abuse back at him, saying the 'painted devils' he depicts are his invention (3.2.147), and querying the terms with which he enacts that abuse, even as she shares and completes his line: 'Whore, what's that?' (3.2.78). Prepared and prejudiced, Monticelso happily provides an answer:

> They are coz'ning alchemy [...]
> They are the true material fire of hell [...]
> They are worse,
> Worse than dead bodies, which are begged at gallows
> And wrought upon by surgeons, to teach man
> Wherein he is imperfect. (3.2.82–99)

There are echoes here of the sexualized 'alchemy' prefigured in the exchange between Camillo and Flamineo (and thus between Webster, Jonson and Aretino) discussed earlier. Furthermore, we can also see that Monticelso's anatomization of Vittoria, and the spiritual, material and ideological horror he perceives her 'character' (3.2.102) to represent, is set on opening things up, laying women bare 'in more natural red and white' (3.2.52), and making matters explicit for everyone's edification and improvement. This is the 'exulceration' or lancing of diseased flesh demanded by the Lawyer (3.2.34). He also advises Monticelso, in his capacity as Vittoria's judge, to turn his eyes upon the plague that she embodies ('*converte oculos in hanc pestem mulierum corruptissimam*', 3.2.10–11). To condemn, Monticelso has to look. In this sense, Monticelso's words and acts repeat models found in pedagogic and scientific woodcut studies of female anatomy featured in texts that would 'reuse' older tropes of arranging the human form for a viewer, taken from pornography, placing 'medical illustrations' in a 'sequence of responses to the possibility of sexual representation initiated by [Aretino]'.[74] To put this another way, Monticelso obsessively, echoically reproduces and animates the very 'character' he seeks to condemn: in the twenty-three lines of the speech including this extract, Monticelso uses the words 'whore' or 'whores' five times, and the near homophone (and perhaps near homonym) 'worse' three times. To make his case against Vittoria all the more compelling, Monticelso insists he is merely echoing others' words:

> Alas I make but repetition,
> Of what is ordinary and Rialto talk,
> And ballated, and would be played o'th'stage (3.2.247–9)

But repeating words or acts does not confirm meanings or identities in this play. The Lawyer's repetitions signal his incomprehensibility and lack of credibility (even as he seeks to be emphatic): 'For to sow kisses (mark what I say), to sow kisses' (3.1.22). His rhetoric rebounds against him, as Flamineo echoes his description of Vittoria (3.2.28) to mock *him* as 'diversivolent' (3.3.21). Such are Flamineo's 'counterpoisons' (3.2.59). So Monticelso's regret at having to resort to such repetitive measures may be fake, and flawed, but it does disclose a recognition that his words are part of a series of echoes, which both do and do not finally determine what Vittoria is and what should be done to or with her. Moreover, even as Monticelso talks of what has been or might be 'played o'th'stage', the conditions of the stage undermine his voyeuristic, invasive critique strategy: 'The paradox is that what [Monticelso] seeks to prove by *sight* can never be *seen*, and must always be subject to doubt'.[75] Despite noting the potential congruences between the play and the social and sexual dynamics of pornography, perhaps this is this one of those places where literature is more subtle and profound than pornography.

Perhaps not: Vittoria's self-defence is unsuccessful. She is constructed as someone who should be in a 'house / Of penitent whores' (3.2.266–7), though she is neither a whore nor penitent. In one of MacKinnon's many influential discussions of the exploitative causes and degrading effects of pornography, she describes what happens to women in pornography, and in a world where it is permissible, profitable and rife: 'You learn that language does not belong to you, that you cannot use it to say what you know, that knowledge is not what you learn from your life, that information is not made out of your experience.'[76] Beyond the physical and psychological violence and contortions pornography enacts, it contributes to a series of strategic silencings of women. This is what Vittoria learns, because in many ways the play conforms to this model. The trial scene attests that what little power women do have is in their words, as Vittoria realizes: 'O woman's poor revenge / Which dwells but in the tongue' (3.2.283–4). However, speech without material agency or political potency is as good as being silent, or dead. In realizing this conjunction Vittoria echoes Isabella, who in her abjection becomes voiceless, enduring 'the killing griefs which dare not speak' (2.1.277), while voicing a common proverb whose words are not even her own. We might remember though that this is a dramatic text, not simply pornography: here silencing is an ambiguous process and does not always work. The Lawyer may say to Vittoria 'Hold your peace' (3.2.33), yet she does the opposite; later, even after stating 'I'll not speak one word more' (4.2.186) in response to Brachiano's contempt, Vittoria will. Moreover, where some women in the play suffer a silencing which is deathly, even some men, like Flamineo, after so many words, anticipate a death which will be 'a long silence' (5.6.199): 'I have lost my voice / Most irrecoverably' (5.6.267–8).

It is precisely because silencing is an uncertain way to control people that Vittoria's enemies in the trial scene insist on others perceiving her as spectators, not hearing her as an audience: 'mark each circumstance' (3.2.119), 'look upon this creature' (3.2.120), 'See my lords' (3.2.129). When what little evidence condemning Vittoria *is* produced we are told to 'view't [...] read it' (3.2.195–7); she is held up as the 'picture' of the 'devil' (3.2.216–7), fulfilling Francisco's earlier injunction Monticelso should 'Come to observe this strumpet' (2.1.389). In Luckyj's words, Monticelso 'insistently foregrounds the visual in a protracted display of misogynistic scopophilia'.[77] But this urge is not Monticelso's alone. Bridling at the pornographic construction by men of women as whores, Zanche will later say to Flamineo: 'A little painting and gay clothes / Make you loathe me' (5.1.161–2). Brachiano will himself mimic Monticelso's anatomizing brutality in his own later attack on Vittoria, when she spurns his advances:

> Ud's death, I'll cut her into atomies [...]
> Where's this whore? [...]
> Where's this changeable stuff? (4.2.40–5)

This obsessive, pornographic viewing, writing and reading of Vittoria as whore in 'picturesque speeches' is meant to reduce what power her words have.[78] So when Brachiano finally decides to 'break silence' (3.2.155) and tries to intervene to save Vittoria, Monticelso questions his legitimacy as 'overseer' (3.2.160), prompting Brachiano to appeal in strategic contrast to the aural, not the visual: 'Do you hear?' (3.2.165). This is a sound move, because, as Francisco is aware, there is 'no sound proof' (3.2.182) to condemn Vittoria. Vittoria herself indicates the 'intelligencing ears' of her attackers have heard little but contrived much (3.2.229).

In its genesis, voyeuristic explication and prosecution, then, the notion of a 'whore' is a male construct, a projection of masculine anxieties and insecurities: women may be painted devils, but men like Monticelso themselves 'paint out' their identity (3.2.51). Vittoria's power and problems arise from knowing this:

> your names
> Of Whore and Murd'ress, they proceed from you,
> As if a man should spit against the wind,
> The filth returns in's face. (3.2.148–51)

But this means male voyeurs, explicators and prosecutors are themselves condemned to keep neurotically looking and pathologically pursuing, just as Monticelso cannot stop looking at the painted plague that is Vittoria: 'no sight can [...] bring about [...] reassurance' for voyeurs, forcing them 'to look again and again, and to see more and more, with an ever increasing intensity'.[79]

Whether in an individual, or as a symptom of a community that loves to look but does not look lovingly, 'a voyeur nation's compulsion with the actions of others' insulates against 'awareness of the fragility of the self'.[80] Men's problem is not women, but men: 'pornography reveals men's insecurities with their own sexuality'.[81] The same could be said of *The White Devil*. From the start, like Monticelso, the play obsesses over nothing, signalled in 'To the Reader' with '*nos haec novimus esse nihil*' (3), [*we know these things are nothing*]. *The White Devil* is *about* nothingness, vulgar and profound: something that cannot be seen or shown; death and decay; the commonplace 'nothing' denoting male comprehension of female genitalia; and a nothingness intrinsic to and emanating from men in a scopophilic and ocularophobic world. As Flamineo realizes: 'There's nothing of so infinite vexation / As man's own thoughts' (5.6.201–2).

In such a world, men see women, and make women, in their own form. Brachiano's description of Vittoria as 'the devil in crystal' (4.2.84), that is, fixed in a 'transparent yet reflective surface', just 'ironically implies that the devil he beholds may be his own mirror image'.[82] Monticelso's construction of Vittoria is thus also a construction of himself: 'both men and women define femininity or manliness through a series of projections and imitations of *each other*'.[83] And yet the terms used to describe her apply to many other women: Flamineo uses 'the language of prostitution to describe all women, even his own mother' (at 1.2.15–21).[84] Flamineo's language describes himself too, though:

> The same motivations of aspiration and achievement, the same willingness to reject traditional moral codes in ascending a social ladder that win Vittoria the label of 'whore,' apply to Flamineo.[85]

Precisely because 'whores' are everywhere, and the whole world revolves around and fixates on them – 'Fortune's a right whore' (1.1.4) – women are hated. Their ascribed priority and imagined power compels misogyny. The play's arguments suggest that men may be 'dissembling', yet they 'sucked' that trait from 'women's breasts' (4.2.177–8), while in turn they accuse women of being destructive dissemblers, and idealized or despised, 'god or [...] wolf' (4.2.87–8). The possibility of an interchange of characteristics is precisely what impels men's need to deny that possibility, by further limiting women's expression, agency and social mobility.

Conclusion

Arthur Golding's 1565 translation of Ovid's *Metamorphoses* contained a story that encapsulates and prefigures many of the issues discussed here. Vulcan, blacksmith to the gods, suspected his wife, Venus, was committing adultery with Mars. To catch them at it, Vulcan 'forged a net of wire so fine and slight', it 'followed every little pull and closed with every touch.' Having found them 'fast in the midst of all their play', Vulcan opened 'the ivory doors' to the bedroom, and 'called all the gods straightaway / To see them.' The crowd of deities do not condemn but enjoy what they see, with one joking they wished they too could be 'shamèd in that sort'.[86] As for Vulcan? His urge to stage what will only appal and shame him suggests the ways he and others – Othello, Flamineo, Monticelso, Brachiano, Webster's audiences, us – can be both disgusted by what they feel the desire to see, and disgusted by their desire itself.

In an influential article, Jonathan Dollimore asked: 'Desire and disgust: just how do they haunt and create each other?'[87] Answering his question, Dollimore reminds us it may be attractive and apparently subversive to suggest that 'disgust always bears the imprint of desire'. Dollimore contends, though, that it is 'wrong' to suggest that disgust is 'always an expression of a repressed desire whose return promises mayhem'. On the contrary, 'aversion is not necessarily about a repressed desire for its object, but about protecting boundaries and maintaining the inner coherence of an existing formation of desire'.[88] By this logic, Vittoria's accusers absolutely do not want her; instead they want to be rid of her, because she disturbs what they say they do want. However, in this play the bond between prohibition and fixation runs deep, and what is denied is desired, or '*quae negata grata*', as Camillo says (1.2.153). This, suggests Dollimore, is as inevitable as it is understandable:

> We desire what is forbidden to us the more because it is forbidden; indeed we may only desire it because it is forbidden. What this means is that to seek security in a social order which one *also* desires to transgress and violate is not just bourgeois hypocrisy or existential bad faith, but the inescapable condition of being human.[89]

For Webster's world is also one where what is desired destroys: 'all delight doth itself soon'st devour' (1.2.186). Destruction can involve or require moral and social punishment, as Francisco says: 'lust carries her sharp whip' (2.1.70). Even when what might be desired disgusts, moral and social prohibitions ensure 'our desire is increased by the difficulty of enjoying' (1.2.20–1). In this sense, restraint increases the possibility of and desire for transgression. Flamineo suggests women are particularly prone to this: 'politic enclosures for paltry mutton makes more rebellion in the flesh' (1.2.90–1). Men like him only say this because they recognize – and repress – what their own 'terrible vision' (5.4.141) does to themselves.

8

Pedagogy and Resources: The *Devil* is in the Details

James Hirsh

Provoking thought: Complexity, curiosity, selectivity

Why bother to teach *The White Devil*? In my own case the main reason is that the play illuminates some fascinating complexities of human experience: the sometimes intricate psychologies of individuals and their sometimes tortuous interactions against a range of challenging and thought-provoking themes. As the saying goes, 'God is in the details'; that is, complexities matter. A disconcerting corollary to that principle is 'the devil is in the details': inattention to complexities can have serious consequences. Many popular forms of entertainment are popular because they depict fantasy worlds in which issues are simple and easy to understand. A teacher might arrive at the pessimistic conclusion that she has a stark choice between assigning works that are accessible because they depict worlds that, unlike the real world, are easy to understand, or works that more accurately reflect the challenging complexities of the real world but that are thereby rendered inaccessible. It is possible, however, to make complexity not merely accessible but engaging. If an author can arouse the *curiosity* of readers or playgoers about characters and their situations, readers and playgoers will be lured into engaging in complex thought even if that was not their prior intention. Exercising one's intellectual capabilities can be as invigorating, pleasurable, and rewarding as engaging in strenuous physical activity. Just as one's physical fitness will atrophy if one does not regularly engage in strenuous physical activities, one's ability to comprehend complexity might stagnate if that ability is not regularly employed. *The White Devil* challenges playgoers to exercise their intellectual capabilities and rewards that effort by leading playgoers (and readers) to a deeper understanding of the human condition. The *Devil* is in the details.

If the value of *The White Devil* derives, in large part, from its dramatization and illumination of complexities, then a well-intentioned teacher who simplified the work to make it more accessible to students would risk eliminating what makes the work valuable. My goal as a teacher is to make *The White Devil* accessible to students, not by reducing its complexities, but rather by raising the abilities of students to understand complexity. I attempt to do this by imitating in my own feeble way the technique employed by Webster, by attempting to arouse the intellectual curiosity of students in order to motivate them to try to understand some of the complexities of the play. In what follows, I will provide detailed illustrations of how I proceed from the analysis of individual details to complex conclusions. As it happens, the impulse to reduce complex experiences to easy-to-understand formulae is a major theme of the play, as demonstrated below.

I do not attempt to cover all elements of this text. To do so would result in a superficial treatment of each element. Instead of improving the skills of students to handle complexity, I would be reinforcing the impulse of students to reduce complexity to simplicity, a practice that would arguably quash the very quality that makes the play valuable. Instead, in both contexts in which I have taught the play (in an undergraduate course on English Renaissance literature and in a graduate course on English Renaissance drama excluding Shakespeare), I have focused on a selection of issues, each of which I have explored in the detail it warrants. At the end of our unit on *The White Devil*, I actively deter students from thinking that we have covered the play, that they now know everything worth knowing about the play. I provide them with a selection of questions that we did not have time to explore. Instead of instilling a sense of closure, I seek to open up the play, to encourage students to reread the play in order to explore issues on their own using the reading skills that they have developed in the course.

Implication and inference: Reading between the lines

Complexity is not the only challenge that readers, playgoers, teachers and students encounter in attempting to understand *The White Devil*; another derives from the fact that Webster frequently employed the technique of implication. Again, a contrast with most forms of popular entertainment of our own time is illuminating. Recognizing implications and making reasonable inferences are forms of intellectual labour, and some authors of popular works avoid placing this burden on their readers on the premise that thinking is an inherently unpleasant task. Such authors make everything explicit or inescapably obvious. In contrast, an author who strives to create genuinely thought-provoking works necessarily employs implication. An author cannot provoke thought in readers if she does all their thinking for them. A major goal of my courses is to improve the abilities of students to read between the lines, that is, to engage in inferential reasoning.

Implication is not only a major technique employed by Webster in *The White Devil*; it is also a major theme and plot element. In the second scene Vittoria tells Brachiano that she had a dream in which his wife (Isabella) and her husband (Camillo) attempted to bury her alive but were themselves killed when a whirlwind collapsed a yew tree on top of them. Flamineo overhears this exchange and draws an inference:

> Excellent devil.
> She hath taught him in a dream
> To make away his Duchess and her husband. (1.2.238–40)

Flamineo's interpretation is a reasonable and seemingly obvious inference. Brachiano himself proceeds to 'interpret' her dream (241) and makes a solemn pledge to 'protect' her from their spouses (242–4). Elsewhere in the play characters are depicted as engaging in the process of drawing inferences, with widely varying degrees of success. After a cryptic remark by Brachiano, Francisco asks himself, 'How strange these words sound? What's the interpretation?' (3.2.301). By means of these depictions, Webster encourages playgoers to reflect on their own procedures of inferential reasoning about elements of the play and, after the performance, about real-life situations. In the case of Vittoria's supposed dream, if the inference that Flamineo and Brachiano both draw about her motive is so obvious, why did she bother to employ implication rather than explicitly urging her lover to murder their inconvenient spouses? Lady Macbeth does not beat around the yew tree in this fashion. Vittoria's use of implication allows her to deceive herself into believing that she is not guilty of the murders because she did not explicitly ask her lover to commit murder. It is her attempt to maintain deniability in her own mind, reminding us of another of the play's key themes: the curious phenomenon of self-deception.

Skill enhancement

My primary goal is to improve each student's intellectual abilities, which include the abilities to understand complexity, to read between the lines, and to engage in rigorous empirical analysis. An analogy should make clear the difference between a course whose main goal is memorization of information and a course whose main goal is the development of skills. One does not learn to play the piano simply by memorizing facts about piano-playing. One does not become an imaginative, rigorous, sophisticated reader of literature simply by memorizing facts. So in order to instill curiosity in students and entice them to read between the lines of a challenging work of literature, I regularly raise questions about plot, characters, relationships between characters, themes, artistic techniques and other features. I do not ask questions that have blatantly obvious answers. Nor do I ask questions that cannot be answered or that encourage pointless speculation. I try to craft questions that have specific answers that can be reached only by a survey of evidence and inferential reasoning.

One usually productive question about a particular character is: 'Do any actions or speeches of this character seem *out of character*?' For example, does the character make an assertion in one situation that is contradicted by what they do or say elsewhere? Does the character do something that seems at odds with their apparent motives in other situations? And so on. In the case of a poor or mediocre dramatist, such discrepancies might be the result of carelessness. Webster was *not* a poor or mediocre dramatist. In his plays such inconsistencies in the speeches and actions of a character are important features of characterization. In some cases, the implication is that the character makes an assertion to mislead the character's onstage interlocutors about the speaker's state of mind. If an incongruity occurs in a soliloquy, a likely implication is that the speaker is engaging in self-deception. In some cases, the implication is that the character has multiple motivations, some of which are at odds with one another. Real people often have conflicting motivations, and so real people often behave inconsistently. An author who seeks to explore how real people think and behave will often intentionally portray characters that speak or behave inconsistently. After our classroom analyses of several such incongruities, students develop the reading habit of consciously looking for such inconsistencies. The attempt to explain an inconsistency draws a student more deeply into the psychology of the character, and this can prompt fascinating issues that can be further explored through essay writing.

An example of an incongruity that might be the basis of a class discussion involves Monticelso. He suspects that Brachiano arranged the murder of the Cardinal's nephew Camillo and exhibits hatred for both Brachiano and Vittoria. His speeches in the arraignment scene (3.2) reveal a profound disregard for justice. He keeps a list of thugs handy and offers the list to Francisco (4.1) in the apparent expectation that he will use it to orchestrate Brachiano's death. And yet, after Monticelso becomes pope, he dissuades Lodovico from pursuing retribution (4.3). In the context of this grim and pessimistic play, it would be naïve to infer that becoming pope has led Monticelso to turn over a new leaf, that he now wants to spread peace on earth. A much more credible inference is that Monticelso is a more deeply committed Machiavellian than Francisco. A true Machiavellian is single-mindedly concerned with the acquisition, maintenance, and extension of political power. Pursuing a private vendetta would not advance this goal, might divert one's time and energies away from it, and might, if something goes wrong, even undermine one's political power. Having arrived at the pinnacle of power in the Catholic Church, a true Machiavellian would exert all his efforts to safeguard and extend that power; indeed one of Machiavelli's most frequent exemplars was a pope (Alexander VI). In contrast, Francisco's single-minded pursuit of personal revenge is distinctly un-Machiavellian. Monticelso knows Francisco well enough to know that he would not abandon the plot simply because one thug got cold feet. Monticelso facilitates Francisco's revenge and yet retains deniability. That the bitter enemies Monticelso and Vittoria are similar in that they both foster violence but attempt to retain deniability is profoundly ironic.

Empirical methodology

Another major goal of all of my courses is to improve each student's skill in conducting rigorous empirical analysis. Improving how students develop that skill will be of great use not merely in analysing works of literature, but in countless other circumstances too. Some students believe that the way to generate the content of an essay about a literary work is to begin by choosing a thesis, to search for evidence within the work that supports the thesis, and (in the case of a research paper) to locate published commentary that supports the thesis. In most other academic fields of study this procedure is condemned as 'confirmation bias,' and students and practitioners are enjoined to avoid it. A student who adopts this strategy ends up where he began and successfully avoids the possibility that he will actually discover anything in the process of writing the paper. I teach students how to produce a paper that is the result of a genuinely empirical investigation. Here is an abbreviated version of these instructions:

1   Locate some aspect of the literary work that really provokes your curiosity; that is, formulate a question that intrigues you but to which you do not at the outset know the answer.

2   Formulate a tentative ('half-baked') hypothesis (a 'hunch').

3   Genuinely test this hypothesis against all the relevant evidence within the literary work; that is, search not only for evidence that supports the hypothesis but

for evidence that conflicts with it. If you discover conflicting evidence, you should be thrilled because this means that you have discovered something that you did not know when you began the process. If your investigation does not uncover any evidence that requires a modification of your initial off-the-top-of-your-head hypothesis, that would be disappointing.

4 Revise the hypothesis in light of the evidence that conflicts with the original. A revised hypothesis is rarely the simple opposite of an original one. Often, all that is needed is the addition of a clause beginning with 'but,' 'although', or some similar word. In other cases, more extensive or more complex additions or modifications are required.

5 Test the revised hypothesis.

6 Repeat this procedure until your most recent hypothesis accounts for all of the relevant evidence that you can locate. That hypothesis thereby becomes a genuine thesis, no longer 'half-' but 'fully-baked' (the testing-and-revising process is the second half of the baking). This thesis will be more accurate than your original hypothesis and more interesting (because it incorporates discoveries that you made during the testing process). It will probably be more complex than your initial hunch and might take the form of several sentences (rather than just one).

Our classroom procedure is also empirical. When a teacher asks students a challenging question about a complex and sophisticated work of literature, the off-the-top-the-head hypotheses proposed by students are often (though not always) simple, superficial and unsophisticated. Instead of treating an initial hunch by a student as an unalterable debate position, we treat it as merely the starting point for a rigorous investigation. We proceed to test each hypothesis against the relevant evidence and modify it to fit the evidence. I do not entirely trust my own ability to recall details of a work, so I prepare for class by cataloguing evidence relevant to each particular question I intend to pose. It is gratifying when a student points out a relevant piece of evidence that had escaped my notice when I prepared for class. This classroom procedure not only illuminates the particular issue under discussion, but gives students practice in empirical methodology. I do not tell students in advance whatever hypothesis about the issue that I reached before coming to class. This has the result of making each class intellectually suspenseful and students listen closely to our survey of evidence to try to independently figure out where the investigation is headed. I am very gratified if our classroom investigation uncovers a piece of evidence that requires a revision of my own preliminary hypothesis.

One beauty of empiricism is that no matter how crude an initial hypothesis might seem the process of testing and revising it will always result in a conclusion that is more accurate. Another beauty is that this conclusion is more interesting than the original hypothesis because it incorporates genuine discoveries. Furthermore, students become more committed to searching for the truth than to defending their own initial opinions. At the outset I do not invite students to share their 'answers' to a question. Instead, I invite them to propose 'preliminary hypotheses'. During the semester, it becomes clear to students that in almost all cases a preliminary hypothesis, an initial guess, needs to be revised to reflect more accurately the complex pattern of evidence. In a gratifying number of cases, the same student who proposed a preliminary hypothesis recalls later in the discussion a piece of evidence that leads to a revision of the hypothesis that they had initially proposed.[1]

An example of the methodology:
The theme of generalizing

The empirical methodology that I employ and that I try to instill in students is illustrated by my approach to a pervasive and conspicuous feature of *The White Devil*: passages in which characters attempt to draw general conclusions from particular experiences. This is such a common intellectual activity that it is rarely isolated as a dramatic theme by commentators on literary works. However, in this play Webster foregrounds the activity and explores a wide range of motives for (and consequences of) particular instances of generalizing. The play contains many aphorisms, succinct generalizations that employ repetitions, balanced phrasing, vivid metaphors or other rhetorical or poetic devices that make them memorable. Some aphorisms are so memorable that they become commonplace in a particular time period. Aphorism usage, of course, varies from age to age, but some have been in wide circulation since ancient times. Some are passed from parents to children, but there are many other means of transmission. For example, catalogues of conventional aphorisms occur in Ecclesiastes and Proverbs, and each fable attributed to Aesop illustrates at least one explicit generalization. An orator or essayist constructs an aphorism to be taken by listeners or readers at face value as a valid insight. A common activity in Webster's time was to catalogue human wisdom by collecting aphorisms into commonplace books. Clever wording of an aphorism not only makes it memorable but also makes it seem true. Conventional aphorisms have an additional ring of truth to them simply because they are familiar. Generalizing is risky behaviour, however, because neither clever wording nor familiarity can make a false or misleading assertion true. William Blake went so far as to declare that 'To Generalize is to be an Idiot.'[2] On the other hand, generalizing is a necessary and unavoidable human activity. Without generalizations, our experience of the world would be utterly atomized and incoherent. As Blake presumably understood, his sweeping dismissal of generalizing is itself a generalization. His implied advice was not *never generalize* (an impossibility), but rather *recognize that, when you do so, you run the risk of being an idiot* because many features of the world are more complex and various than can be captured by a generalization. In composing this essay I have formulated numerous generalizations and quoted a number of commonplace maxims and thereby run the risk of being an idiot.

The aphorisms in *The White Devil* should not be taken at face value as expressions of the author's point of view. Each aphorism in the play is, first and foremost, used as an expression of the subjective point of view of the *character* who articulates it. It is an expression of that particular character's temperament, situation, point of view, motivations, and idiosyncrasies. In response to a painful, frightening, or disturbing experience, a character might formulate or recall a reassuring or comforting generalization. A character might resign him or herself to a devastating setback by formulating or recalling a fatalistic generalization. Some aphorisms are attempts to make sense of – to confer sense upon – a senseless circumstance and thereby give the aphorist an illusion of control over the situation. In other situations, characters use aphorisms to justify their actions. A discrepancy between an aphorism and the actions of the character who speaks it might indicate hypocrisy or self-deception. At times the activity of aphorizing becomes an explicit issue, as in the following passage by Flamineo:

And of all axioms this shall win the prize:
''Tis better to be fortunate than wise.' (5.6.173–8)

An axiom is an aphorism that has become widely repeated and conventional. Collectively, the aphorisms dramatize the nearly universal impulse of individuals to confer meaning – even, as a last resort, a painful meaning – on an experience, by formulating or recalling a pithy generalization that supposedly sums up the experience.

These features of Webster's dramatization of the theme of generalizing do not mean that the aphorisms in the play are all false or worthless. It does mean that each well-turned generalization needs to be scrutinized and tested individually. Rather than searching through the play only for ratifications of an aphorism (an activity that would constitute confirmation bias), my students and I search just as diligently for discrepancies of the kinds catalogued above. Conflict is the soul of drama, and hence a conflict between a generalization articulated by a character and either the behaviour of the character, or other elements of the dramatized action, is more dramatic (and more interesting) than simple agreement. *The White Devil* is a laboratory for the testing of aphorisms. In a classroom lecture discussion of generalizing as a theme and as a technique of characterization, my students and I proceed empirically by exploring the implications of particular aphorisms. We consider the psychological state or motivation of the speaker, the thematic implications of the generalization, and the possible dramatic ironies it sets up. A few cases will illustrate the classroom methodology of analysing individual passages and recognizing larger patterns in the evidence.

The third speech of the play contains three aphorisms that are not intended by Webster to be taken at face value as wise insights, but rather as features of the very particular psychology of their speaker, Lodovico; he employs them in an attempt to come to terms with his banishment:

> [1] Ha, ha. O Democritus, thy gods
> That govern the whole world: courtly reward,
> And punishment. [2] Fortune's a right whore:
> If she gave ought, she deals it in small parcels,
> That she may take away all at one swoop [...]
> [3] Your wolf no longer seems to be a wolf
> Than when she's hungry. (1.2–9)

In the first generalization Lodovico projects onto 'the whole world' his own personal concern with 'courtly reward, /

And punishment.' The play dramatizes the idea that other motivations, such as sexual desire, might 'govern' a person's behaviour. The second aphorism reflects Lodovico's bitter disappointment and egotism. The thought that one is not the only victim of cruel fate, that others suffer similar fates, is comforting to a selfish person. It is dramatic irony that Lodovico here inadvertently illustrates an aphorism that was familiar in Webster's time and in our own: 'misery loves company'. That Lodovico's generalization is prompted by the speaker's particular and subjective situation undermines its objectivity and validity. As in the case of the first aphorism, in the second Lodovico projects his own situation onto mankind in general.

Lodovico's third aphorism is cryptic. He presumably means that *a wolf never seems more wolfish (predatory) than when she's hungry*. But Webster's syntax makes this meaning difficult to process. Hearing the line 'Your wolf no longer seems to be a wolf,' one would expect the second line to consist of words meaning *when her belly is full*. Like Lodovico, playgoers try to make sense of their experience, so they translate what Lodovico says into what he presumably meant to say. Another complication is the relationship between the third aphorism and the previous ones. Who might the hungry wolf represent? The allusion to Fortune of the second aphorism and the wolf of the third are both female and predatory. Unlike the wolf of the third, who is only at times hungry and predatory, however, the Fortune described in the second aphorism is unrelentingly predatory. Later in the scene Lodovico explains that the person he holds most directly responsible for his banishment is the Duke (Brachiano), who has refused to grant him a pardon; but a female wolf would be an incongruous metaphor for the Duke, and a refusal to grant an acknowledged murderer a pardon does not seem particularly wolfish. Lodovico does hold a woman indirectly responsible for his situation:

Vittoria, she that might have got my pardon
For one kiss to the Duke. (43–4)

Playgoers whose curiosities were aroused by Lodovico's earlier cryptic reference to a female wolf might conclude in retrospect that Lodovico had her in mind. But Vittoria's refusal to cajole her lover into pardoning a murderer is, again, not particularly wolfish. In some respects the metaphor is a more appropriate description of Lodovico himself than of Fortune or those he hates. He is an impoverished and outcast nobleman who has lost courtly favour and so is *hungry*, desperate for employment and advancement. The metaphor might simply be bravado, implying that he is dangerous and capable of violence (wolf-like). But the wolf of the metaphor is female. Another possibility is that the metaphor constitutes dramatic irony. In attempting to describe his enemies, he has inadvertently described a feature of his own psychology. By intentionally making Lodovico's aphorism cryptic, Webster dramatizes the abnormality and obscurity of the character's thought processes. All three aphorisms dramatize the twisted and irrational hypothetical psychology of a professional henchman. The psychology and behaviour of henchmen is another major theme of the play.

Later in the scene Antonelli tries to cheer Lodovico up with a sentimental platitude at odds with his friend's earlier cynical aphorisms. Antonelli tells Lodovico:

> Perfumes, the more they are chafed, the more they render
> Their pleasing scents; and so affliction
> Expresseth virtue fully. (47–9)

Affliction does bring out the best in some people. But that is far from a universal or inevitable response. Affliction sometimes brings out the worst in people. Many people who suffer become bitterly fixated on their own pain and (if they can find someone to blame for their suffering) they might become vengeful; so Antonelli's generalization is misleading. This aphorism sets up a moment of dramatic irony. The later behaviour of the person to whom this platitude is directed, Lodovico, vividly refutes it; his affliction leads him to commit gruesome murders.

Brachiano's first generalization, 'But all delight doth itself soon'st devour' (1.2.186), is incongruously gloomy for a man at the outset of a love affair. Cornelia's subsequent condemnation of her daughter and Brachiano also includes the formulation of a general principle:

> Earthquakes leave behind,
> Where they have tyrannized, iron, or lead, or stone,
> But, woe to ruin, violent lust leaves none. (1.2.201–3)

Like many aphorisms in the play, this one is not a credible extrapolation from the evidence of human experience. Earthquakes are generally more destructive than sexual desire. Cornelia's fanaticism discredits her point of view. In an extended aphorism in a soliloquy at the very end of the scene, Flamineo, another unscrupulous henchman, attempts to confer dignity, grandeur, and a dangerous beauty on the machinations of politicians and their henchmen ('those who know policy'):

> As rivers, to find out the ocean
> Flow with crook bendings beneath forced banks,
> Or as we see, to aspire some mountain's top,
> The way ascends not straight but imitates
> The subtle folding of a winter's snake,
> So, who knows policy and her true aspect,
> Shall find her ways winding and indirect. (1.2.330–6)

Webster here dramatizes how a clever, imaginative henchman might attempt to maintain a semblance of self-respect by romanticizing his sordid profession. It is significant that this passage occurs in a soliloquy. Flamineo attempts to talk himself into believing he is a member of a worthy profession. Once again, a character uses an aphorism to manipulate himself. This attempt fails in the long run; elsewhere in the play Flamineo exhibits and expresses self-contempt.

In descriptions that resemble Cornelia's fanatical condemnation of sexual desire in Act 1, Scene 2, Monticelso unleashes a torrent of aphorisms in the arraignment scene that take the form of metaphors to describe 'whores':

> They are first
> Sweetmeats which rot the eater: in man's nostril
> Poisoned perfumes. They are coz'ning alchemy,
> Shipwrecks in calmest weather! What are whores?
> Cold Russian winters, that appear so barren
> As if that nature had forgot the spring. (3.2.80–5)

Although Monticelso presumably intends this torrent of insults (which continues for another seventeen lines) to generate unmitigated disgust and contempt for the women so described in his onstage listeners, his metaphors are so vicious, so over-the-top, and so numerous that they should generate sceptical resistance on the part of playgoers, and sympathy for the women so relentlessly castigated. Moreover, if all of these metaphors were valid, 'whores' would be a powerful, awe-inspiring group of people. The tirade reveals much more about the speaker than about the women described. It reveals Monticelso's pathological misogyny, disgust with sexuality, blind hatred of Vittoria, and utter lack of an impartial judicial temperament.

In an apostrophe (in the sense of an address to an imaginary audience) in his soliloquy after the exit of Monticelso in 4.1, Francisco deploys a maxim to express pride in his own implacable hatred of Brachiano and Vittoria, and his contempt for the Cardinal's supposedly less enduring enmity toward the couple:

> Your flax soon kindles, soon is out again,
> But gold slow heats, and long will hot remain. (41–2)

Flax is not only quickly consumed by fire but nearly worthless; gold not only retains heat but is the gold standard (so to speak) for material value. By a kind of alchemy, Francisco turns implacable hatred and bloodthirsty vengefulness into gold. Francisco's grief for his sister Isabella has not brought out his virtues, and so his response to suffering is another refutation of Antonelli's sentimental generalization.

A dramatic character might be particularly tempted to 'sum up' (or speak reflectively) when their death is imminent. Instead of drawing a generalization from a particular occurrence, a character facing death might try to formulate overarching conclusions about his or her entire personal experience, or the experience of humanity at large. The threat of imminent death brings out the aphorist in Flamineo:

> [1] Fate's a spaniel,
We cannot beat it from us [...]
[2] Let all that do ill take this precedent:
'Man may his fate foresee, but not prevent.'
[3] And of all axioms this shall win the prize:
''Tis better to be fortunate than wise.' (5.6.173–8)

In the first two generalizations, Flamineo consoles himself with the thought that his early death was fated, inevitable. By convincing himself that nothing he did or failed to do could have changed his destiny, he can relieve himself of tormenting regrets. The third aphorism is a corollary of the first two. It is ironic that the wisdom Flamineo has derived from his experience dismisses the value of wisdom. A moment later he articulates another sweeping generalization:

> There's nothing of so infinite vexation
As man's own thoughts. (201–2)

This is another instance in which a character projects his own very subjective perspective onto humankind in general. In fact, most people have far less weighing on their consciences than Flamineo has on his, and so their thoughts are less vexatious.

In her dying words, Vittoria articulates a generalization that conspicuously employs balanced phrasing and rhyme

– techniques that, as in earlier cases, give the assertion a bogus ring of truth:

> O happy they that never saw the court,
> 'Nor ever knew great man but by report'. (5.6.257–8)

This is a demonstrably false subjective opinion. Absence from the court is not the sole key to happiness, as poverty-stricken people could have attested. Moreover, it is shocking that this is Vittoria's summary judgement of her life and of life in general. She here implies that she would have been 'happy' if she had never met Brachiano. She also implies that the 'great man' was responsible for her suffering and death. She wishes away her love for him and his for her. Her final generalization seems disloyal to the man who committed crimes for love of her, who suffered and died for love of her, and to whom she had pledged her love.

In the final lines of the play, Giovanni, who is the new Duke of Brachiano and the highest ranking character on stage, tries to draw a moral from recent events. His well-turned generalization is embedded in a warning:

> Let guilty men remember their black deeds
> Do lean on crutches, made of slender reeds. (5.6.296–7)

In a play in which characters have very frequently reflected upon the implications of individual experiences, this is the final reflection: a moment of exaggerated closure and 'summing up'. Once again, rhyme gives an assertion a bogus ring of validity, and coming as it does at the very end of the play, the couplet contributes to a superficial impression of closure. Playgoers who take the trouble to test Giovanni's generalization against the dramatized events they have just witnessed, however, will recognize a conspicuous refutation. Francisco, the powerful Duke of Florence, has not been brought to justice for his crimes, and the play does not dramatize any means likely to bring him to justice in the future. Webster slyly prompts playgoers to make the connection by having Giovanni use the term 'black deeds,' a subtle reminder fact that Francisco spent part of the play in blackface. The final generalization is an example of wishful thinking. It would be nice if the 'black deeds' of 'guilty men' really did 'lean on crutches, made of slender reeds.' In fact, some guilty men, such as Francisco, occupy positions of immense power and are never brought to justice for their heinous crimes. The fact that the action of the play conspicuously contradicts the closing generalization is not a flaw. It was a daring and brilliant move by Webster to end his tragedy with a demonstrably false, intentionally unsatisfying, generalization. What is the motive of the character who articulates it? It might be that young Giovanni naively believes the sentimental notion he espouses. That would not bode well for his dominion. A prince who naively believes that guilty men are ipso facto weak will not be an effective ruler. On the other hand, a Machiavellian prince might choose to project a public image of simple piety, as Shakespeare's Richard of Gloucester does in Act 2, Scene 7. of *Richard III*. That the final generalization in *The White Devil* might be insincere, that it might be a ploy by the speaker to manipulate public opinion, is a chillingly ironic conclusion to the play's sophisticated and disturbing use of generalization.

Other issues and approaches

In another instance of employing empiricism as a teaching methodology, I begin by asking students for an explanation of the play's title. What is a 'white devil' and to which character in the play does it refer? Every time I have taught the play a bright student offers the preliminary hypothesis that the title means a person who seems innocent, but who is actually evil – and that it refers to Vittoria. As a class, we then catalogue evidence supporting this hypothesis. Rather than moving on to another issue, I then ask students if Vittoria is the *only* character in the play to whom the term might be attached. One of the main tasks of a devil is to inflict suffering, and other characters – Brachiano, Francisco, Lodovico, and Flamineo – fulfil this job description more conspicuously than Vittoria. Vittoria is not the only character who is labelled a devil by other characters or who is associated with whiteness.

That still is not the end of our empirical investigation of the title. The fact that characters in the play frequently accuse one another of being devils is profoundly disturbing. If one's enemies are not human beings but utterly evil and irredeemable nonhuman beings, it would not be a crime to inflict any kind of suffering on them. In Christian mythology, a devil *deserves* whatever suffering it receives. The play vividly dramatizes the fact that, if one regards other people as devils, one thereby metaphorically turns one's own life into a living hell. Most of the characters in the play are nominal Christians, but treating one's fellow human beings as if they were devils is profoundly and conspicuously at odds with explicit teachings of Jesus. For example, Matthew 5.44 instructs the Christian to: 'Love your enemies, bless them that curse you, do good to them that hate you, and pray for them which despitefully use you, and persecute you.' The notion that one can solve problems by eradicating supposed demons disguised as human beings may, according to Christian logic, seem good, but is actually evil. Demonization itself is a metaphorical white devil; it is a problem masquerading as a solution. Ironically, if at some point during the play, playgoers make the seemingly obvious connection between the title of the play and Vittoria, they themselves engage in the practice of demonization. After witnessing characters accuse one another of being devils and using that designation to justify the infliction of pain or death, playgoers should become squeamish about engaging in the practice themselves.[3] The forgoing discussions of the theme of generalizing and the title are merely two examples of how issues raised in *The White Devil* might be explored in detail in a classroom lecture-discussion. There are an unlimited number of other issues raised by the play that become more interesting the more deeply one analyses individual passages relevant to the issue. For example, the surviving text of *The White Devil* came into existence as the script for a theatrical performance. Some features of this text will be missed or misconstrued if that provenance is disregarded. Students should be encouraged to imagine not simply characters, but actors portraying those characters on stage. A complicating factor is that stage conditions are not transhistorical; they change from one period to another. A teacher or student who projects current theatrical practices onto the play will misunderstand or entirely miss important features of the play. Conversely, an understanding of stage practices of late Renaissance theatres can bring to light elements not apparent without such an understanding.[4] A teacher might decide to explore implications and ramifications of the work's theatricality, such as doubling.

The theatrical practice of doubling, whereby a single actor plays more than one character in a performance of a play was nearly ubiquitous in late Renaissance professional theatres. A practical function of this was to allow the performance of plays with more characters than there were actors available. (Two characters could not have been doubled if they ever appear on stage at the same time.) Rather than hoping that playgoers would not notice the practice, good dramatists actively employed it to serve artistic purposes. Doubling is an implicit invitation for playgoers to ponder the similarities and differences between the two characters played by the same actor, and thereby to understand each character more deeply. The fact that one actor plays multiple roles was also a meta-dramatic extension of the theme that, in reality, all people inevitably perform. Doubling can serve other functions, and in some cases multiple functions. A teacher can invite students to consider the implications of possible doublings in the play. For example, the Conjurer, who appears in Act 2, Scene 2, could have been doubled as the Armorer in Act 5, Scene 3; both episodes depict the poisoning of a character. In the first, the victim is Isabella, Brachiano is the instigator and the Conjurer his guilty henchman. In the second, Brachiano is the victim. Because he is poisoned by his helmet,

Brachiano assumes that the Armorer is guilty and peremptorily condemns him to torture without a fair trial (at line 6). Sympathy for Brachiano is undercut both by the reminder that Brachiano is suffering a fate similar to the one he inflicted on his wife and also by his unjust treatment of the Armorer. Doubling the role might heighten irony of one character's guilt, against another's apparent innocence.

A teacher might also lead a discussion of soliloquies in the play. Evidence from plays of the period demonstrates that soliloquies represented self-addressed speeches by characters (not either interior monologues or audience-addressed speeches) as a matter of convention.[5] A soliloquy represents how characters interact with themselves. Dramatists and playgoers were evidently fascinated by the prospect of eavesdropping on a character's most private moments. Like Shakespeare, Webster often used soliloquys to depict characters engaging in the curious and convoluted process of self-deception. Duke Francisco even catches himself in the act. After praising himself in a soliloquy for the cleverness of his machinations, he says, 'I am so used to frequent flattery / That being alone, I now flatter myself' (4.1.123–4).

A teacher might help students, some of whom have rarely or never attended a live performance by a professional acting company, to develop their ability to turn a reading experience into a hypothetical theatrical experience by having students act out episodes of the play. Like a professional actor, each student who volunteers to play a part will have to re-imagine the situation from the subjective point of view of the character she is playing. A teacher interested in this approach can develop their approach by using various studies in this area.[6] A teacher interested in other features of Webster's artistry might also consult the studies by Ralph Berry (on baroque style), Lee Bliss (on alienation effects,), Katherine M. Carey (on the dumb shows), Charles R. Forker (on 'the aesthetics of chaos'), Dena Goldberg (on the manipulation of audience response) and Christina Luckyj (on repetition, non-linear development, parallels and subplots).[7]

Furthermore, approaching this play from the perspective of genre poses several challenges for a conscientious educator. Generic formulae tend to be lowest common denominators because they are found in mediocre examples of the genre. *The White Devil* is not generic in the pejorative sense. Human experience is far more complex and diverse than simple and narrow generic formulae. Focusing attention on those elements of the play that it shares with run-of-the-mill tragedies (for example, that characters die) distracts the attention of students away from the complexities that make *The White Devil* worth studying. Instead of focusing on what the play shares with more conventional examples of the genre, a teacher could show how the play violates or transcends its own generic formulae. This will bring out what makes the play distinctive as opposed to what makes it generic. If conflict is the soul of drama, a classroom exploration of conflicts between the play and generic formulae will itself be dramatic, as several sophisticated accounts show.[8]

Themes of gender and sexuality pose similar challenges. Sophisticated writers, including Webster, recognized that real men and women are more complex and diverse than those simple, narrow, set patterns of thought and behaviour and that departures from conventionality are not necessarily immoral or shameful. In general, the more fully developed a character in a play by Webster is, the more complex and individualized that character's interaction with perceived gender norms will be. A teacher and students can test gender norms of the period against the behaviour of individual characters. A conventional notion of the time was that women should be demure, but Vittoria's eloquent and robust defence of herself in the arraignment scene should arouse the admiration of playgoers. These issues have provoked stimulating scholarly discussions of gender and sexuality.[9] The play raises, moreover, other social and political issues – some of which are explored in the chapter on the play in Jonathan Dollimore's provocative and influential *Radical Tragedy*.[10] Race is also a core theme of the play, highlighted by the title, by the pattern of white and black imagery, and by the appearance in the play of a Moorish servant (Zanche) who is a substantial character in her own right; a European character (Duke Francisco) who adopts a Moorish disguise (Mulinassar); as well as a Moorish child servant who does not speak but whose presence in Act 2, Scene 1 would have been conspicuous. A teacher who wishes to explore the issue of race might prepare by consulting Virginia Mason Vaughan's *Performing Blackness on English Stages, 1500–1800*.[11]

Another pedagogical approach would be to integrate one or more literary or sociological theories into a lecture-discussion of *The White Devil*. A teacher interested in this approach might consult *Renaissance Drama and Contemporary Literary Theory* by Andy Mousley, which includes chapters on semiotics, structuralism, poststructuralism, psychoanalysis, historicism, feminism, and Marxism.[12] (The chapter on historicism includes a section on *The White Devil*.) If a teacher and students simply look for evidence in the play that illustrates a particular theory, that procedure would be an example of confirmation bias. It would also place the theory rather than the play in the foreground. An empirical approach, one that genuinely tests a theory and the play against one another, would result in a deeper understanding of both the theory and the play.

Editions

The best currently available, reasonably priced, free-standing edition of the play is the latest version (2008) prepared by Christina Luckyj. The text of the play is reliable and the introduction and notes are informative and astute. The play is also available in a paperback anthology of Webster's plays edited by René Weis and in *Three Plays* edited by David Gunby. *Selected Plays by John Webster* (edited by Dollimore and Alan Sinfield) and Volume 1 of *The Works of John Webster*, edited by Gunby, et al. are too expensive to assign as course texts, but contain annotations and other material that might interest a teacher. Furthermore, *The White Devil* is included in a Kindle anthology of plays by Webster and John Ford, edited by Jane Kingsley-Smith, and in two anthologies of revenge tragedies, a Kindle version edited by Gāmini Salgādo (which also includes *The Revenger's Tragedy* and *The Changeling*), and a print version edited by Janet Clare (which also includes *The Spanish Tragedy*, *The Revenger's Tragedy*, and *'Tis Pity She's a Whore*). A course on English Renaissance drama or one more narrowly focused on revenge tragedies of the period could be based on a combination of one of the above anthologies with a selection of individual plays or a selective anthology of plays by Marlowe, Jonson and/or Middleton. Alternatively, a teacher might assign *English Renaissance Drama: A Norton Anthology*, edited by David Bevington, which includes twenty-seven plays, including *The White Devil*.[13]

A course exploring the diversity of portrayals of women in Renaissance drama could be built on one of the above Webster anthologies in combination with the anthology *Plays on Women*, edited by Kathleen McLuskie (the four plays included in the anthology are all Renaissance works) and *The Tragedy of Mariam* by Elizabeth Cary, edited by Karen Britland.[14]

Internet resources

Early English Books Online. eebo.chadwyck.com. Searchable facsimiles and transcriptions of early modern printed works. Limited access, subscription required.

Early Modern London Theatres. www.emlot.kcl.ac.uk. A valuable online resource that offers access to the use of pre-1642 documents relevant to professional performance in London.

Folger Shakespeare Library. www.folger.edu. The site contains materials about the culturalcontext which are relevant to the study of Webster.

Luminarium: An Anthology of English Literature. www.
    luminarium.org. A collection of texts, scholarship, links to other
    sites, etc.
This Rough Magic. www.thisroughmagic.org. A peer-reviewed,
    online academic journal dedicated to the teaching of medieval
    and Renaissance literature.
Royal Shakespeare Company. http://www.rsc.org.uk/whats-on/
    the-white-devil. Information about the 2014 RSC production of
    the play.

NOTES

Introduction

1 Raymond Williams, *Marxism and Literature* (Oxford: Oxford University Press, 1977), 129.

2 *The White Devil*, ed. Christina Luckyj, 3rd edn (London: Methuen, 2008). Unless otherwise stated, all essays in this collection use this edition.

3 *OCR A Level English Literature: Introduction and guided reading, The White Devil*, 10. Available online: http://www. ocr.org.uk/Images/72976-unit-f663-the-white-devil-webster-introduction-and-guided-reading.pdf.

4 *OCR A Level English Literature*, 10–11.

5 *Get Carter* (dir. Mike Hodges: MGM, 1971).

6 Steve Chibnall, *Get Carter* (London and New York: I.B. Tauris, 2003), 14; see Jonathan Dollimore, *Radical Tragedy: Religion, Ideology and Power in the Drama of Shakespeare and his Contemporaries*, 3rd edn (Durham: Duke University Press, 2010), 83–108, 231–46.

7 Chibnall, 7; see also Robert Murphy, 'A Revenger's Tragedy – Get Carter', in Steve Chibnall and Robert Murphy, eds, *British Crime Cinema* (London and New York: Routledge, 1999), 132.

8 Mathias Enard, *Zone* (2008), trans. Charlotte Mandell (London: Fitzcarraldo Editions, 2014), 249, 284, 76, 451.

9 Erica Whyman, *The White Devil programme notes* (Stratford-upon-Avon, Royal Shakespeare Company, 2014), 1. Aberg's production continued a development in stagings of the play typified by Philip Franks' version for the Lyric Hammersmith, London (2000), which referenced *The Sopranos* and *The*

Godfather, and Jonathan Munby's 2008 production at the Menier Chocolate Factory, London, which sought to establish 'a contemporary context that felt recognizable'; see Stephen Purcell, *The White Devil: A Guide to the Text and Play in Performance* (Basingstoke: Palgrave Macmillan, 2012), 116.

10 Michael Day, 'Berlusconi's 'White Lady' Jailed for Three Years', *The Independent* (30 November 2015). Available online: http://www.independent.co.uk/news/world/europe/federica-gagliardi-berlusconi-s-white-lady-jailed-for-3-years-for-cocaine-smuggling-a6754966.html.

11 Darryll Grantley, *London in Early Modern English Drama: Representing the Built Environment* (Basingstoke: Palgrave Macmillan, 2008), 5.

12 *1611: Authority, Gender & The Word in Early Modern England* (Chichester: Wiley Blackwell, 2014), 211.

13 *John Webster's Borrowing* (Berkeley and Los Angeles: University of California Press, 1960), 5.

14 Emma Rhatigan, 'Reading the White Devil in Thomas Adams and John Webster', in Adrian Streete, ed., *Early Modern Drama and the Bible: Contexts and Readings, 1570–1625* (Basingstoke: Palgrave, 2012), 176–94, 177. See also Alison Shell, *Catholicism, Controversy and the English Literary Imagination, 1558–1660* (Cambridge: Cambridge University Press, 1999), 26.

15 Rhatigan, 179.

16 'A Darker Shade of Pale: Webster's Winter Whiteness', *E-rea* 12(2) (2015): §1–54. Available online: https://erea.revues.org/4483.

17 William Shakespeare, *Hamlet*, eds Ann Thompson and Neil Taylor, 3rd edn (London: Arden, 2005).

18 Thomas Rist, *Revenge Tragedy and the Drama of Commemoration in Reforming England* (Aldershot: Ashgate, 2008), 121–34.

19 *The Duchess of Malfi by John Webster*, ed. Leah S. Marcus (London: Arden, 2009).

20 Connolly and Hopkins touch upon this connection (§§17–18), but on the details of James VI/I's transference of his mother's remains see Peter Sherlock, 'The Monuments of Elizabeth

Tudor and Mary Stuart: King James and the Manipulation of Memory', *Journal of British Studies* 46(2) (2007): 263–89.

21 Sherlock, 272.

22 Kieran Hickey, *Wolves in Ireland: A Natural and Cultural History* (Dublin: Open Air Press, 2011), 14.

23 *The White Devil*, 85, n.80.

24 *An Itinerary* (1617) trans. and cited in Joep Leersen, *Meer Irish and FíorGhael: Studies in the Idea of Irish Nationality, its Development and Literary Expression prior to the Nineteenth Century* (Cork University Press, 1996), 56.

25 Thomas J. Morrissey, 'Father David Wolfe', *Oxford Dictionary of National Biography*. Available online at: http://oxforddnb.com. See also Cyril Falls, *Elizabeth's Irish Wars* (London: Methuen & Co. Ltd, 1950), 123.

26 Willy Maley and Andrew Hadfield, eds, *A View on the Present State of Ireland: From the first printed edition of 1633* (Oxford: Blackwell, 1997), 57.

27 *Staging Ireland: Representations of Shakespeare and Renaissance Drama* (Dublin: Four Courts Press, 2007), 18.

28 *The Bible: The King James Authorized Version* (Oxford: Oxford University Press, 1997; rpr. 2008). All references to this version unless otherwise stated.

29 Dena Goldberg, '"By Report": The Spectator as Voyeur in Webster's The White Devil', *English Literary Renaissance*, 17(1) (1987): 67–84.

30 See, for example, John Lanchester, 'The Snowden Files: Why the British Public Should be Worrying about GCHQ', *The Guardian* (3 October 2013). Available online: http://www.theguardian.com/world/2013/oct/03/edward-snowden-files-john-lanchester.

31 Cited in Arundhati Roy, 'When Arundhati Roy met John Cusack met Edward Snowden', *The Guardian* (28 November 2015), 62.

32 Katherine M. Carey, 'The Aesthetics of Immediacy and Hypermediation: the Dumb Shows in Webster's *The White Devil*', *New Theatre Quarterly*, 23.1 (2007): 73–80.

33 J. W. Lever, *The Tragedy of State: A Study of Jacobean Drama* (London, Methuen: 1971), 1.

34   Jonathan Dollimore and Alan Sinfield, 'Introduction', *The Selected Plays of John Webster* (Cambridge: Cambridge University Press, 1983), xvi.

35   Jessica Ringrose, *Postfeminist Education?: Girls and the Sexual Politics of Schooling* (London and New York: Routledge, 2013), 93; see also F. Attwood, 'Sluts and Riot Grrrls: Female identity and Sexual Agency', *Journal of Gender Studies*, 16(3) (2007): 233–47.

36   On the Indignados, and their influence beyond Spain, see Olga Abasolo, Jeremy Gilbert and Hilary Wainwright, 'The Indignados and Us', *Soundings* 57 (2014): 35–49; Alberto Castañeda, 'The Indignados of Spain: A Precedent to Occupy Wall Street', *Social Movement Studies: Journal of Social, Cultural and Political Protest* 11 (2012): 309–19; and Neil Hughes, '"Young People Took to the Streets and all of a Sudden all of the Political Parties Got Old": The 15M Movement in Spain', *Social Movement Studies: Journal of Social, Cultural and Political Protest* 10 (2011): 407–13.

37   William Shakespeare, *Romeo and Juliet*, ed. René Weis (London: Arden, 2012).

38   Achille Mbembe, trans. Libby Meintjes, 'Necropolitics', *Public Culture* 15(1) (2003): 11–40, 16.

39   Ibid., 11.

40   Ibid., 40. For an invigorating application of Mbembe's ideas to the work of another early modern dramatist, see also Patricia Cahill, 'Marlowe, Death-worlds, and Warfare', in *Christopher Marlowe in Context* (Cambridge: Cambridge University Press, 2013), 169–80.

41   J. R. Brown, '*The White Devil* as Tragedy' (1960), in G. K. and S. K. Hunter, eds, *John Webster: A Critical Anthology* (Harmondsworth: Penguin, 1969), 241

42   Charles R. Forker, *Skull Beneath the Skin: The Achievement of John Webster* (Carbondale and Edwardsville: Southern Illinois University Press, 1986), 295.

43   *John Webster, Renaissance Dramatist* (Edinburgh University Press, 2010), 57; see Coleman 60–9. Indeed, as the chapters here from long-standing Websterians like Christina Luckyj and James

Hirsh show, this is a play whose individual critics can and do change their mind about as they work and work again on it.

44   *Between Worlds: a Study of the Plays of John Webster* (Waterloo, Ontario: Wilfrid Laurier University Press: 1987), 5.

45   'The Case of John Webster', *Scrutiny* (1949), in Hunter and Hunter,158.

46   Travis Bogard, 'Tragic Satire' (1955), in Hunter and Hunter, 175.

47   Hereward T. Price 'The Function of Imagery in Webster' (1955), in Hunter and Hunter, 177.

48   Dollimore and Sinfield, 'Introduction', xvi; Dollimore and Sinfield cite Jack, 164.

49   Coleman, 2.

50   Purcell, 155.

51   Samuel Sheppard, 'On Mr. Webster's Most Excellent Tragedy Called "The White Devil"' (1651), in Don D. Moore, ed., *Webster: The Critical Heritage* (London: Routledge and Kegan Paul, 1981), 36.

52   Andrew Strycharski, 'Ethics, Individualism, and Class in John Webster's *The White Devil*', *Criticism* 54(2) (Spring 2012): 291.

53   Strycharski, 291.

54   Ibid., 310.

55   Ibid., 311.

56   Terry Eagleton, *Sweet Violence: The Idea of the Tragic* (Oxford: Blackwell, 2003), xvi.

Chapter 1

1   John Webster, *The White Devil*, ed. Christina Luckyj (London: Bloomsbury, 2008).

2   Ibid., 5

3   Ibid.

4   Zachary Lesser, *Renaissance Drama and the Politics of*

Publication: Readings in the English Book Trade (Cambridge: Cambridge University Press, 2007); Douglas A. Brooks, *From Playhouse to Printing House: Drama and Authorship in Early Modern England* (Cambridge: Cambridge University Press, 2000).

5   G. K Hunter and S. K. Hunter, eds, *John Webster: A Critical Anthology* (Harmondsworth: Penguin, 1969), 36.

6   Don D. Moore, ed., *Webster: The Critical Heritage* (London: Routledge and Kegan Paul, 1981), 60.

7   Moore, Webster, 51–2.

8   Ibid., 67.

9   Ibid. xiv.

10 Ibid.

11 Ibid.

12 Charles Kingsley, *The Works of Charles Kingsley: Volume XVI, Plays and Puritans* (London: Macmillan and Co., 1885), 50.

13 Ibid.

14 Algernon Charles Swinburne, *The Age of Shakespeare* (London: Chatto and Windus, 1908), 39.

15 Ibid., 50.

16 Rupert Brooke, *John Webster and the Elizabethan Drama* (London: Sidgwick and Jackson, 1917), 94.

17 Clifford Leech, *John Webster: A Critical Study* (New York: Hogarth Press, 1951), 44.

18 R. V. Holdsworth, ed., *Webster: The White Devil and The Duchess of Malfi, A Casebook* (London: Palgrave Macmillan, 1971), 150.

19 Ibid.

20 Ibid., 151.

21 Ibid., 154.

22 Ibid.

23 Ibid., 155.

24 M. C. Bradbrook, *John Webster, Citizen and Dramatist* (London: Weidenfeld and Nicolson, 1980), 131.

25   Ibid., 132.

26   Ibid.

27   Ibid.

28   Jonathan Dollimore, *Radical Tragedy: Religion, Ideology and Power in the Drama of Shakespeare and his Contemporaries*, 3rd edn (Basingstoke: Palgrave Macmillan, 2010).

29   Ibid., 235.

30   Ibid.

31   Ibid., 236.

32   Dympna Callaghan, *Women and Gender in Renaissance Tragedy: A Study of King Lear, Othello, The Duchess of Malfi and The White Devil* (London: Harvester Wheatsheaf, 1989)

33   Catherine Belsey, *The Subject of Tragedy: Identity and Difference in Renaissance Drama* (London: Methuen, 1985).

34   Callaghan, *Women and Gender*, 64.

35   Ibid., 65, 68.

36   Ibid., 65

37   Ibid., 65, 67.

38   Ibid., 76.

39   Ibid.

40   Ann Rosalind Jones, 'Italians and Others', in David Scott Kastan and Peter Stallybrass, eds, *Staging the Renaissance* (London and New York: Routledge, 1991), 251–62.

41   Ibid., 256.

42   Ibid.

43   Ibid., 257.

44   Moore, *Webster*, 55.

45   Ibid., 56.

46   J. A. Symonds, ed., *Webster and Tourneur: The Best Plays of the Old Dramatists* (London: Mermaid, 1888).

47   Ibid., xix.

48   Ibid.

49   Ibid., xx.

50   Ibid.

51   Ibid.

52   F. L. Lucas, *The Complete Works of John Webster, Volume I, General Introduction and The White Devil* (London: Chatto and Windus, 1927).

53   Ibid., 21.

54   Ibid., 17.

55   Ibid.

56   Ibid.

57   Ibid., 21.

58   E. M. W. Tillyard, *The Elizabethan World Picture: A Study of the Idea of Order in the Age of Shakespeare, Donne and Milton* (London: Chatto and Windus, 1943).

59   Una Ellis-Fermor, *The Jacobean Drama: An Interpretation* (London: Methuen and Co., 1936, repr. 1958), 187.

60   Ibid.

61   Ibid., 189.

62   Ibid., 190.

63   Ibid.

64   Hunter and Hunter, *John Webster*, 146.

65   Ibid.

66   Ibid.

67   Ralph Berry, *The Art of John Webster* (Oxford: Clarendon, 1972), 5.

68   Ibid., 6.

69   Ibid., 15.

70   Ibid., 70.

71   Ibid.

72   Bradbrook, *John Webster*, 7.

73   Ibid.

74   Ibid.

75   Ibid., 6.

76   Ibid., 7.

77 Christina Luckyj, *A Winter's Snake: Dramatic Form in the Tragedies of John Webster* (Athens, GA: University of Georgia, 1989), xvi.

78 Ibid., xv.

79 Ibid., 149.

80 Ibid., xxiv.

81 Ibid., xxv.

82 Ibid., 149.

83 Jacqueline Pearson, *Tragedy and Tragicomedy in the Plays of John Webster* (Manchester: Manchester University Press, 1980).

84 Ibid., 56. Her category of grotesque tragedy draws on Nicholas Brooke's *Horrid Laughter in Jacobean Tragedy* (London: Open Books, 1979).

85 Ibid., 62.

86 Ibid., 66.

87 Ibid.

88 Ibid., 71.

89 Ibid., 79.

90 Hunter and Hunter, *John Webster*, 266.

91 Hazlitt, *Lectures*, 9.

92 Ibid., 95.

93 Ibid.

94 Ibid.

95 Moore, *Webster*, 54.

96 Ibid.

97 Ibid., 55

98 Ibid.

99 Ibid.

100 Ibid., 56.

101 Ibid.

102 Ibid.

103 Ibid., 141.

104 Algernon Charles Swinburne, *The Age of Shakespeare*, (London: Chatto and Windus, 1908), 45.

105 Ibid.

106 Hereward T. Price, 'The Function of Imagery in Webster', *PMLA*, 70(4) (September 1955), 717–39, 717.

107 Ibid.

108 Ibid., 718.

109 Ibid.

110 Ibid., 739

111 Ibid., 738–9.

112 Ibid., 739.

113 Ibid.

114 Ibid., 739

115 See, for example, Susan Bennett's *Performing Nostalgia: Shifting Shakespeare and the Contemporary Past* (London: Routledge, 1996); Pascale Aebischer's *Jacobean Drama* (Basingstoke: Palgrave Macmillan, 2012) and *Screening Early Modern Drama: Beyond Shakespeare* (Cambridge University Press, 2013); and Sarah Werner's *New Directions in Renaissance Drama and Performance Studies* (Basingstoke: Palgrave Macmillan, 2010).

Chapter 2

1   This research was made possible with an award from the Society for Theatre Research, enabling visits to the Royal Shakespeare Company archives at the Shakespeare Centre Library, Stratford-upon-Avon, the Royal National Theatre Archives at the NT Studio, The Cut and the V&A Theatre and Performance Archives, Blythe House (hereinafter, 'V&A').

2   Luckyj, 'Introduction', *The White Devil*, ix–x.

3   No Stationers' Register date exists for the first edition of 1612.

4   Concerning the first company that performed the play, their audience and their venues, see Eva Griffith, *A Jacobean Company and Its Playhouse: the Queen's Servants at the Red Bull Theatre c.1605–1619* (Cambridge: Cambridge University Press, 2013).

5   Ibid., 152.

6   William Shakespeare, *Hamlet*, eds Ann Thompson and Neil Taylor (London: Bloomsbury Arden Shakespeare, 2006).

7   David Mateer, 'Edward Alleyn, Richard Perkins and the Rivalry between the Swan and Rose Playhouses', *Review of English Studies* 60 (2009): 61–77.

8   He was given fifteen shillings to buy things for a Heywood play and ten for travelling with the company to the country. See Philip Henslowe, *Henslowe's Diary* ed. R. A. Foakes, 2nd edn (Cambridge: Cambridge University Press, 2002), 213.

9   For Perkins' parts, see Gerald Eades Bentley, *The Jacobean and Caroline Stage*, 7 vols (Oxford: Clarendon Press, 1941–68), II: 528.

10   See, for example, National Theatre programme notes (1991 production, V&A) by John Russell Brown; *The White Devil*, ed. Luckyj, 166 n.305. For his programme notes for the 1925 production, Montague Summers guessed that Brachiano was Perkins' 'rôle'. The title page does not mention Flamineo, only 'Vittoria Corombona' and 'Paulo Giordano Ursini, Duke of Brachiano'.

11   British Library edition 644.a.7.

12   Perkins was given the King's livery in 1623/4 and received black cloth in 1625 for James I's funeral procession. He was then included in the cast list for James Shirley's *The Wedding* (licensed 1626; published 1629) which is known to have been performed by Queen Henrietta Maria's Men; see Bentley, *Jacobean and Caroline Stage*, II: 527–8.

13   Samuel Pepys, entry for 30 October 1662, *The Diary of Samuel Pepys*, eds Robert Latham and William Matthews, 11 vols (London: Bell & Hyman, 1983), III: 243–4.

14   Pepys, *Diary*, Vol. II: 190.

15   Ibid., 191.

16   Bentley, *Jacobean and Caroline Stage*, II: 360–2.

17   Ibid., 377–9.

18   Ibid., 511–12; and 571–2 for the Shatterells.

19   William Van Lennep, *The London Stage 1660–1800 Part I: 1660–1700* (Carbondale, IL: Southern Illinois University Press, 1965), 36, 81.

20   John Downes, *Roscius Anglicanus* (London, 1708), 9, 15.

21   David Hopkins, 'Tate, Nahum (c.1652–1715)', *Oxford Dictionary of National Biography* (Oxford: Oxford University Press, 2004). Available online: http://www.oxforddnb.com/.

22   Tate's *Injur'd Love* is found at BL 644.i.64.

23   Ibid., B1/page 5.

24   Ibid.

25   Ibid., B1v/page 6.

26   Tate, *Injur'd Love*, B1v/page 6.

27   Ibid.

28   Ibid., B1v-B2/pages 6–7.

29   Ibid., B2/page 7.

30   Peter Thomson, 'Garrick, David (1717–79)', *Oxford Dictionary of National Biography*; online edn [January 2008]. The David Garrick/British Library editions are 1612: BL C.34.e.18; 1631: BL 644.a.7; 1665: BL 644.f.76; 1672 (as 'Vittoria Corombona'): BL 644.f.77.

31   Frances Anne Kemble, *Record of a Girlhood*, 3 vols (London: Richard Bentley & Son, 1878), II: 260.

32   Ibid., 276.

33   Ibid., 277.

34   Ibid., 277–8.

35   Charles Lamb, *Specimens of English Dramatic Poets who Lived about the time of Shakespeare* (1808); Hazlitt, in 1821, wrote that his tragedies 'come the nearest to Shakespear[e] of any things we have upon record'. See David Coleman, *John Webster, Renaissance Dramatist* (Edinburgh: Edinburgh University Press, 2010), 56–9. The play was also published during the eighteenth century

in R. Dodsley, *A Select Collection of Old Plays*, 12 vols (London, 1744), III.

36 An *Observer* article of 4 October 1835 describes under the title 'Dramatic Intelligence' that the Drury Lane theatre was reopening after a refurbishment and that 'Mr. Proctor' had 'an alteration of Webster's *Vittoria Corombona*' ready. In the same column on 24 January 1836 it was reported that expectations had 'revived' respecting 'Barry Cornwall's alteration of Webster's *Victoria* [*sic*] *Corombona*, an old play to which he has written nearly three new acts'.

37 For more information about the Society, see their website: http://www.themarlowesociety.com/.

38 12 March 1920. *The White Devil* was to be reprised several times by the Society: 1931 (dir. G. H. W. Rylands); 1937 (for the 30th-anniversary tour, dir. Donald Beves); 1948 (taken to Berlin, again by Beves); and 1967 (dir. [?] Peter Watson). *The Duchess of Malfi*, in comparison, has only been produced twice by them.

39 T. S. Eliot, 'Whispers of Immortality', in *T. S. Eliot: The Complete Poems and Plays* (London: Faber, 1969), 52. See Coleman, *John Webster*, 60–2.

40 Taken from the programme (V&A) where Fredman and Grein are described as the directors and Craig as producer. The terms were exchanged during the twentieth century.

41 She was also the daughter of the actor Dame Ellen Alice Terry. Katharine Cockin, 'Craig, Edith Ailsa Geraldine (1869–1947)', *ODNB* [January 2011]. Jacob Thomas Grein was the Dutch critic and impresario who first produced Ibsen's *Ghosts*, for example, in 1891 and G. B. Shaw's first play, *Widowers' Houses*, in 1892. See J. P. Wearing 'Grein, Jacob Thomas (1862–1935)', *ODNB*; online edn [January 2008].

42 For further material on Craig, her feminism, pageants and theatre activities, see Michael Holroyd, *A Strange Eventful History: The Dramatic Lives of Ellen Terry, Henry Irving and their remarkable families* (London: Vintage Books, 2009), 426–8, 498–9.

43 Andrew Cowie, http://bloggingshakespeare.com/reviewing-shakespeare/. The two recent female directors are: Maria

Aberg and, previously, also for the RSC, Gale Edwards, in 1996. Before this, Celia Bannerman directed the play for the Bristol Old Vic in 1983.

44 'The New Star of Revue Whose Acting is an Outstanding Feature of "Bubbly"', *The Tatler*, 11 July 1917 (V&A).

45 *Sketch*, 9 March 1932 (V&A).

46 Hayes was born in 1909 and played child parts from six years old. During a long career, she won a Bafta for her role as *Edna the Inebriate Woman*, a 1971 BBC Play for Today.

47 'H. G.' from an unidentified newspaper (V&A).

48 *Observer*, 24 March 1935 (V&A).

49 V&A. Future production plans listed in the programme included Dekker's *The Honest Whore*, Middleton's *Women Beware Women*, Farquhar's *The Recruiting Officer* and Fletcher's *The Island Princess* for their 'First Season', October 1935–March 1936.

50 V&A.

51 Kenneth Tynan, *A View of the English Stage 1944–1965* (London: Methuen, 1975), 46; Anna Bemrose, *Robert Helpmann: a Servant of the Art* (St Lucia, Queensland, Australia: University of Queensland Press, 2009), 76–7.

52 Harold Hobson, *The Sunday Times*, 9 March 1947 (V&A). For the use of colour in *The White Devil*, see Annaliese Connolly and Lisa Hopkins, 'A Darker Shade of Pale: Webster's Winter Whiteness', *E-rea* 12(2) (2015) Available online: https://erea.revues.org/4483?lang=en.

53 James Agate, *The Sunday Times*, 25 May 1947 (V&A).

54 See Eric Salmon, 'Monck, (Walter) Nugent Bligh (1878–1958)', *ODNB*, online edn [May 2015].

55 Programme, V&A.

56 Philip Hope-Wallace, 6 March 1961. Barbara Leigh-Hunt played Isabella. Stephen Moore, who played Lodovico, provided the music for the production (programme, V&A).

57 David Carnegie, 'Theatrical Introduction to *The White Devil*', in David Gunby, David Carnegie and Antony Hammond, eds, *The Works of John Webster: An Old Spelling Critical Edition*,

3 vols (Cambridge: Cambridge University Press, 1995), I: 109–10.

58 At The Stables in October (Carnegie, 95). The Everyman, Liverpool, also put on a production in 1969.

59 Broadcast 19 November 1969. Transcript taken from RNT Archives.

60 Trewin had been a critic for *Observer* however this review is from an unidentified newspaper dated 29 November 1969 (V&A).

61 14 November 1969 (V&A).

62 *Daily Telegraph*, 14 November 1969 (V&A).

63 www.edwardbond.org.

64 Glenda Jackson played Vittoria; James Villiers, Brachiano; Jonathan Pryce, Lodovico; Jack Shepherd, Flamineo; Frances de la Tour, Isabella; and Miriam Margolyes, Zanche.

65 *The Times*, 13 July 1976 (V&A).

66 *Daily Telegraph*, 13 July 1976 (V&A). See also Richard Allen Cave, *Text and Performance: The White Devil and The Duchess of Malfi* (Basingstoke: Palgrave Macmillan, 1988), 45–6 and 53–9. For Edward Bond's adaptation, see David L. Hirst, *Edward Bond* (Basingstoke: Macmillan, 1985), 19–23.

67 In 1977, the play was put on at the Guthrie Theatre, Minneapolis, again giving a 1930s' gangland spin. In 1979, a much cut touring production was mounted by Michael Kahn and the Acting Company at the Houseman Theatre, Saratoga Springs, New York, channelling punk rock music. The production toured America and Australia, but was felt to be misguided. See Carnegie, 113–14.

68 Flyers and programmes, V&A.

69 See Stephen Purcell, *The White Devil: A Guide to the Text and the Play in Performance* (Basingstoke: Palgrave Macmillan, 2012), 110.

70 It was one of a three-play group headed by Prowse and Giles Havergal.

71 5 February 1984 (V&A).

72 *Guardian*, 3 February 1984 (V&A).

73   *The Times*, 6 February 1984 (V&A).

74   Michael Arditti, 19 June 1991 (V&A).

75   20 June 1991 (V&A).

76   *Independent*, 24 April 1996; see Purcell, 110.

77   *Telegraph* 29 April 1996 (V&A).

78   29 April 1996 (V&A).

79   Interview with Franks, in Purcell, 111.

80   Purcell, '120.

81   Ibid., 116–17.

82   See http://www.whatsonstage.com/london-theatre/news/06–2014/maria-aberg-interview-hotel-white-devil_34711.html.

83   The RSC claims to operate a system of casting that is meant to ignore, for example, skin colour. Aberg has freely described, however, that there must also be 'an artistic reason for doing it that comes from inside each concept or production in a different way' (*WhatsOnStage* article). She is not just radicalizing the casting of plays for the sake of it; she is making entertainment immediate for today's audience by so doing.

Chapter 3

1   Douglas A. Brooks, From *Playhouse to Printing House: Drama and Authorship in Early Modern England* (Cambridge: Cambridge University Press, 2000), 46.

2   Ibid., 49.

3   Ibid., 46.

4   Zachary Lesser, *Renaissance Drama and the Politics of Publication: Readings in the English Book Trade* (Cambridge: Cambridge University Press, 2006), 66.

5   Ibid., 116.

6   Ibid., 116–17.

7   Ibid., 139.

8   Ibid., 146.

9   Ibid., 149, 148. See also Christina Luckyj's chapter in this volume for a critique and extension of Lesser's reading.

10   John Webster, *The White Devil*, ed. Jackie Moore (Oxford: Oxford University Press, 2011). Recent A–level syllabi in English Literature offered by various exam boards, such as AQA, OCR and Pearson Edexcel include *The White Devil* as a set text or recommended reading.

11   John Webster, *The Duchess of Malfi*, ed. Jackie Moore (Oxford: Oxford University Press, 2007).

12   John Webster, *The White Devil*, ed. David Bevington, in David Bevington et al., eds, *English Renaissance Drama: A Norton Anthology* (New York: W. W. Norton, 2002), 1659–1748.

13   John Webster, *The White Devil*, ed. Christina Luckyj, rev. 3rd edn (London: Bloomsbury, 2008).

14   John Webster, *The White Devil*, ed. Benedict S. Robinson (London: Bloomsbury, forthcoming).

15   Webster, *The White Devil*, ed. John Russell Brown, 2nd edn (London: Methuen, 1966).

16   See Gabriel Egan, *The Struggle for Shakespeare's Text: Twentieth-Century Editorial Theory and Practice* (Cambridge: Cambridge University Press, 2010).

17   D. F. McKenzie, *Bibliography and the Sociology of Texts* (London: British Library, 1986); Jerome J. McGann, *Critique of Modern Textual Criticism* (Chicago: University of Chicago Press, 1983), and *The Textual Condition* (Princeton: Princeton University Press, 1991).

18   Stanley Wells, 'General Introduction', in *William Shakespeare: The Complete Works* (Oxford: Oxford University Press, 1986), xxxv.

19   David Gunby, David Carnegie and Antony Hammond, eds, *The Works of John Webster*, 3 vols (Cambridge: Cambridge University Press, 1995–2007).

20   Antony Hammond and Doreen DelVecchio, 'General Textual Introduction', it is Gunby et al., eds, *The Works of John Webster*, 3: 40.

21   R. A. Foakes, 'The Need for Editions of Shakespeare:
      A Response to Marvin Spevack', *Connotations* 6 (1996–7):
      326.

22   On digital editions of early modern drama, see Francis X.
      Connor, '*The Cambridge Edition of the Works of Ben Jonson
      Online* and the Utility of the Digital Edition', *Papers of the
      Bibliographical Society of America* 109 (2015): 247–63; and
      Brett D. Hirsch, 'The Kingdom has been Digitized: Electronic
      Editions of Renaissance Drama and the Long Shadows
      of Shakespeare and Print', *Literature Compass* 8 (2011):
      568–91.

23   Mary Floyd-Wilson, 'Moors, Race, and the Study of English
      Renaissance Literature: A Brief Retrospective', *Literature
      Compass* 3 (2006): 1044.

24   Representative studies include Daniel J. Vitkus, *Turning
      Turk: English Theater and the Multicultural Mediterranean,
      1570–1630* (New York: Palgrave Macmillan, 2003); and,
      Jean E. Feerick, *Strangers in Blood: Relocating Race in the
      Renaissance* (Toronto: University of Toronto Press, 2010).

25   Such as Imtiaz Habib, *Black Lives in the English Archives,
      1500–1677: Imprints of the Invisible* (Aldershot: Ashgate,
      2008). For an important critique of Habib, see Miranda
      Kaufmann, '"Making the Beast with two Backs": Interracial
      Relationships in Early Modern England', *Literature Compass*
      12 (2015): 22–37.

26   Francesca Royster, '"Working Like a Dog": African Labor and
      Racing the Human-Animal Divide in Early Modern England',
      in Philip D. Beidler and Gary Taylor, eds, *Writing Race Across
      the Atlantic World, Medieval to Modern* (New York: Palgrave
      Macmillan, 2005), 113–15.

27   Virginia Mason Vaughan, *Performing Blackness on English
      Stages, 1500–1800* (Cambridge: Cambridge University Press,
      2005), 107–8.

28   Celia R. Daileader, *Racism, Misogyny, and the 'Othello'
      Myth: Inter-racial Couples from Shakespeare to Spike Lee*
      (Cambridge: Cambridge University Press, 2005), 16–17, 32.
      Kaufman, cited above, provides a necessary corrective to
      Daileader in light of recent archival research.

29   Matthew Steggle, 'Othello, the Moor of London: Shakespeare's Black Britons', in Robert C. Evans, ed., *Othello: A Critical Reader* (London: Bloomsbury, 2015), 115–16.

30   Lara Bovilsky, 'Black Beauties, White Devils: The English Italian in Milton and Webster', *English Literary History* 70 (2003): 637.

31   Ibid., 639, 646–7.

32   Sujata Iyengar, *Shades of Difference: Mythologies of Skin Color in Early Modern England* (Philadelphia: University of Pennsylvania Press, 2005), 136.

33   Ibid., 138–9.

34   Farah Karim-Cooper, *Cosmetics in Shakespeare and Renaissance Drama* (Edinburgh: Edinburgh University Press, 2006), 89, 108.

35   Ibid., 92.

36   Ibid., 98–9.

37   Amelle Sabatier, 'White or/and Red? Defining and Re-Defining the Colour of Corruption in John Webster's *The White Devil*', *Interfaces* 33 (2012): 135.

38   Natascha Wanninger, 'Theatrical Colours: Cosmetics, Rhetoric and Theatre in Webster's *The White Devil*', *E-rea* 12(2) (2015): §§1–54.

39   Subha Mukherji, *Law and Representation in Early Modern Drama* (Cambridge: Cambridge University Press, 2006), 135.

40   Annaliese Connolly and Lisa Hopkins, 'A Darker Shade of Pale: Webster's Winter Whiteness', *E-rea* 12(2) (2015): §9.

41   Ibid., §§14–15.

42   Ibid., §18.

43   Ibid., §§19–20, §22.

44   Luke Wilson, '*The White Devil* and the Law', in Garrett A. Sullivan, Jr, Patrick Cheney and Andrew Hadfield, eds, *Early Modern English Drama: A Critical Companion* (Oxford: Oxford University Press, 2006), 230–31.

45   Ina Habermann, '"She has that in her belly will dry up your ink": Femininity as Challenge in the "Equitable Drama" of John Webster', in Erica Sheen and Lorna Hutson, eds,

Literature, Politics, and Law in Renaissance England (New York: Palgrave Macmillan, 2005), 100.

46   Ibid., 100, 110.

47   Wilson, *The White Devil* and the Law', 233–4.

48   Alastair Bellany, 'The Court', in Suzanne Gossett, ed., *Thomas Middleton in Context* (Cambridge: Cambridge University Press, 2011), 121.

49   Stevie Simkin, *Cultural Constructions of the Femme Fatale: From Pandora's Box to Amanda Knox* (New York: Palgrave Macmillan, 2014), 74.

50   On these events, see David Lindley, *The Trials of Frances Howard: Fact and Fiction at the Court of King James* (London: Routledge, 1993).

51   Simkin, *Cultural Constructions*, 75–7.

52   Carol Blessing, 'The Trials of Mary Stuart: Anxious Circulation in John Webster's Drama', in Andrew Majeske and Emily Detmer-Goebel, eds, *Justice, Women, and Power in English Renaissance Drama* (Madison: Fairleigh Dickinson University Press, 2009), 85.

53   See Retha M. Warnicke, *Mary, Queen of Scots* (London: Routledge, 2006), 135–55.

54   Blessing, 'The Trials of Mary Stuart', 85–6.

55   Lou Taylor, *Mourning Dress: A Costume and Social History* (London: Allen & Unwin, 1983), 52–4.

56   Blessing, 'The Trials of Mary Stuart', 86–8.

57   *Shakespeare in Love*, dir. John Madden (Universal, 1998).

58   T. S. Eliot, 'Whispers of Immortality', *Little Review* 5(5) (1918): 11.

59   Julie Sanders, *The Cambridge Introduction to Early Modern Drama, 1576–1642* (Cambridge: Cambridge University Press, 2014), 197.

60   William E. Engel, *Death and Drama in Renaissance England: Shades of Memory* (Oxford: Oxford University Press, 2002), 66–7.

61   Zoltán Márkus, 'Violence in Jacobean Drama: *Macbeth*, *The Revenger's Tragedy*, *The White Devil*, and *The Changeling*',

in Robert DeMaria, Heesok Chang, Samantha Zacher, *A Companion to British Literature*, 4 vols (Malden: John Wiley & Sons, 2014), 2: 273, 275.

62   Katherine M. Carey, 'The Aesthetics of Immediacy and Hypermediation: The Dumb Shows in Webster's *The White Devil*', *New Theatre Quarterly* 23 (2007): 74.

63   David Coleman, *John Webster, Renaissance Dramatist* (Edinburgh: Edinburgh University Press, 2010), 70.

64   David K. Anderson, *Martyrs and Players in Early Modern England: Tragedy, Religion and Violence on Stage* (Farnham: Ashgate, 2014), 124.

65   Roberta Barker, '"Another Voyage": Death as Social Performance in the Major Tragedies of John Webster', *Early Theatre* 8 (2005): 36.

66   Ibid., 36, 41.

67   Lisa Dickson, 'Theatrum Mundi: Performativity, Violence, and Metatheater in Webster's *The White Devil*', in Allie Terry-Fritsch and Erin Felicia Labbie, eds, *Beholding Violence in Medieval and Early Modern Europe* (Farnham: Ashgate, 2012), 163.

68   Ibid., 163, 172.

69   'Nasty', *The Young Ones*, BBC2, 29 May 1984. The present author has taken the liberty of transcribing the dialogue – written by Ben Elton, Rik Mayall and Lise Mayer – from the 2007 DVD release of the series, lineated to approximate blank verse. I thank Gabriel Egan for introducing the show to me.

70   Ceri Sullivan, 'John Webster', in David Scott Kastan, ed., *The Oxford Encyclopedia of British Literature*, 5 vols (Oxford: Oxford University Press, 2006), 5: 260.

71   See Jennifer Clement, 'Beyond Shakespeare: Early Modern Adaptation Studies and Its Potential', *Literature Compass* 10 (2013): 677–87.

72   Representative studies include: Marcia Lee Anderson, 'Hardy's Debt to Webster in *The Return of the Native*', *Modern Language Notes* 54 (1939): 497–501; Hennig Cohen, 'Melville and Webster's *The White Devil*', *ESQ: A Journal of the American Renaissance* 8 (1963): 33; Linda Costanzo Cahir,

'T. S. Eliot's *The Waste Land* and John Webster's *White Devil*: An Explication of Two Poetic Lines', *Yeats Eliot Review* 14 (1997): 43–4; Jane de Gay, *Virginia Woolf's Novels and the Literary Past* (Edinburgh: Edinburgh University Press, 2006), 207–8; Lyon D. Evans, Jr, 'The Source of Melville's "The Little Good Fellows"', *Melville Society Extracts* 49 (1982): 13; Henry Hart, 'For the Confederate and Union Dead: Reflections on Civil War Poetry', *Sewanee Review* 121 (2013): 214; and Patricia Waugh, '1963, London: The Myth of the Artist and the Woman Writer', in Brian McHale and Randall Stevenson, eds, *The Edinburgh Companion to Twentieth-Century Literatures in English* (Edinburgh: Edinburgh University Press, 2006), 177.

73 Melvin B. Rahming, '"Goodbye to All That!" Engaging the Shift of Sensibility between John Webster's *The White Devil* and Amiri Baraka's *Dutchman*', *CLA Journal* 46 (2002): 72–97; and, Jeanette Roberts Shumaker, 'The *White Devil* in *Orley Farm*: Trollope, Webster, and Degeneracy', *Readerly/Writerly Texts* 10 (2002–3): 79–87.

74 Pascale Aebischer, *Screening Early Modern Drama: Beyond Shakespeare* (Cambridge: Cambridge University Press, 2013), 140.

75 Nonetheless, Alan Taylor has offered an unpersuasive and ahistorical comparative study of Webster's art and *The White Devil*, in particular, and the filmic techniques of Alfred Hitchcock; see Alan Taylor, *Jacobean Visions: Webster, Hitchcock and Google Culture* (Frankfurt: Peter Lang, 2007).

76 Hazelton Spencer, 'Tate and *The White Devil*', *English Literary History* 1 (1934): 235–49.

77 Justin Evans, *The White Devil: A Ghost Story* (London: Weidenfeld & Nicolson, 2011).

78 'Under God's Power She Flourishes', *Boardwalk Empire*, HBO, 4 December 2011.

79 James Shapiro, *Contested Will: Who Wrote Shakespeare?* (New York: Simon & Schuster, 2010), 238.

80 Elli Abraham Shellist, 'John Webster', in Arthur F. Kinney, *A Companion to Renaissance Drama* (Malden: Blackwell, 2002), 560.

81 Gunnar Boklund, *The Sources of The White Devil* (Uppsala: Lundequist, 1957); and, R.W. Dent, *John Webster's Borrowing* (Berkeley: University of California Press, 1960).

82 Dent, *John Webster's Borrowing*, 13.

83 See Brett D. Hirsch and Laurie Johnson, 'Shakespeare Source Study in the Age of Google: Revisiting Greenblatt's Elephants and Horatio's Ground', in Dennis Austin Britton and Melissa Walter, eds, *Rethinking Shakespeare Source Study: Audiences, Authors, and Digital Technologies* (London: Routledge, 2016).

84 MacDonald P. Jackson, 'The Webster Canon: A Reassessment', in Gunby et al., eds, *The Works of John Webster*, 3: xxx–xli; 'John Webster, James Shirley, and the Melbourne Manuscript', *Medieval and Renaissance Drama in England* 19 (2006): 21–44.

85 For example, Jonathan Hope and Michael Witmore, 'The Hundredth Psalm to the Tune of "Green Sleeves": Digital Approaches to Shakespeare's Language of Genre', *Shakespeare Quarterly* 61 (2010): 357–90.

86 Quoted in Chris Adams, *Turquoise Days: The Weird World of Echo and the Bunnymen* (New York: Soft Skull Press, 2002), 102.

87 Ibid.

88 H[enry] F[itzgeffrey], *Satires and Satirical Epigrams* (London, 1617), F7r. I have silently modernized spelling and punctuation.

89 Echo and the Bunnymen, 'My White Devil', *Porcupine* (Korova, 1983). I am indebted to Laurie Johnson for introducing me to this song.

Chapter 4

1 See Emma Rhatigan, 'Reading the White Devil in Thomas Adams and John Webster', in Adrian Streete, ed., *Early Modern Drama and the Bible: Contexts and Readings, 1570–1625* (Basingstoke: Palgrave Macmillan, 2011), 176–94.

2   Charles R. Forker, *Skull Beneath the Skin: The Achievement of John Webster* (Carbondale: Southern Illinois University Press, 1986), 289.

3   Martin Wiggins, 'Conjuring the Ghosts of *The White Devil*', *The Review of English Studies* 48 (1997): 448–70, 470.

4   James R. Hurt, 'Inverted Rituals in Webster's *The White Devil*', *The Journal of English and Germanic Philology* 61 (1962): 42–7, 42.

5   Ibid., 42, 47.

6   Sigmund Freud, *The Uncanny*, translated by David McLintock (London: Penguin, 2003), 145.

7   Nicholas Royle, *The Uncanny* (Manchester: Manchester University Press, 2003), 1.

8   Lara Bovilsky, 'Black Beauties, White Devils: The English Italian in Milton and Webster', *English Literary History* 70 (2003): 625–51, 638.

9   Andrew Strycharski, 'Ethics, Individualism, and Class in John Webster's *The White Devil*', *Criticism* 54 (2012): 291–315, 294.

10   Ibid., 299.

11   Ibid., 300.

12   Ibid., 304.

13   Ibid., 309.

14   Raymond Williams, *Marxism and Literature* (Oxford: Oxford University Press, 1977), 123.

15   Elizabeth Williamson, 'The Domestication of Religious Objects in *The White Devil*', *Studies in English Literature 1500–1900* 47 (2007): 473–90, 477.

16   See, for example: Sarah Beckwith, *Christ's Body: Identity, Culture and Society in Late Medieval Literature* (London: Routledge, 1993); Huston Diehl, *Staging Reform, Reforming the Stage: Protestantism and Popular Theatre in Early Modern England* (Ithaca: Cornell University Press, 1997); and Michael O'Connell, *The Idolatrous Eye: Iconoclasm and Theatre in Early Modern England* (Oxford: Oxford University Press, 2000).

17 Williamson, 'The Domestication of Religious Objects', 477.

18 Ibid., 475.

19 Holger Schott Syme, '(Mis)Representing Justice on the Early Modern Stage', *Studies in Philology* 109 (2012): 63–85.

20 For an extensive outline of the theological debates, see Thomas N. Tentler, *Sin and Confession on the Eve of the Reformation* (Princeton: Princeton University Press, 1977); and Jaroslav Pelikan, *Reformation of Church and Dogma (1300–1700)* (Chicago: University of Chicago Press, 1984).

21 Marlowe's Abigail, in *The Jew of Malta*, for example, confesses sins, noting that 'one offence […] torments me […] To work my peace, this I confess to thee' (see *The Jew of Malta*, in David Bevington and Eric Rasmussen, eds, *Doctor Faustus and Other Plays* (Oxford: Clarendon Press, 1995), 3.6.19, 31); while Shakespeare's *Hamlet* presents the ghost of the Old King bewailing the fact that he has died without confession, 'sent to my account / With all my imperfections on my head' (in Stephen Greenblatt, et al., eds, *The Norton Shakespeare* (New York: Norton, 1997), 1.5.75–6).

22 For an example of the first viewpoint, see John Bale's play *King Johan* (1538): 'by confession the Holy Father knoweth / Throughout all Christendom what to his holiness groweth' (in Peter Happé, ed., *The Complete Plays of John Bale Volume Two* [Cambridge: Brewer, 1986], 272–3).

23 Bovilsky, 'Black Beauties', 637.

24 Tentler, *Sin and Confession*, 144.

25 Brian Chalk, 'Webster's "Worthyest Monument": The Problem of Posterity in *The Duchess of Malfi*', *Studies in Philology* 108 (2011): 379–402, 386.

26 Freud, *The Uncanny*, 244.

27 Royle, *The Uncanny*, 142.

28 Hurt, 'Inverted Rituals', 42.

29 Ibid., 44.

30 Williamson, 'The Domestication of Religious Objects', 478.

31 Ibid.

32 Ibid., 486.

33   Bovilsky, 'Black Beauties', 638.

34   John R. Ziegler, 'Irish Mantles, English Nationalism: Apparel
     and National Identity in Early Modern English and Irish
     Texts', *Journal for Early Modern Cultural Studies* 13 (2013):
     73–95, 80.

35   Bovilsky, 'Black Beauties', 642.

36   Ibid.

37   Thomas Rist, *Revenge Tragedy and the Drama of
     Commemoration in Reforming England* (Aldershot: Ashgate,
     2009), 129.

38   Michael Neill, *Issues of Death: Mortality and Identity in
     English Renaissance Tragedy* (Oxford: Oxford University
     Press, 1997), 299.

39   Strycharski, 'Ethics', 310.

40   Williamson, 'The Domestication of Religious Objects', 487.

41   Syme, '(Mis)Representing Justice', 70.

42   Bovilsky, 'Black Beauties', 646.

43   Michael Cordner, '*The Malcontent* and the *Hamlet*
     Aftermath', *Shakespeare Bulletin* 31 (2013): 165–90, 165.

44   *Hamlet*, 3.3.90, 3.4.87.

45   Royle, *The Uncanny*, 2.

46   Ibid.

Chapter 5

1   Jean Calvin, *Institutes of the Christian Religion*, ed. John
     T. McNeill, trans. Ford Lewis Battles, 2 vols (London:
     S.C.M. Press, Ltd, 1961), I.6. This is the first line in Calvin's
     Institutes.

2   Michel de Montaigne, 'That to Philosophise Is To Learn How
     To Die', *Essays of Michael Lord of Montaigne*, trans. John
     Florio, 3 vols (London: Grant Richards, 1898), I.19.86

3   The most extensive study of Webster's use of Montaigne is
     J. W. Dent's *John Webster's Borrowings* (Berkeley: University

of California Press, 1960). See also Peter Mack, 'Marston and Webster's use of Florio's Montaigne', *Montaigne Studies* 24 (2012): 67–82.

4   Most recently, see Robert Ellrodt, *Montaigne and Shakespeare: The Emergence of Modern Self-Consciousness* (Manchester: Manchester University Press: 2015). For a cognate reading to this essay's interest in Webster's use of Montaigne and Calvin, see Susan E. Schreiner, 'Appearances and Reality in Luther, Montaigne, and Shakespeare', *The Journal of Religion* 83(2) (2003): 345–80.

5   Lisa Hopkins's pioneering study *Shakespeare on the Edge: Border Crossing in the Tragedies and the Henriad* (Aldershot: Ashgate, 2005) has unpacked ways in which Shakespearean plays (including plays which *The White Devil* was overtly emulating and appropriating, such as *Othello* and *Hamlet*) were obsessed by issues of physical movement and spirituality. See also Hopkins, *Renaissance Drama on the Edge* (Farnham: Ashgate, 2014).

6   See Thomas Rist, *Revenge Tragedy and the Drama of Commemoration in Reforming England* (Aldershot: Ashgate, 2013), 121–34; and Elizabeth Williamson, 'The Domestication of Religious Objects in *The White Devil*', *Studies in English Literature 1500–1900* 47 (2007): 473–90. See also David Coleman's revision and development of Williamson's thesis in this volume.

7   *Issues of Death: Mortality and Identity in English Renaissance Tragedy* (Oxford: Clarendon, 2001), 3.

8   *Radical Tragedy: Religion, Ideology and Power in the Drama of Shakespeare and his Contemporaries*, 3rd ed. (Basingstoke: Palgrave, 2004; rpr. 2010), 83–108, 231–46.

9   On predestination and early modern tragedy see John Stachniewski, *The Persecutory Imagination: English Puritanism and the literature of Religious Despair* (Oxford: Oxford University Press, 1991).

10 *The Geneva Bible: A Facsimile of the 1560 Edition* (Peabody, MA: Hendrickson Bibles, 1969; rpr. 2007).

11 Augustine, *Confessions*, trans. Henry Chadwyck (Oxford:

Oxford University Press, 1998). Hereafter cited in-text, according to the 1679 chapter and paragraph divisions.

12   See for example *Institutes* I.15.4: 'For that speculation of Augustine, that the soul is the reflection of the Trinity because in it reside the understanding, will, and memory, is by no means sound.'

13   On English Protestantism and the paradigm of faithful ambulation, see Neil Keeble '"To be a pilgrim": Constructing the Protestant Life in Early Modern England', in Colin Morris and Peter Roberts, eds, *Pilgrimage: The English Experience from Beckett to Bunyan* (Cambridge: Cambridge University Press, 2002), 178–98.

14   This phrase litters almost of all of Calvin's writings; see Arthur Golding's 1577 translation of Calvin's sermons: 'so long as God letteth us alone in our own state and plight, wee be blind wretches wandering in darkness' (33v); 'if the poor ignorant sort, which never had any certain way, but have been as blind wretches wandering here and there too seek God, and yet he hath not showed himself unto them, have none excuse at all, but are condemned at Gods hand, because they had not a true root' (86v); 'that Reason hath nothing in it but vanity, untruth, and deceitfulness: and again, that all that ever men can conceive, is but a maze of vain fancies, and that they do but overthrow themselves more and more, as if a blind wretch should wander abroad in the dark' (200). *The Sermons of M. John Calvin*, trans. Arthur Golding (London: 1577).

15   Samuel Sheppard, *Epigrams Theological, Philosophical, and Romantic* (1651), cited in Don D. Moore, ed., *John Webster: The Critical Heritage* (London: Routledge, 1981), 134.

16   Drawn from Augustine, the idea of the reprobate's slippery footing was prominent in English Calvinist works such as exegete Andrew Willet's 1611 guidance to be charitable and accept our 'Our weak brother, though he have many infirmities […] seeing God hath received him: this makes against those, which upon every slip and infirmity are ready to censure their brethren, as reprobates and castaways'. Hexapla, that *is, A Six-fold Commentary upon the most Divine Epistle of the Holy Apostle S. Paul to the Romans* (London: 1611), 668.

17 Plato, *Complete Works*, ed. John M. Cooper (Indianapolis, IN: Hackett Publishing, 1997).

18 'you'll have your daughter covered with a Barbary horse, you'll have your nephews neigh to you, you'll have coursers for cousins and jennets for germans!' (1.1.109–12). *Othello*, ed. E. A. J. Honigmann 3rd edn (London: Bloomsbury Arden Shakespeare, 1999; rpr. 2003).

19 On the use of colour-imagery in this play, and its religious significances, see Annaliese Connolly and Lisa Hopkins, 'A Darker Shade of Pale: Webster's Winter Whiteness', *E-rea* 12(2) (2015) http://erea.revues.org /4483.

20 Elizabeth Anne Socolow, 'Letting Loose the Horses: Sir Philip Sidney's Exordium to The Defence of Poesie', in Peter Edwards, Karl A. E. Enenkel, and Elspeth Graham, *The Horse as Cultural Icon: The Real and Symbolic Horse in the Early Modern World* (Leiden: Brill, 2012), 121–42; 138.

21 See, for example, Nicholas de Nicolay's contemporary description of Barabary equestrianism: 'I have also seen diverse Moors mounted on Barbary horses without saddle, bridle, stirrups or spurs, having only a string in the mouth to stay them withall. And as for the men they are altogether naked, having only about their middle part to cover their privities, some piece of a white sarge or blanket in manner of an apron, and about their head a linen cloth rolled, which they bring about and under their chin' (8). *The Navigations, Peregrinations and Voyages made into Turkey by Nicholay Daulphinois*, trans. T. Washington (London: 1585).

22 Bruce Boehrer, 'Shakespeare and the Social Devaluation of the Horse', in Karen Raber and Treva J. Tucker, eds, *The Culture of the Horse: Status, Discipline, and Identity in the Early Modern World* (Basingstoke: Palgrave, 2005), 91–112, 95.

23 It is worth noting that the play's other 'revenger', Francisco, is also variously associated with onward motion and questions of fate. See for instance, where he warns Lodovico to 'Divert me not' (4.3.75); his aside regarding Flamineo: 'I pity thy sad fate. Now to the barriers. / This shall his passage to the black lake further' (5.2.80–2); and his use of the phrase 'O the fate of princes!' at 4.1.122.

24 On 'crowner' - 'coroner' see Luckyj (77n); and also F. L. Lucas, ed., *The White Devil* (London: Chatto and Windus, 1958), 235.

25 Reformed Catholic (London: 1598), 13. Emphasis in copy. *On Perkins's importance to English Calvinism and the Calvinist doctrine of faith*, see R. T. Kendall, *Calvin and English Calvinism to 1649* (Oxford: Oxford University Press, 1979), 51–78.

26 Rist, *Revenge Tragedy and the Drama of Commemoration* (5). See also Neil, *Issues of Death* (38–42).

27 See, for example, the 1534 print of Richard Rolle's influential theorization of Purgatory: 'in purgatory the souls dwelleth still / Till they ben cleansed of all manner ill' (Sig. A2r); 'the souls uncleansed should there dwell / Still in purgatory and be bound fast / With bonds of sin to make them aghast / And as many souls as be in that prison' (Sig. B3v). *Here beginneth a little book, that speaketh of purgatory, what purgatory is, in what place* (London: 1534).

28 On contemporary understanding of e/motions see Bridget Escolme, *Emotional Excess on the Shakespearean Stage: Passion's Slaves* (London: Bloomsbury, 2014), xxi–xxiii.

29 On Augustine's influence over Montaigne, see Andrée Comparot, *Augustinisme et Aristotélisme de Sebon à Montaigne* (Paris: Editions du Cerf, 1984).

30 On the stylistics of what she terms 'Montaigne's 'cultivation of a wayward style', see Margaret McGowan, 'The Art of Transition in the Essais', in I. D. MacFarlane and Ian Maclean, *Montaigne: Essays in Memory of Richard Sayce* (Oxford: Clarendon, 1982), 35–56.

31 As with most early modern plays, there are distinct subtexts of homoeroticism which Flamineo's 'backward' movement might correlate with. See, for instance, Flamineo's insult of Cardinal Monticelso: 'Wheresoever he comes to doe mischief, he comes with his backside towards you' (3.3.16–17).

32 See Alan James Hogarth, '"Hide and be hidden, ride and be ridden": The Coach as Trangressive Space in the Literature of Early Modern London', *EMLS* 17 (2) (2014). Available online: https://extra.shu.ac.uk/emls/journal/index.php/emls/article/view/98/134.

33 Henry Fitzgeffrey famously termed Webster 'Crabbed (Websterio)/The Play-wright, *Cart-wright*' in his 1617 *Satyres: and satyricall epigrams* (Sigs. F6v–F7r). For details on the Webster coach business, see M. C. Bradbrook, *John Webster: Citizen and Dramatist* (London: Weidenfeld & Nicholson, 1980), 10–26.

34 The term carried political currency, and was used by reformers such as William Wilkinson to deplore papists 'abusing the pretence of the Gospel as a stalking horse to level at others by' (Sig. U1v). *A Confutation of Certain Articles* (London: 1579).

35 Flamineo also uses the 'horse leech' insult at 5.6.162.

36 Thomas Beard, *A retractive from the Romish religion* (London: 1616), 428. John White's *The Way to the True Church* also made passing reference to the saint, glossing 'That Antony of Padua converted an heretic, by making *his horse adore the host*' (London: 1608), 305 (emphasis in copy). See also later allusions to the miracle: in William Lloyd, *A Sermon preached before the King at White-Hall* (London, 1668), 29; Edward Stillingfleet, *A Discourse concerning the idolatry practised in the Church of Rome* (London, 1671), 252; and Anthony Horneck, *The Crucified Jesus* (London, 1695), 128.

37 *John Webster, Renaissance Dramatist* (Edinburgh University Press, 2010), 48.

38 See Christopher Elwood, *The Body Broken: The Calvinist Doctrine of the Eucharist and the Symbolization of Power in Sixteenth-Century France* (Oxford: Oxford University Press, 1999).

39 'Appendix II', *An Apology for Raymond Sebond*, ed. and trans. M. A. Screech (London: Penguin, 1989; rpr. 1993), xli.

40 For one modern critic, the impression of Montaigne himself was related to equestrianism: 'when we view his life as a whole, our most constant image of him is on horseback', and 'Montaigne on horseback is symbolic of man continually in movement not only between public and private domains but also between different social roles' (10, 11). Frederick Rider, *The Dialectic of Selfhood in Montaigne* (Stanford University Press, 1973).

41   'Pedagogy and the Art of Dressage in the Italian Renaissance',
      Animals and Early Modern Identity, eds. Pia F. Cuneo and
      Alison G. Stewart (Burlington, VT: Ashgate, 2014), 375–90;
      376–77.

42   Also note Flamineo's use of 'I recover like a spent taper for a
      flash' (259) against Montaigne's 'me seemed it was a flashing
      or lightning' (quoted above).

43   David Gunby, 'John Webster', *Oxford Dictionary of National
      Biography*. Available online: http://www.oxforddnb.com.

Chapter 6

1   Jonathan Dollimore, *Radical Tragedy: Religion, Ideology and
     Power in the Drama of Shakespeare and his Contemporaries*
     (Chicago: University of Chicago Press, 1984), 59, 231–4; J. W.
     Lever, *The Tragedy of State* (London: Methuen, 1971), 78–86.

2   *The White Devil*, ed. John Russell Brown (Manchester:
     Manchester University Press, 1996), 4. Brown is in the curious
     position of countering his own earlier view of the play's
     representation of a 'fragmentary, decentred world' with his
     later political reading of the play. See his critique of his own
     earlier view, 9–10.

3   The exception to this vagueness is Brown, who associates
     Flamineo with Jacobean courtiers like Sir Thomas Overbury,
     Vittoria with Frances Howard, and Giovanni with Prince
     Henry (see 7–9). His brief and suggestive remarks do
     not, however, lead to a sustained political reading of the
     play. Unlike Brown, Lever and Dollimore avoid drawing
     connections between the play and specific political figures and
     events in Jacobean England, though Dollimore does tie the
     generalized political critique he finds in Jacobean drama to the
     ferment that preceded the English civil war (4).

4   Bovilsky, 'Black Beauties, White Devils: The English Italian in
     Milton and Webster', *English Literary History* 70(3) (2003):
     625–51, 638.

5   Emma Rhatigan, 'Reading 'The White Devil' in Thomas

Adams and John Webster', in Adrian Streete, ed., *Early Modern Drama and the Bible: Contexts and Readings 1570–1625* (London: Palgrave, 2011), 193.

6　Bovilsky, 638; Anthony Ellis, 'The Machiavel and the Virago: The Use of Italian Types in Webster's *The White Devil*', *Journal of Dramatic Theory and Criticism* 20 (2006): 49–74, 59; June Waudby, 'Contextualizing Vittoria: Subjectivity and Censure in *The White Devil*', *This Rough Magic* 1(2) (June 2010): 1–24, 14. Dympna Callaghan, *Woman and Gender in Renaissance Tragedy: A Study of King Lear, Othello, The Duchess of Malfi, and The White Devil* (Atlantic Highlands, NJ: Humanities Press, 1989), 76.

7　This odd symmetry between the play's misogyny and that of some of its critics has been noted in passing by Martin Orkin, '"As If a Man Should Spit Against the Wind"', in Naomi Conn Liebler, ed., *The Female Tragic Hero in English Renaissance Drama* (London: Palgrave, 2002), 150. For another exception to the general critical censure of Vittoria, see Andrew Strycharski, 'Ethics, Individualism and Class in John Webster's *The White Devil*', *Criticism* 5(2) (2012): 291–315, 299. *The Duchess of Malfi*, ed. Leah Marcus (London: Bloomsbury, 2013), 388. For a list of such critics, see Frances E. Dolan, 'Can This Be Certain?:' *The Duchess of Malfi*'s Secrets', in Christina Luckyj, ed., *The Duchess of Malfi: A Critical Guide* (London: Bloomsbury, 2011), 133 n.7.

8　Brown, 8.

9　'A London citizen with an Inns of Court education and family ties to the London business community, Webster lived in a milieu closely associated with both puritan and common law interests'; see Luke Wilson, 'The White Devil and the Law', in Garret A. Sullivan Jr., Patrick Cheney, and Andrew Hadfield, *Early Modern English Drama: A Critical Companion* (Oxford: Oxford University Press, 2006), 231. Webster's contributions to the second edition of Overbury's Characters (1614) place him in the company of other 'literati members of the Protestant faction at court under the patronage of William Herbert, Earl of Pembroke', according to Donald Beecher; see *Characters, together with Poems, News, Edicts and Paradoxes based on the eleventh edition of A Wife Now the Widow of Sir Thomas Overbury* (Ottawa: Dovehouse, 2003), 57. Most studies of Webster's hyper-Protestant politics have focused on *The Duchess of Malfi*: see, for example, Leah Marcus, 'Introduction', *The Duchess of Malfi*, ed. Marcus (London: Bloomsbury, 2013); and Curtis Perry and Melissa Walter, 'Staging Secret Interiors: *The Duchess of Malfi* as Inns of Court and Anticourt Drama', in Luckyj, ed., *The Duchess of Malfi: A Critical Guide* (London: Bloomsbury, 2011), 87–105.

10 On the commonplace analogy between domestic and political spheres, according to which a woman (normally a wife) stood in the same relation to man as subject to king, see Melissa Sanchez, *Erotic Subjects: The Sexuality of Politics in Early Modern English Literature* (Oxford: Oxford University Press, 2011).

11 For further discussion of the controversy, see Katherine Usher Henderson and Barbara F. McManus, *Half Humankind: Contexts and Texts of the Controversy about Women, 1540–1640* (Urbana, IL: University of Illinois Press, 1985); and Linda Woodbridge, *Women and the English Renaissance: Literature and the Nature of Womankind 1540–1620* (Urbana, IL: University of Illinois Press, 1984). For Webster's engagement with the 'Elizabethan feminist controversy' see Dollimore, 239–40, and Waudby, 2–4; see also the 'Introduction' to my edition of *The White Devil* (London: Methuen, 2008), xviii.

12 Orkin, 145.

13 Henderson and McManus, *Half Humankind*, 181.

14 Sowernam, *Esther Hath Hanged Haman*, excerpted in *Half Humankind*, 220.

15 Admittedly, Vittoria's line is open to interpretation; as the note in my edition remarks, 'blood' could also signify sexual passion (24n).

16 David Gunby, David Carnegie and Antony Hammond, eds, *The Works of John Webster*, 3 vols (Cambridge: Cambridge University Press, 1995), I: 271.

17 Gunnar Boklund, *The Sources of The White Devil* (New York: Haskell House, 1966), 42.

18 R. W. Dent, for example, dwells on Vittoria's admission that she 'could not pray' (1.2.232), and compares it with similar moments in *Macbeth* and *Hamlet* to argue that 'there appears to have been an established convention by which the audience could recognize the devil in Vittoria's dream without Flamineo's assistance'; see *John Webster's Borrowing* (Berkeley, CA: University of California Press, 1960), 88.

19 William Heale, *An Apologie for Women* (London, 1609), 13.

20 See my edition on this point: 'Because Webster chooses to suppress knowledge that Isabella has been murdered until after Vittoria's trial, Vittoria's victimization by masculine authority in 3.2 is juxtaposed with Isabella's treatment by those who "wrapped her in a cruel fold of lead" (3.2.331)' (xxiii).

21 Lever, 81.

22 Belinda Roberts Peters observes: 'when rulers in Jacobean tragedy usurped the rights of marriage and, especially, subjected wives to seduction, rape or dishonor, they stripped their subjects of political liberties'; see *Marriage in Seventeenth-Century English Political Thought* (London: Palgrave, 2004), 161.

23 For a detailed account of the rebellions, see Gordon McMullan, *The Politics of Unease in the Plays of John Fletcher* (Amherst: University of Massachusetts Press, 1994), 37–84.

24 Jack Landau, 'Elizabethan Art in a Mickey Spillane Setting', *Theatre Arts* (1955), reprinted in R. V. Holdsworth, ed., *Webster: 'The White Devil' and 'The Duchess of Malfi': A Casebook* (London: Macmillan, 1975), 234; For the former, see Madeleine Doran, *Endeavors of Art: A Study of Form in Elizabethan Drama* (Madison: University of Wisconsin Press, 1954), 118; for the latter, see Catherine Belsey, *The Subject of Tragedy: Identity and Difference in Renaissance Drama* (London: Methuen, 1985), 163.

25 See Waudby, who declares that Vittoria 'invites condemnation as a 'public' woman, which in Webster's culture attested her guilt' (11), and Bovilsky, who contends that 'Vittoria's defence

does not fundamentally rework the terms Monticelso has set up' (643).

26   Alison Shell, *Catholicism, Controversy and the English Literary Imagination* (Cambridge: Cambridge University Press, 1999), 47. Rhatigan concurs with her view: 'Vittoria is clearly associated with the Whore of Babylon' (192).

27   H. Bruce Franklin first pointed out that 'Webster's thinly-veiled, point-by-point ironic character of the 'Whore of Babylon [...] articulates almost every contemporary accusation hurled against the Church;' he remarks that the Cardinal's first figure ('Sweetmeats which rot the eater') comes from 'Dekker's virulently anti-Catholic *Whore of Babylon*' where it 'refers to rhetoric'. He nonetheless perceives that 'Vittoria's simple reply, "This character 'scapes me" (105) deflates the cardinal's overblown harangue'; see 'The Trial Scene of Webster's *The White Devil* Examined in Terms of Renaissance Rhetoric', *Studies in English Literature 1500–1900* 1(2) (1961): 35–51, 41–2.

28   Webster, 'A Jesuit', *Characters*, 276.

29   *The Examinations of Anne Askew*, ed. Elaine Beilin (Oxford: Oxford University Press, 1996).

30   Jennifer Summit, *Lost Property: The Woman Writer and English Literary History, 1380–1589* (Chicago: University of Chicago Press, 2000), 149.

31   David Colclough notes that 'the martyr's speech required validation from a larger community in order to attain the status of true religious parrhesia'; see *Freedom of Speech in Early Stuart England* (Cambridge: Cambridge University Press, 2005), 92.

32   Franklin, 42–3. 'At the core of the Reformation was not only the idea that the dogma, hierarchy and services of the church universal should be cleansed, but also the proposition that the undefiled truth of scripture should be propagated in the clear vernacular to the people'; see John Morgan, *Godly Learning: Puritan Attitudes towards Reason, Learning and Education, 1560–1640* (Cambridge: Cambridge University Press, 1986), 121.

33   Compare Askew: 'That for as much as I am by the law

condemned for an evil doer, Here I take heaven and earth to record, that I shall die in my innocence[…] But look what God hath charged me with his mouth, that have I shut up in my heart' (*Examinations*, 117–18.)

34 The title page of the quarto reads 'The White Divel or, The Tragedy of Paulo Giordano Ursini, Duke of Brachiano, with the Life and Death of Vittoria Corombona the famous Venetian Curtizan'.

35 See Boklund, 138.

36 Anne M. Haselkorn, 'Sin and the Politics of Penitence: Three Jacobean Adulteresses', in Anne M. Haselkorn and Betty Travitsky, *The Renaissance Englishwoman in Print* (Amherst, MA: University of Massachusetts Press, 1990), 124.

37 The play was performed and printed in 1612, but Webster admits in his preface to the reader that he was 'a long time in finishing this tragedy' (6). Since he borrows from Tofte's 1610 translation of Nicolas de Montreux's *Honour's Academy*, we may imagine him writing the play during the years 1610–12.

38 James Doelman, *King James I and the Religious Culture of England* (Cambridge: D. S. Brewer, 2000), 105.

39 Spenser's poem of praise prefaces Lewkenor's work. Contarini describes the equitable justice system in Venice at length, specifically its insistence on provisions for defence as well as prosecution at trial. In particular, Advocates should 'refrain from unseemly railing and so not digress or wander out of the matter with extremity of spiteful words. For whosoever maliciously raileth, seemeth rather to betray a mind intemperate and hateful, then any way to advance the commonwealths cause […] [T]he matter is far otherwise among the Venetians, then it was times passed among the Romans'; see Lewis Lewkenor, *The Commonwealth and Government of Venice* (London, 1599), 86–88.

40 See Lewkenor, A2r-v.

41 Mark Matheson, 'Venetian Culture and the Politics of Othello', in Catherine M. S. Alexander, ed., *Shakespeare and Politics* (Cambridge: Cambridge University Press, 2004), 170.

42 Cited in Colclough, 155, 150.

43 See Colclough for a discussion of the 1610 Parliament, in which 'the links between freedom of speech and the liberties of the subject were asserted in a far more sophisticated way than they had been in 1604' (158).

44 In his *History of Italy* (1549), traveller William Thomas observed, "their principal profession is liberty, and he that should usurp upon another should incontinently be reputed a tyrant, which name of all things they cannot abide"'; cited in Graham Holderness, *Shakespeare and Venice* (Farnham: Ashgate, 2010), 26.

45 See my essay, '*A Mouzell for Melastomus* in Context: Rereading the Swetnam/Speght Debate', *English Literary Renaissance* 40(1) (Winter 2010): 113–31.

46 Chris R. Kyle, *Theater of State: Parliament and Political Culture in Early Stuart England* (Stanford University Press, 2012), 85.

47 Within a few years of *The White Devil*, Archer's publications included Middleton's *The Roaring Girl* (1611), as well as both Swetnam's *Arraignment of Lewd, Idle Forward and Unconstant Women* (1615) and Speght's *Mouzell for Melastomus* (1617). See Lesser, 116.

48 Constance Jordan, *Renaissance Feminism: Literary Texts and Political Models* (Ithaca: Cornell University Press, 1990), 20.

49 Julie Crawford, *Mediatrix: Women, Politics and Literary Production in Early Modern England* (Oxford: Oxford University Press, 2014), 38.

50 James Knowles remarks, 'In contrast to Elizabeth's reign where one power centre dominated, the Jacobean court boasted three royal households or courts, each with its own structures and policies'; see '"Tied to rules of flattery"?: Court Drama and the Masque', in Michael Hattaway, ed., *A New Companion to English Renaissance Literature and Culture*, 2 vols (Chichester: Wiley Blackwell, 2010), II: 109.

51 Eva Griffith, *A Jacobean Company and its Playhouse: The Queen's Servants at the Red Bull Theatre* (Cambridge: Cambridge University Press, 2013), 108.

52 See Jonson's *Masque of Queens*, ed. David Lindley, in
    David Bevington, Martin Butler and Ian Donaldson, eds,
    The Cambridge Edition of the Works of Ben Jonson, 7 vols
    (Cambridge: Cambridge University Press, 2012), III: 281–349,
    302.

53 Kathryn Schwarz, 'Amazon Reflection in the Jacobean Queen's
    Masque', *Studies in English Literature 1500–1900* 35(2)
    (1995): 293–319, 296.

54 Knowles, 112.

55 Schwarz, 307.

56 'Tyrants, Love and Ladies' Eyes: The Politics of Female/Boy
    Alliance on the Jacobean Stage', in Christina Luckyj and
    Niamh O'Leary, eds, *The Politics of Female Alliance* (under
    submission).

57 Alastair Bellany, *The Politics of Court Scandal in Early
    Modern England* (Cambridge: Cambridge University Press,
    2002), 37.

58 The connection between Giovanni and Prince Henry was
    first suggested by F. L. Lucas, and has been developed by the
    editors of the new Cambridge edition (see note to 2.1.108ff.),
    who claim that 'Webster's portrayal of Giovanni as a prince
    devoted to an ideal of warlike leadership and the hard work
    of practising with his pike [...] may have been influenced
    by Prince Henry's barriers' (*Works*, 106). However, the
    Cambridge editors are primarily interested in the theatrical,
    not the political, implications of Webster's likely debt to Prince
    Henry's Barriers.

59 For the question of the ages of boys in the companies see
    David Kathman, 'How Old Were Shakespeare's Boy Actors?',
    Shakespeare Survey 58 (2005): 220–46, 220.

60 On the notion of the Stuart royal family as a 'living text,
    write large in the public consciousness', see David Bergeron,
    Shakespeare's Romances and the Royal Family (Lawrence, KS:
    University Press of Kansas, 1985), 20.

61 See Robin Headlam Wells, '"Manhood and Chevalrie":
    Coriolanus, Prince Henry and the Chivalric Revival', *The
    Review of English Studies* n.s. 51.203 (August 2000):
    395–422.

62 I am arguing here against my own earlier work, 'Gender, Rhetoric and Performance in *The White Devil*', in which I suggest that 'the play's most obvious exposure of masculinity as a precarious and risible construction comes [...] when Bracciano's son, the young prince Giovanni, dons a suit of armor and tosses his "pike" (2.1.110) [...] Giovanni makes the swaggering Bracciano of the second act by analogy look like a child'; see Viviana Comensoli and Anne Russell, eds, *Enacting Gender on the English Renaissance Stage* (Urbana and Chicago: University of Illinois Press, 1999), 224.

63 The editors of the Cambridge edition similarly contrast the source material with Webster's complex portrait of Giovanni: 'In *The White Devil* [...] he is portrayed as a boy-prince of considerable emotional and moral strength, capable of providing, at the last, a symbol of hope and renewal, however fragile'; see Gunby et al., *Works of John Webster: An Old Spelling Critical Edition* (Cambridge: Cambridge University Press, 1995), 366.

64 *Works*, 373.

65 Ibid., 60.

66 Ibid., 107, for a reproduction of the engraving.

67 Compare Swetnam's *The school of the noble and worthy science of defence* (1617): 'it behooveth Kings being challenged by their equals for the safeguard and good of their subjects and country, to adventure and hazard their own lives in hope of a conquest, so that thereby the wars may cease' (C2v), emphasis added. See my essay, 'A Mouzell for Melastomus', for an argument aligning Swetnam with hyper-Protestantism critical of the King.

68 *A Monumentall Column erected to the living memory of the ever-glorious Henry, late Prince of Wales* (London, 1613), Bʳ.

69 Roy Strong, *Henry, Prince of Wales and England's Lost Renaissance* (New York: Thames and Hudson, 1986), 151.

70 David Carnegie, 'Theatrical Introduction', *The White Devil* in *Works*, 103, 106.

71 On this point, and for evidence that Giovanni has been cut in modern productions, see Carnegie, 96.

72 See Leeds Barroll, *Anna of Denmark Queen of England: A Cultural Biography* (Philadelphia: University of Pennsylvania Press, 2001), esp. Ch. 5, 'Masquing and Faction: Prince Henry and After'.

73 'To the Reader', I. 6.

Chapter 7

1 Contributor to online forum, Women Online Worldwide, cited in Pamela Paul, *Pornified: How Pornography is Transforming our Lives, Our Relationships, and Our Families* (New York: Henry Holt, 2005), 167.

2 Pietro Aretino, Letter (c. 11 December 1537), cited in Bette Talvacchia, *Taking Positions: On the Erotic in Renaissance Culture* (Princeton University Press, 1999), 85.

3 Henry Fitzjeffrey, 'Notes from Blackfriars' (1617), in Don D. Moore *Webster: The Critical Heritage* (London: Routledge and Kegan Paul, 1981), 33.

4 Frank Marcus, 'The White Devil' (review of the production, dir. Frank Dunlop), *Sunday Telegraph* (16 November 1969).

5 Jonathan Munby, director of the Menier Chocolate Factory production of *The White Devil* (2008), interview cited in Stephen Purcell, *The White Devil: A Guide to the Text and the Play in Performance* (Basingstoke: Palgrave, 2012), 111.

6 T. S. Eliot, 'Whispers of Immortality' (1919), in G. K. and S. K. Hunter, eds, *John Webster: A Critical Anthology* (Harmondsworth: Penguin, 1969), 111–12.

7 See https://digitalshakespeares.wordpress.com/2014/08/20/visualizing-the-white-devil/ (accessed 25 June 2015).

8 Maria Aberg, interviewed by Catherine Love, *What'sOnStage* (11 June 2014). Available online: www.whatsonstage.com/london-theatre/news/06–2014/maria-aberg-interview-hotel-white-devil_34711.html.

9 Kat Banyard, 'What the Powerful Want to See', *The White*

Devil programme notes (Stratford-upon-Avon, Royal Shakespeare Company, 2014), 3–5.

10   Christina Luckyj, *A Winter's Snake: Dramatic Form in the Tragedies of John Webster* (Athens, GA: The University of Georgia Press, 1989), 39.

11   Forker, 19.

12   Dena Goldberg, '"By Report": The Spectator as Voyeur in Webster's *The White Devil*', *English Literary Renaissance* 17(1) (1987): 67–84.

13   Lord Thomas Howard, letter to Sir John Harrington, cited in Katherine M. Carey, 'The Aesthetics of Immediacy and Hypermediation: the Dumb Shows in Webster's *The White Devil*', *New Theatre Quarterly* 23 (1) (February 2007): 75.

14   Sarah Toulalan, *Imagining Sex: Pornography and Bodies in Seventeenth-Century England* (Oxford: Oxford University Press, 2007), 161.

15   David O. Frantz, *Festum Voluptatis: A Study of Renaissance Erotica* (Columbus, OH: Ohio State University Press, 1989), 1.

16   Mary Joe Frug, 'The Politics of Postmodern Feminism: Lessons from the Anti-Pornography Campaign', in Drucilla Cornell, ed., *Feminism and Pornography* (Oxford: Oxford University Press, 2000), 256. See also Douglas A. Hughes, ed., *Perspectives on Pornography* (New York: Macmillan, 1970); Roger Thompson, *Unfit for Modest Ears* (London: Macmillan, 1979); Walter Kendrick, *The Secret Museum: Pornography in Modern Culture* (Berkeley: University of California Press, 1996).

17   Paul, *Pornified*, 276.

18   *Before Pornography: Erotic Writing in Early Modern England* (Oxford: Oxford University Press, 2000), 5.

19   Diana E. H. Russell, 'Pornography and Rape: A Causal Model', in *Feminism and Pornography* 48. Italics in original.

20   Lynn Hunt, 'Obscenity and the Origins of Modernity, 1500–1800', in *Feminism and Pornography*, 355.

21   Patrick J. Kearney, *A History of Erotic Literature* (Hong Kong: Parragon, 1982), 90.

22 David Foxon, *Libertine Literature in England, 1660–1745* (New York: University Books, 1965), ix.

23 Kendrick, 11.

24 Gail Dines, *Pornland: How Porn has Hijacked Our Sexuality* (Boston: Beacon Press, 2010), 86.

25 See Jonathan Dollimore, *Sex, Literature and Censorship* (Cambridge: Polity, 2001), 95–106.

26 Thomson, ix.

27 Angela Carter, 'Pornography in the Service of Women', in *Feminism and Pornography*, 535.

28 Carter, 534.

29 J. G. Ballard, 'Introduction' (1995), in Ballard, *Crash* (1973; London: Vintage, 1995), 3.

30 David Mura, *A Male Grief: Notes on Pornography and Addiction* (Minneapolis: Thistle, 1987), 16.

31 Moulton, *Before Pornography*, 11.

32 Laura Mulvey, *Visual and Other Pleasures* (Basingstoke: Palgrave, 1989), 16.

33 Frantz, 230.

34 Dollimore, *Sex*, 132.

35 Stuart Clark, *Vanities of the Eye: Vision in Early Modern European Culture* (Oxford: Oxford University Press, 2007), 28, 21.

36 George Hakewill, *The Vanity of the Eye* (Oxford: 1615), 27, 5, 4, 6, 12, 6, 10. Spelling modernized.

37 Saint Augustine, *Confessions*, translated by Henry Chadwick (Oxford: Oxford University Press, 1998), 211.

38 Hakewill, 38–9.

39 Anthony Munday, *A Second and Third Blast of retrait from plaies and Theaters* (1580), 95–6; cited in Michael O'Connell, *The Idolatrous Eye: Iconoclasm and Theater in Early Modern England* (Oxford: Oxford University Press, 2000), 19.

40 William Prynne, *Histrio-Mastix, the Players Scourge, or actors tragoedie* (London, 1633; New York: Garland, 1973), 929–31; cited in O'Connell, 34.

41 O'Connell, 33.

42 Phillip Stubbes, *The Anatomie of Abuses* (1583), cited in Jonathan Goldberg, *Sodometries: Renaissance Texts, Modern Sexualities* (New York: Fordham University Press, 1992), 118.

43 Peter Stallybrass, 'Transvestism and the "Body Beneath": Speculating on the Boy Actor', in Susan Zimmerman, ed., *Erotic Politics: Desire on the Renaissance Stage* (New York and London: Routledge, 1992), 64–83, 78.

44 Michael Neill, 'Unproper Beds: Race, Adultery, and the Hideous in *Othello*', *Shakespeare Quarterly* 40(4) (Winter 1989): 400.

45 *Othello*, ed. E. A. J. Honigmann (London: Bloomsbury Arden Shakespeare, 2003).

46 Dollimore, *Sex*, 132.

47 Lynda Boose, '"Let it be Hid": The Pornographic Aesthetic of Shakespeare's *Othello*', in Linda Woodbridge and Sharon A. Beehler, eds, *Women, Violence, and English Renaissance Literature* (Tempe: Arizona Center for Medieval and Renaissance Studies, 2003), 246.

48 Neill, 385.

49 Ibid., 390.

50 Ibid., 384, n.5.

51 Harold Jenkins, 'Revenge in Shakespeare and Webster' (1961), in *Webster: A Critical Anthology*, 264; Forker, 262.

52 Purcell, 12.

53 Ibid., 126.

54 Ibid., 12.

55 Forker, 262.

56 Christopher Marlowe, *Hero and Leander*, 2.71–4; see *The Complete Poems and Translations*, ed. Stephen Orgel (Harmondsworth: Penguin, 2007), 20.

57 Frantz, 3.

58 Boose, 252–3. On English appropriations of Aretino, see Frantz 140–58, 186–207.

59 Moulton, 137.

60 Ibid., 128.

61 Pietro Aretino, letter to Battista Zatti, cited in Frantz, 50.

62 Ben Jonson, *The Alchemist*, ed. F. H. Mares (London: Methuen, 1971).

63 Notably, neither of the major authorities on Webster's borrowings point to any debt he might have to Aretino (or *The Alchemist* or *Othello*, for that matter). See R. W. Dent, *John Webster's Borrowing* (Berkeley, CA: University of California Press, 1960); and Gunnar Boklund, *The Sources of The White Devil* (New York: Haskell House, 1966).

64 Moulton, 6.

65 Toulalan, 278.

66 Ibid., 9.

67 Andrea Dworkin, 'Pornography and Grief', in *Feminism and Pornography*, 41.

68 Moulton, 3–4.

69 Ibid., 11.

70 David Coleman, *John Webster, Renaissance Dramatist* (Edinburgh: Edinburgh University Press, 2010), 40.

71 Kay Stanton, *Shakespeare's 'Whores': Erotics, Politics and Poetics* (Basingstoke: Palgrave Macmillan, 2014), 3.

72 Dines, xxii, xxiv.

73 Andrea Dworkin and Catharine A. MacKinnon, *Pornography and Civil Rights: A New Day* (Minneapolis: Organizing Against Pornography, 1988), cited in Drucilla Cornell, 'Introduction', in *Feminism and Pornography*, 3–4.

74 Talvacchia, 161.

75 Luckyj, 'Introduction', xxii.

76 Catharine A. MacKinnon, 'Only Words', in *Feminism and Pornography*, 96.

77 Christina Luckyj, 'Gender, Rhetoric, and Performance in John Webster's *The White Devil*', in Viviana Comensoli and Anne Russell, eds, *Enacting Gender on the English Renaissance Stage* (Urbana and Chicago: University of Illinois Press, 1998), 225.

78 Dena Goldberg, *Between Worlds: A Study of the Plays of John Webster* (Waterloo, ON: Wilfrid Laurier University Press: 1987), 56.

79 Otto Fenichel, *The Psychoanalytic Theory of Neurosis* (New York: W. W. Norton, 1945), 348.

80 Jonathan M. Metzl, 'From Scopophilia to *Survivor*: A Brief History of Voyeurism', *Textual Practice* 18(3) (2004): 419.

81 Paul, *Pornified*, 32.

82 Sheryl A. Stevenson, '"As Differing As two Adamants": Sexual Difference in *The White Devil*', in Carole Levin and Karen Robertson, eds, *Sexuality and Politics in Renaissance Drama* (Lewiston, Queenston and Lampeter: Edwin Mellen Press, 1991), 159.

83 Ibid., 162, 168.

84 Coleman, 39.

85 Andrew Strycharski, 'Ethics, Individualism, and Class in John Webster's *The White Devil*', *Criticism* 54(2) (Spring 2012): 308.

86 Ovid, *Metamorphoses* (4:210–28), translated by Arthur Golding (1565), ed. Madeline Forey (Harmondsworth: Penguin, 2002), 127

87 Jonathan Dollimore, 'Sexual Disgust', *Oxford Literary Review* (1998): 47.

88 Ibid., 55.

89 Ibid., 67.

Chapter 8

1 For a further discussion of empirical methodology in relation to literary study, see James Hirsh '*Hamlet* and Empiricism', *Shakespeare Survey* 66 (2013): 330–43.

2 William Blake, 'Annotations to the *Works of Sir Joshua Reynolds*', in David V. Erdman, *The Complete Poetry and Prose of William Blake* (Berkeley, CA: University of California Press, 1982), 635–2, 641.

3   For a more extensive discussion of the title, see James Hirsh,
    'Vittoria's Secret: An Approach to Teaching John Webster's
    The White Devil', in Karen Bamford and Alexander Leggatt,
    eds, *Approaches to Teaching English Renaissance Drama*
    (New York: Modern Language Association, 2002), 73–9.

4   See Andrew Gurr, *Playgoing in Shakespeare's London*
    (Cambridge: Cambridge University Press, 2004), for a wealth
    of information about late Renaissance stage conditions in
    general.

5   For explorations of the artistic implications of the conventions
    governing soliloquies in the period, an interested teacher might
    consult the following works by the present author: *Shakespeare
    and the History of Soliloquies* (Madison, NJ: Fairleigh
    Dickinson University Press, 2003); 'Dialogic Self-Address in
    Shakespeare's Plays', *Shakespeare* 8 (2012): 312–27; 'Guarded,
    Unguarded, and Unguardable Speech in Late Renaissance
    Drama', in Laury Magnus and Walter W. Cannon, *Who
    Hears in Shakespeare? Auditory Worlds on Stage and Screen*
    (Madison, NJ: Fairleigh Dickinson University Press, 2012),
    17–40; 'Late Renaissance Self-Address Fashioning: Scholarly
    Orthodoxy versus Evidence', *Medieval and Renaissance Drama
    in England* 27 (2014): 132–60; and 'The Origin of the Late
    Renaissance Dramatic Convention of Self-Addressed Speech',
    Shakespeare Survey 68 (2015): 131–45.

6   See Richard Cave, *The White Devil and The Duchess of
    Malfi: Text and Performance* (Basingstoke: Macmillan, 1988);
    Stephen Purcell, *Webster: The White Devil: A Guide to the
    Text and Performance* (Basingstoke: Palgrave Macmillan,
    2012); Helen Ostovich, '"Our Sport Shall Be to Take What
    They Mistake": Classroom Performance and Learning', in
    Bamford and Leggatt, 87–94; and Milla Cozart Riggio, ed.,
    Teaching Shakespeare through Performance (New York:
    Modern Language Association, 1999).

7   See Ralph Berry, *The Art of John Webster* (Oxford: Clarendon
    Press, 1972); Lee Bliss, *The World's Perspective: John Webster
    and the Jacobean Drama* (New Brunswick, NJ: Rutgers
    University Press, 1983); Katherine M. Carey, 'The Aesthetics
    of Immediacy and Hypermediation: The Dumb Shows in
    Webster's *The White Devil*', *New Theatre Quarterly* 23

(2007): 73–80; Charles R. Forker, *Skull Beneath the Skin: The Achievement of John Webster* (Carbondale, IL: Southern Illinois University Press, 1986); Dena Goldberg, '"By Report": The Spectator as Voyeur in Webster's *The White Devil*', *English Literary Renaissance* 17 (1987): 67–84; and Christina Luckyj, *A Winter's Snake: Dramatic Form in the Tragedies of John Webster* (Athens, GA: University of Georgia Press, 1989).

8   See Nicholas Brooke, *Horrid Laughter in Jacobean Tragedy* (New York: Barnes & Noble, 1979); Travis Bogard, *The Tragic Satire of John Webster* (Berkeley, CA: University of California Press, 1955); and Jacqueline Pearson, *Tragedy and Tragicomedy in the Plays of John Webster* (Totowa, NJ: Barnes & Noble, 1980).

9   See Laura L. Behling, '"S/He Scandles Our Proceedings": The Anxiety of Alternative Sexualities in *The White Devil* and *The Duchess of Malfi*', *English Language Notes* 33 (1996): 24–43; Laura G. Bromley, 'The Rhetoric of Feminine Identity in *The White Devil*', in Dorothea Kehler and Susan Baker, eds, *In Another Country: Feminist Perspectives on Renaissance Drama* (Metuchen, NJ: Scarecrow, 1991), 50–70; Dympna Callaghan, *Women and Gender in Renaissance Tragedy: A Study of King Lear, Othello, The Duchess of Malfi, and The White Devil* (Atlantic Highlands, NJ: Humanities Press International, 1989); Ina Habermann,'"She has that in her belly will dry up your ink": Femininity as Challenge in the "Equitable Drama" of John Webster', in Erica Sheen and Lorna Hutson, eds, *Literature, Politics and Law in Renaissance England* (Basingstoke: Palgrave Macmillan, 2005), 100–20; Christina Luckyj, 'Gender, Rhetoric and Performance in John Webster's *The White Devil*', in Viviana Comensoli and Anne Russell, eds, *Enacting Gender on the English Renaissance Stage* (Urbana, IL: University of Illinois Press, 1988), 190–207; Sara Mendelson and Patricia Crawford, *Women in Early Modern England, 1550–1720* (Oxford: Oxford University Press, 1998); and Mary Beth Rose, *The Expense of Spirit: Love and Sexuality in English Renaissance Drama* (Ithaca, NY: Cornell University Press, 1988).

10 Jonathan Dollimore, *Radical Tragedy: Religion, Ideology and Power in the Drama of Shakespeare and His Contemporaries*, 3rd edn (London: Palgrave Macmillan, 2010).

11 Virginia Mason Vaughan, *Performing Blackness on English Stages, 1500–1800* (Cambridge: Cambridge University Press, 2005).

12 Andy Mousley, *Renaissance Drama and Contemporary Literary Theory* (New York: St Martin's, 2000).

13 *The Duchess of Malfi and Other Plays*, ed. Réne Weis (Oxford: Oxford University Press, 1996); *Three Plays: The White Devil, The Duchess of Malfi [and] The Devil's Law Case*, ed. David Gunby (Harmondsworth: Penguin, 1972); *The Selected Plays of John Webster*, Jonathan Dollimore and Alan Sinfield, eds (Cambridge: Cambridge University Press: 1983); *The Works of John Webster*, Gunby et al., eds, 3 vols (Cambridge: Cambridge University Press, 1995–2003); *The Duchess of Malfi, The White Devil, The Broken Heart* and *'Tis Pity She's a Whore*, ed. Jane Kingsley Smith (London: Penguin, 2014); *Three Revenge Tragedies*, ed. Gāmini Salgādo (Cambridge: Proquest LLC, 2011), ebook edn; *Four Revenge Tragedies: The Spanish Tragedy, The Revenger's Tragedy, 'Tis Pity She's a Whore, The White Devil*, ed. Janet Clare (London: Methuen Drama, 2014), ebook edn, David Bevington et al. *English Renaissance Drama: A Norton Anthology* (New York: W. W. Norton, 2002).

14 *Plays on Women*, Bevington and Kathleen McLuskie, eds (Manchester University Press, 1999); Elizabeth Carey, *The Tragedy of Mariam, the fair queen of Jewry*, ed. Karen Britland (London: Methuen, 2010).

SELECT BIBLIOGRAPHY

Anderson, David K. (2014). *Martyrs and Players in Early Modern England: Tragedy, Religion and Violence on Stage*. Farnham: Ashgate.

Barker, Roberta (2005). '"Another Voyage": Death as Social Performance in the Major Tragedies of John Webster', *Early Theatre* 8: 35–56.

Behling, Laura L. (1996). '"S/He Scandles Our Proceedings": The Anxiety of Alternative Sexualities in *The White Devil* and *The Duchess of Malfi*', *English Language Notes* 33: 24–43.

Berry, Ralph (1972). *The Art of John Webster*. Oxford: Clarendon Press.

Blessing, Carol (2009). 'The Trials of Mary Stuart: Anxious Circulation in John Webster's Drama', in Andrew Majeske and Emily Detmer-Goebel, eds, *Justice, Women, and Power in English Renaissance Drama*. Madison: Fairleigh Dickinson University Press.

Bliss, Lee (1983). *The World's Perspective: John Webster and the Jacobean Drama*. New Brunswick, NJ: Rutgers University Press.

Boklund, Gunnar (1957). *The Sources of the White Devil*. Cambridge, MA.: Harvard University Press.

Bovlisky, Lara (2003). 'Black Beauties, White Devils: The English Italian in Milton and Webster', *English Literary History* 70: 625–51.

Bradbrook, M. C. (1980). *John Webster: Citizen and Dramatist*. London: Weidenfeld & Nicholson.

Bromley, Laura G. (1991). 'The Rhetoric of Feminine Identity in *The White Devil*', in Dorothea Kehler and Susan Baker, eds, *In Another Country: Feminist Perspectives on Renaissance Drama*. Metuchen, NJ: Scarecrow.

Callaghan, Dympna (1989). *Women and Gender in Renaissance*

Tragedy: A Study of King Lear, Othello, The Duchess of Malfi, and The White Devil. Atlantic Highlands, NJ: Humanities Press.

Carey, Katherine M. (2007). 'The Aesthetics of Immediacy and Hypermediation: The Dumb Shows in Webster's *The White Devil*', *New Theatre Quarterly* 23: 73–80.

Cave, Richard (1988). *The White Devil and The Duchess of Malfi: Text and Performance.* Basingstoke: Macmillan.

Coleman, David (2010). *John Webster: Renaissance Dramatist.* Edinburgh: Edinburgh University Press.

Comensoli, Viviana and Anne Russell, eds (1998). *Enacting Gender on the English Renaissance Stage.* Urbana, IL: University of Illinois Press.

Conn Liebler, Naomi, ed. (2002). *The Female Tragic Hero in English Renaissance Drama.* London: Palgrave.

Connolly, Annaliese and Lisa Hopkins (2015). 'A Darker Shade of Pale: Webster's Winter Whiteness', *E-Rea* 12.2 §§1–31. Available online: http://erea.revues.org/4483.

Den, F. Lehman (2011). '"We confound knowledge with knowledge": Posthumanism and Sensory Encounter in John Webster's *The White Devil*', *Cashiers Elisabethains* 80: 35–46.

Dent, R. W. (1960). *John Webster's Borrowing.* Berkeley, CA: University of California Press.

Dickson, Lisa (2012). 'Theatrum Mundi: Performativity, Violence, and Metatheater in Webster's *The White Devil*', in Allie Terry-Fritsch and Erin Felicia Labbie, eds, *Beholding Violence in Medieval and Early Modern Europe.* Farnham: Ashgate.

Dollimore, Jonathan (2010). *Radical Tragedy: Religion, Ideology and Power in the Drama of Shakespeare and his Contemporaries*, 3rd edn. Basingstoke: Palgrave.

Engel, William E. (2002). *Death and Drama in Renaissance England: Shades of Memory.* Oxford: Oxford University Press.

Forker, Charles (1986). *Skull Beneath the Skin: The Achievement of John Webster.* Carbondale, IL: Southern Illinois University Press.

Goldberg, Dena (1987). *Between Worlds: A Study of the Plays of John Webster.* Waterloo, ON: Wilfrid Laurier University Press.

Griffith, Eva (2013). *A Jacobean Company and its Playhouse: The Queen's Servants at the Red Bull Theatre.* Cambridge: Cambridge University Press.

Habermann, Ina (2005). '"She has that in her belly will dry up your ink": Femininity as Challenge in the Equitable Drama of John Webster', in Erica Sheen and Lorna Hutson, eds, *Literature, Politics and Law in Renaissance England*. New York: Palgrave.

Habib, Imtiaz (2008). *Black Lives in the English Archives, 1500–1677: Imprints of the Invisible*. Aldershot: Ashgate.

Hirsh, James (2002). 'Vittoria's Secret: An Approach to Teaching John Webster's *The White Devil*', in Karen Bamford and Alexander Leggatt, eds, *Approaches to Teaching English Renaissance Drama*. New York: Modern Language Association.

Hunter, G. K. and S. K. Hunter, eds (1969). *John Webster: A Critical Anthology*. Harmondsworth: Penguin.

Iyengar, Sujata (2005). *Shades of Difference: Mythologies of Skin Color in Early Modern England*. Philadelphia: University of Pennsylvania Press.

Klein, Bernhard (2001). *Maps and the Writing of Space in Early Modern England and Ireland*. New York: St Martin's Press.

Levin, Carole and Karen Robertson, eds (1991). *Sexuality and Politics in Renaissance Drama*. Lewiston, Queenston and Lampeter: Edwin Mellen Press.

Lindley, David (1993). *The Trials of Frances Howard: Fact and Fiction at the Court of King James*. London: Routledge.

Luckyj, Christina (1989). *A Winter's Snake: Dramatic Form in the Tragedies of John Webster*. Athens, GA: University of Georgia Press.

Márkus, Zoltán (2014). 'Violence in Jacobean Drama: *Macbeth, The Revenger's Tragedy*, *The White Devil*, and *The Changeling*', in Robert DeMaria, Jr., Heesok Chang and Samantha Zacher, eds, *A Companion to British Literature*. 4 vols. Malden, MA: John Wiley & Sons. II.

Mason Vaughan, Virginia (2005). *Performing Blackness on English Stages, 1500–1800*. Cambridge: Cambridge University Press.

Moore, Don D., ed. (1981). *John Webster: The Critical Heritage*. London: Routledge.

Neill, Michael (2001). *Issues of Death: Mortality and Identity in English Renaissance Tragedy*. Oxford: Clarendon.

O'Connell, Michael (2000). *The Idolatrous Eye: Iconoclasm and Theatre in Early Modern England*. Oxford: Oxford University Press.

Pearson, Jacqueline (1980). *Tragedy and Tragicomedy in the Plays of John Webster*. Totowa, NJ: Barnes & Noble.

Purcell, Stephen (2012). *Webster: The White Devil: A Guide to the Text and Performance*. Basingstoke: Palgrave Macmillan.

Rahming, Melvin B. (2002). '"Goodbye to All That!" Engaging the Shift of Sensibility between John Webster's *The White Devil* and Amiri Baraka's *Dutchman*', *CLA Journal* 46: 72–97.

Rhatigan, Emma (2011). 'Reading the White Devil in Thomas Adams and John Webster', in Adrian Streete, ed., *Early Modern Drama and the Bible: Contexts and Readings 1570–1625*. London: Palgrave.

Rist, Thomas (2013). *Revenge Tragedy and the Drama of Commemoration in Reforming England*. Aldershot: Ashgate.

Sabatier, Armelle (2012). 'White or/and Red? Defining and Re-Defining the Colour of Corruption in John Webster's *The White Devil*', *Interfaces* 33: 135–48.

Sanchez, Melissa (2011). *Erotic Subjects: The Sexuality of Politics in Early Modern English Literature*. Oxford: Oxford University Press.

Schuman, Samuel (1985). *John Webster: A Reference Guide*. Boston, Mass.: G. K. Hall & Co., 1985.

Shell, Alison (1999). *Catholicism, Controversy and the English Literary Imagination*. Cambridge: Cambridge University Press.

Spencer, Hazelton (1934). 'Tate and *The White Devil*', *English Literary History* 1: 235–49.

Stanton, Kay (2014). *Shakespeare's 'Whores': Erotics, Politics and Poetics*. Basingstoke: Palgrave.

Strycharski, Andrew (2012). 'Ethics, Individualism, and Class in John Webster's *The White Devil*', *Criticism* 54 (2): 291–315.

Taylor, Alan (2007). *Jacobean Visions: Webster, Hitchcock and Google Culture*. Frankfurt: Peter Lang.

Vitkus, Daniel (2003). *Turning Turk: English Theatre and the Multicultural Mediterranean, 1570–1630*. New York: Palgrave.

Wanninger, Natascha (2015). 'Theatrical Colours: Cosmetics, Rhetoric and Theatre in Webster's *The White Devil*', *E-rea* 12 (2): §1–54. Available online: https://erea.revues.org/4475.

Waudby, June (2010). 'Contextualising Vittoria: Subjectivity and Censure in *The White Devil*', *This Rough Magic* 1 (2): 1–24.

Wilcox, Helen (2015). *1611: Authority, Gender & the Word in Early Modern England*. London: Wiley Blackwell.

Wilson, Luke (2006). '*The White Devil* and the Law', in Garrett A. Sullivan, Jr., Patrick Cheney and Andrew Hadfield, eds, *Early*

Modern English Drama: A Critical Companion. Oxford: Oxford University Press.

Williamson, Elizabeth (2007). 'The Domestification of Religious Objects in *The White Devil*'. *Studies in English Literature 1500–1900* 47: 473–90.

Woodbridge, Linda and Sharon A. Beehler, eds (2003). *Women, Violence, and English Renaissance Literature*. Tempe: Arizona Center for Medieval and Renaissance Studies.

INDEX